The Role of the Arab-Islamic World in the Rise of the West

The Role of the Arab-Islamic World in the Rise of the West

Implications for Contemporary Trans-Cultural Relations

Edited by

Nayef R. F. Al-Rodhan
Senior Member of St Antony's College, University of Oxford, UK, and Senior Scholar in Geostrategy and Director of the Geopolitics of Globalisation and Transnational Security Programme at the Geneva Centre for Security Policy, Switzerland

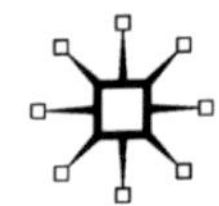

First published 2012 by
PALGRAVE MACMILLAN

Palgrave Macmillan in the UK is an imprint of Macmillan Publishers Limited, registered in England, company number 785998, of Houndmills, Basingstoke, Hampshire RG21 6XS.

Palgrave Macmillan in the US is a division of St Martin's Press LLC, 175 Fifth Avenue, New York, NY 10010.

Palgrave Macmillan is the global academic imprint of the above companies and has companies and representatives throughout the world.

Palgrave® and Macmillan® are registered trademarks in the United States, the United Kingdom, Europe and other countries.

ISBN: 978–0–230–39320–2

This book is printed on paper suitable for recycling and made from fully managed and sustained forest sources. Logging, pulping and manufacturing processes are expected to conform to the environmental regulations of the country of origin.

A catalogue record for this book is available from the British Library.

A catalog record for this book is available from the Library of Congress.

10 9 8 7 6 5 4 3 2 1
21 20 19 18 17 16 15 14 13 12

Transferred to Digital Printing in 2012

Contents

Acknowledgements

The editor would like to thank his colleagues at St Antony's College, Oxford University and the Geneva Centre for Security Policy for their continued support. He is especially grateful for the assistance of Lisa Watanabe of the Geneva Centre for Security Policy and Christina Brian of Palgrave Macmillan.

The views expressed in this book are entirely those of the editor and the authors of individual chapters, and do not necessarily reflect those of their respective institutions.

Contributors

Mohammed Abattouy is Senior Scholar at the Foundation for Science, Technology and Civilization, Manchester, UK and Head of the Philosophy Department, Mohammed Vth University, Rabat, Morocco.

Nayef R. F. Al-Rodhan is Senior Member of St Antony's College, University of Oxford, UK, and Senior Scholar in Geostrategy and Director of the Geopolitics of Globalisation and Transnational Security Programme at the Geneva Centre for Security Policy, Switzerland. He is a philosopher, neuroscientist and geostrategist. A prize-winning scholar, he has published 19 books proposing many innovative concepts and theories in global politics, security, philosophy and history. He was educated at Yale University, the Mayo Clinic and Harvard University. He is best known for several philosophical and analytic books on global politics that include *Symbiotic Realism* (2007), *Emotional Amoral Egoism* (2008), *Neo-Statecraft and Meta-Geopolitics* (2009), *Sustainable History and the Dignity of Man* (2009), *The Politics of Emerging Strategic Technologies* (2011).

Samar Attar is an independent scholar, who has taught English, Arabic and comparative literature in the USA, Canada, Algeria, Germany, Australia and Turkey. She has published extensively in both English and Arabic in the fields of literary criticism, philosophy, migration and gender studies.

Jack Goody is Emeritus Professor in Social Anthropology at the University of Cambridge and Fellow of St John's College, Cambridge University, UK.

Frédérique Guerin is Research Fellow and Programme Coordinator of the Geopolitics of Globalisation and Transnational Security Programme, Geneva Centre for Security Policy, Switzerland.

John M. Hobson is Professor of Politics and International Relations at the Department of Politics, University of Sheffield, UK.

Mohammad-Mahmoud Ould Mohamedou is Visiting Professor in the International History and Politics and Development departments of the Graduate Institute of International and Development Studies in

Geneva, and Head of the Middle East and North Africa Programme at the Geneva Centre for Security Policy, Switzerland.

Lisa Watanabe is Research Fellow of the Geopolitics of Globalisation and Transnational Security Programme, Geneva Centre for Security Policy, Switzerland.

1

Introduction: A Thousand Years of Amnesia

Nayef R. F. Al-Rodhan

Islam in Europe is often considered a relatively recent phenomenon. Political discourse in many European countries presents Islam as a foreign presence in Europe that is incompatible with societal values and a threat to people's way of life. Yet, far from being incompatible, the West and the Muslim world have a shared heritage that represents something positive upon which to build. The presence of Islam in Europe has far more profound roots than is commonly imagined, not simply because the Arab-Islamic Empire at one time included Spain, southern Italy, Sicily and the Balkans, but also due to the transmission of knowledge and techniques to non-Muslim areas of Europe from the Arab-Islamic Empire. While early Arab and Berber invaders did not initially belong to an obviously higher culture, they were not organized on a tribal basis and their capacity to embrace the contributions and advances in knowledge of Ancient Greece, China and India meant that the impact of the Arab-Islamic Empire on Europe had a very special character, and an important part to play in the rise of Europe.[1] While the Islamic geo-cultural domain comprised a number of ethnic and religious communities, I employ the term Arab-Islamic Empire, because Arab culture provided the cultural framework of the Empire and Arabic the backbone of intellectual endeavour, and Arabs also provided for the most of the political leadership during the golden age of the Empire.

The transmission of knowledge, techniques and institutions to Europe was particularly important during the medieval period. While trade had collapsed and non-religious learning and scientific inquiry had been stifled in Christian Europe during the so-called Dark Ages, the Arab-Islamic Empire flourished. While Europe was plunged into 'darkness' following the collapse of the Roman Empire, this was not the case in the Arab-Islamic world. Trade between the Arab-Islamic Empire and the East continued following the fall of the Roman Empire, and scientific and philosophical inquiry thrived, particularly in the ninth and tenth centuries. In Baghdad a centre for rationalist learning was created by the Abbasid caliph, Al-Mamum (786–833) in ninth century, based on the earlier Persian Academy of Gundeshapur. Emissaries were dispatched to find seminal texts in a variety of areas of learning, including mathematics, astronomy, science and philosophy. The best translators and scholars were brought to what became known as the 'House of Wisdom' or *bayt al hikma*. Among the many scholars assembled at the university was Mohamed Al-Khwarizmi (c.780–850), the father of algebra and the algorithm. In the eleventh century, the House of Knowledge in Cairo attracted the brilliant minds of the age, including Ibn Al-Haytham (965–1039), who developed theories of optics that laid the foundation for our understanding of human vision. Intellectual pursuits and discoveries were also taking place in the far west of the Empire where Muslim Spain (Al-Andalus) was home to numerous centres of learning[2] in Cordoba, Toledo, Seville and Granada. The Arab-Islamic Empire possessed translations of Aristotle, the neo-Platonic commentators, some of Plato's works, a large part of Galen's body of work, as well as other Greek scientific works.[3]

Reflecting the tremendous intellectual achievements occurring at the time in the Arab-Islamic Empire, Arabic became the lingua franca in Medieval Europe, as Latin would later become during the Renaissance. Hungry for knowledge, European scholars sought to familiarize themselves with Ancient Greek texts that were translated and commented on, as well as the cutting edge studies of Muslim scholars. Among these works were the texts of Aristotle, Al-Razi (Rhazes), Al-Kindi, Euclid, Archimedes, Al-Haytham, Galen, Appollionios, Hypsicles, Theodosios, Menalaos, Ptolemy, Al-Khwarizmi, Al-Farghani, Al-Naiziri, Thabit Ibn Qurra, Ibn Sina (Avicenna) and Abul-Qasim[4] and Ibn Rushd (Averroes), among others. Al-Khwarizmi's work would only be translated for Europeans 300 years after it was undertaken.[5] Muslim Spain, known as the 'ornament of the world' at one time, Sicily and southern Italy were key points for the transmission of knowledge and practices to Europe from the Arab-Islamic world, partly as a result of scholars, translators, pilgrims and traders travelling between Europe and the Arab-Islamic Empire and partly because of the fall of Al-Andalus to Catholic Spain and of Sicily to the Normans. When Toledo fell to Catholic Spain in 1085, one of the most significant translations of scientific work was undertaken.[6] With the fall of other major centres of learning, such as Cordoba, Seville and Granada, in 1236, 1248 and 1492 respectively, transfers of knowledge and institutions took place. In Sicily, which fell to the Normans between 965 and 1061, exchanges between Arab and Norman culture would continue to take place over several centuries, with Islamic legal concepts, it is believed, making their way further west, as far as England.[7] Indeed, other institutions of governance may also have been transmitted to Europe via the island of Sicily.

The myriad forms in which the Arab-Islamic world influenced Europe's development has been documented by a number of scholars.[8] However, to the great detriment to history and to contemporary relations between the West and the Muslim world, such positive encounters are little known in the West today and are no longer part of the collective memory of Westerners. Why this is so is a complex and fascinating question. It has much to do with the construction of an identity, first of Latin Christendom and then of Europe, that coincided with that continent's rise and eventual triumph. This process involved a juxtaposition of a positive Self identity for the West against a negative Other, with the Arab-Islamic world falling into the latter category along with the East in general. Despite the great attraction of the cultural riches of Arab-Islamic lands, Latin Christendom was being constructed against Islam. Later, during the Renaissance, emphasis was placed on Greek rather than Arab heritage.[9] As Europe became more powerful, eventually becoming dominant, this polarization continued, but in a slightly different way. Orientalism, as Edward Said called it, assumed the inherent superiority of the West in relation to the East.[10] In relation to Europe, Eurocentrism – the tendency to view the world from the viewpoint of European dominance and an implied assumption of European uniqueness and superiority – infused Europe's account of its own historical development and place in world history. In these accounts, the role of the Arab-Islamic world in the rise of the West is obscured. The aim of this book is to recapture some of this history of cultural borrowing and exchange and, it is hoped that by so doing, it may contribute in a small way to a better understanding of relations between the West and the Arab-Islamic world. Acknowledging the West's debt to the Arab-Islamic world is vital in an era of increased global interconnectedness and pluri-cultural societies, when relations between the West and the Muslim world can often be characterized by an interplay of negative images of the Other. However, let us begin by briefly surveying how dominant accounts of the rise of the West tend to depict its historical trajectory.

The rise of the West – the dominant narrative

Modern Europe is often conceived as an exceptional case in terms of its development, moving along a linear, progressive path from Antiquity through feudalism, followed by the Renaissance and capitalism.[11] The revival of its Ancient Greek heritage following the Dark Ages is believed to have paved the way for the Renaissance, from which the Scientific Revolution and the Enlightenment are thought to have emerged. Similarly, the rise of capitalism and the expansion of the European world system are often thought to have taken place as a result of uniquely European attributes and it is often viewed as a transitional phase within a linear, progressive path towards modernity, containing within it the seeds of first mercantile and later industrial capitalism.[12] Max Weber's characterization of the West assumed that its superiority vis-à-vis other civilizations was its rationalism.[13] Indeed, the uniqueness of the European state was believed to lie in its distinctly rational nature. This, in turn, is thought to have laid dependable legal foundations upon which commercial affairs could be based. The type of capitalism that emerged in the West was thought to have been possible only in Christian lands,[14] the Protestant work ethic being viewed as particularly significant for its emergence.[15] For Karl Marx, the classical and feudal periods were necessary precursors of capitalism in the West. Asia was seen as the exception to the rule.[16] Marx, at least in his early writings, viewed the East as backward and stagnant due to oriental despotism that was believed to have stifled the emergence of private ownership. Capitalist relations in the East could, in his view, only materialize as a result of Western influence.[17] Indeed, the rest of the world was thought to have remained despotic and stagnant until incursions were made by the West.[18] Within this distinctly Eurocentric historiography, a dynamic West is frequently juxtaposed with a static East, with the achievements of non-Europeans assessed from the viewpoint of European dominance and its presumed uniqueness. Weber too approached non-European civilizations in terms of their perceived lack of Western attributes, in this case rationalism.[19] The dice were, therefore, loaded against them from the outset. Non-European civilizations have tended to be ascribed less positive roles in world history, which itself becomes identical with Western history, with the characteristics attributed to the West being frequently associated with positive human development and progress.[20]

That said, philosophers of history, who have sought to compare Western civilization with that which went before have, at times, adopted a more nuanced view. Oswald Spengler's *Decline of the West*, for example, proposed a cultural cyclical notion of history that differed from the traditional linear interpretation of Western history:[21]

> Thanks to the sub-division of history into 'Ancient', 'Medieval' and 'Modern' – an incredibly jejune and *meaningless* scheme, which has, however, entirely dominated our historical thinking – we have failed to perceive the true position in the general history of higher mankind of the little part-world which has developed on West European soil from the time of the German-Roman Empire, to judge of its relative importance and above all to estimate its direction.... It is not only that the scheme circumscribes the area of history. What is worse, it rigs the stage. The Western European area is regarded as a fixed pole, a unique patch chosen on the surface of the sphere for no better reason it seems, than because we live on it – and great histories of millennial duration and mighty faraway Cultures are made to revolve around this pole in all modesty.[22]

Nevertheless, Spengler does seem to assume that modernity is an essentially Western phenomenon, driven by a spirit of discovery and a Faustian desire to master nature.[23] Arnold Toynbee's liberal analysis of the rise and fall of civilizations did not, by contrast, try to paint a different picture of Western civilization. He sought to examine history in a way that did not place Europe and the rise of the West at the centre, his conceptualization of history being cyclical.[24]

In answer to the specific question 'why Europe?' Fernand Braudel's examination of capitalism within a broader world history attributed Europe's success to the key characteristic of liberty, in the sense of privileges or rights that protected one group from the abuses of another. The development of towns is conceived as central to the growth of such liberties. Towns are believed to have fostered freedom, provided markets for rural artisans and given birth to finance capital. The growth of towns increased production and the revenue of peasants, allowing peasants greater freedom as land became more abundant. Material prosperity earned cities independence and private liberties. This situation is contrasted with despotism in the East. Yet, as Braudel notes, towns were not unique to the West. They were also crucial to the development of the Arab-Islamic Empire, where the combination of production and distribution, whatever form it took, also required finance. Indeed, he recognizes that trade and finance developed together in the Arab-Islamic Empire. While in Braudel's account, Europe appears to have autonomously charted its course to industrialization, he does acknowledge the role that colonialism post-1492 played in the development of industrialism and the rise of Europe.[25]

The importance of towns to Europe's revival after the Dark Ages, during which urban life and the money economy collapsed, is also emphasized by Carlo Cipolla in *Before the Industrial Revolution: European Society and Economy 1000–1700*.[26] After lengthy struggles with the nobility and bishops, towns became the domains of the business and professional classes. The socially prominent position that these classes achieved, is believed to be what distinguished European towns from those that existed elsewhere in the medieval period. Towns are conceived as critical to Europe's development, because they stimulated demand and greater equality. Indeed, the urban revolution is believed to have laid the foundations of the Industrial Revolution.[27] In the field of enterprise and credit, Cipolla cites the *contratto di commenda* as a critical innovation that enabled savings to be transformed into productive investment. The *commenda*, or *collegantia* as it was known in Venice, enabled merchants to finance the purchase of goods for sale on their voyages as well as the trips themselves.[28] Again, there is no mention that this technique originated in the Near East. In his view, these were, among a myriad other innovations and inventions, 'the original product of European experimental curiosity and imagination'.[29]

David Landes has sought to understand the main 'stream' of economic development and modernization by asking the following questions: 'How and why did we get where we are? How did the rich countries get so rich? Why are poor countries so poor? Why did Europe (the West) take the lead in changing the world?'[30] These questions are posed by Landes, because '[a]s the historical record shows, for the last thousand years, Europe (the West) has been the prime mover of development and modernity'.[31] Among the factors thought to affect a nation's destiny is climate (geography). Europe is believed to have been blessed with the most temperate climate. The Middle Ages are conceived as an intervening period connecting the ancient with the modern world. During this interregnum, a new society is believed to have emerged that set a course unique to this civilization. Greek democracy, albeit with its shortcomings, is contrasted with oriental despotism. The separation of the secular and the religious is also thought to have contributed to Europe's rise in that it enabled popular initiative and decentralized authority. Inventiveness is also a factor considered crucial for increases in productivity in Europe. 1492 is understood as a key factor in Europe's rise. In response to the question 'Why Europe?', Landes cites what he views as specifically European sources of success: intellectual freedom, a common language of proof, the routinization of research and its spread.[32]

In relation to the Scientific Revolution, Toby Huff has employed a comparative framework in *Intellectual Curiosity and the Scientific Revolution: A Global Perspective*[33] to examine the historical, deep structures of the developments that together formed the Scientific Revolution in order to understand the cultural and intellectual starting points that were in place in Europe as opposed to Mughal India, China and the Ottoman Empire. The specific window through which he seeks to do this is through the development of the telescope and its transmission around the world in the first two decades of the seventeenth century. He argues that in Europe the 'surplus of *human capital* was singular and did set the West on a unique developmental trajectory... the unique Western system of education and the abundant fruit spawned by the scientific revolution created a level of human capital unmatched anywhere in the world until the end of the twentieth century'.[34] In his view, modern science did not develop elsewhere in the world due to an absence of 'supportive social and cultural conditions'.[35] The scientific ethos of intellectual curiosity was, in Huff's view, simply unrivalled beyond Europe during this period. Indeed, that the telescope, when taken around the world, failed to trigger similar developments outside Europe was ultimately due to a deficit of scientific curiosity.[36] Moreover, while he acknowledges that there were earlier scientific discoveries, especially in the Middle East, that 'built on the Greek legacy of a still earlier age', little evidence is believed to exist to support the idea that scientific developments of China or Mughal India gave momentum to the European scientific revolution of the seventeenth century.[37]

The dominant narrative of Europe's rise, therefore, depicts Europe as possessing unique characteristics, whether it be rationalism, liberty or intellectual curiosity. Moreover, within this overarching narrative, Europe is portrayed as having charted its course largely autonomously, owing very little to other geo-cultural domains. The Arab-Islamic Empire, which itself drew upon Chinese, Indian and Ancient Greek contributions to knowledge and practices, is often seen as little more than a 'holder' of Ancient Greek manuscripts. Its own contributions to the developmental trajectory of the West is rarely acknowledged.

Towards a more holistic approach to Europe's rise

Despite the entrenched nature of the dominant narrative of Europe's success, some scholars have argued that the rise of the West needs to be rephrased and rethought to capture mutual influences between civilizations at every stage of history. In recent times, historians have attempted to understand European dominance and the rise of the West within the context of global history, calling into question European exceptionalism. André Gunder Frank, for example, adopts a materialist approach that emphasizes the global context rather than focusing on specific cultural and/or institutional features ascribed to the West. In *ReOrient*, Gunder Frank questions the notion that modern history is essentially European history. He challenges Eurocentric historiography by providing a different version of history between the fifteenth and eighteenth centuries. In Gunder Frank's view, Europe employed its American money to make gains from Asian trade, production and markets. By implication, Europe is considered as neither more important than other regions of the world nor at the centre of a developing global economic system. Neither capitalist relations in Europe nor European exceptionalism are believed to be the source of the modern economic and social system.[38]

A similar approach is employed by Janet Abu-Lughold in *Before European Hegemony*. The world system as a whole is examined, of which Europe was but a peripheral economic system before it came to dominate. Between 1250 and 1350, the world system is thought to have reached a critical turning point when the Middle East linked the Mediterranean and the Indian Ocean, and East and West became more or less balanced. In fact, she argues that before this shift in global power occurred, Asian, Arab and Western forms of capitalism were very alike and, where differences did exist, it was the West that was the least advanced. Geographic, political and demographic factors are thought to be more important and determining in the rise of the West than any unique inventiveness or institutions. The demise of the Middle Eastern monopoly of the trade route to the East, caused by the opening up of the Atlantic sea routes is also believed to have played a significant role in the growth of European trade.[39] Thus, contingency is given greater explanatory power than specific forms of capitalism or cultural traits in Abu-Lughold's account.

The role of contingency has also been emphasized by a number of other scholars. In *The Colonizer's Model of the World: Geographical Diffusionism and Eurocentric History*, James Blaut claims that Europeans had no superiority over non-Europeans prior to 1492. Processes taking place in Europe pre-1492 were also taking place elsewhere. In this interpretation, it was Europe's colonial riches that propelled its advance after 1492.[40] As in other accounts, the discovery of the Americas is thought to have played a critical role in the rise of the West. Kenneth Pommeranz has gone further in arguing that there is nothing to indicate that Europe held a comparative advantage in being able to amass capital stock before 1800. What altered the odds in Europe's favour is believed to have been innovations in Europe that enabled land saving, especially those linked to fossil fuels that did not rely on forests for energy. European advantages in transportation and technological sophistication need to be severely qualified. In his view, non-European societies retained advantages in technological sophistication in many areas up to the eighteenth century.[41] Cultural agency in conjunction with contingency has also been highlighted by some scholars. Jack Goldstone, for example, claims that the rise of Europe was not due to any overarching superiority vis-à-vis other regions of the globe. In his view, the answer to the question 'Why Europe?' may be found in a combination of factors: discoveries that led to the questioning of ancient and religious texts; experimental science and mathematical analysis of the natural world; scientific method; an instrument-driven approach to experiment and observation; tolerance and pluralism; and close social relations between entrepreneurs, scientists, engineers and artisans.[42]

Similar factors are also identified by H. Floris Cohen in *How Modern Science Came into the World: Four Civilizations, One 17th-Century Breakthrough*.[43] Cohen examines how modern science emerged and why this occurred in Europe rather than in Chinese or Islamic civilizations. Rather than conceiving of the Scientific Revolution of the seventeenth century as one event, Cohen identifies six distinct, but interconnected revolutionary transformations that together comprised what we tend to think of as the Scientific Revolution. With this interpretation of the Scientific Revolution, Cohen offers an explanation of why modern science came about in Europe and not in Greece, China or the Islamic world. Rather than a unidirectional sequencing, a number of episodes gave rise to a comparative approach, with modes of 'nature-knowledge' or approaches to natural phenomena forming the 'entities' compared. In Cohen's view, Greece offered a non-modern corpus of nature-knowledge, which ultimately experienced a decline. In contrast to the master narrative of the Scientific Revolution, Cohen argues that medieval nature-knowledge did not serve as a preparatory stage for modern science, but as an exceptional case in which the revival of a Greek corpus of knowledge ultimately remained blocked. Both Islamic civilization and Renaissance Europe were two other recipients of the Greek body of knowledge and are perceived by Cohen as similar enough to be compared.[44] Within the Ottoman Empire, reliance on established modes of nature-knowledge impeded the uptake of new and innovative thinking that had emerged within European nature-knowledge structures. The latter is also believed to have been too incompatible with Ancient Chinese conceptual frameworks to be adopted in China.[45] In Renaissance Europe, by contrast, three simultaneous transformations are believed to have enabled modern science to come into the world. First, the Greek mathematical tradition was turned into a mathematization of nature, sustained by experimentation, by Galileo and Kepler. Second, the Aristotelian philosophy of nature was replaced by an atomist natural philosophy and a novel conception of movement provided by Galileo and Descartes. Third, practice-orientated inquiry and fact finding with regards to the natural world, consolidated by Galileo and Francis Bacon.[46] While a decline in nature-knowledge occurred in Europe halfway to the Scientific Revolution, royal confidence, Baconian optimism and religious sanctioning, out of which freedom of investigation could flourish, came together in the 1660s to give momentum to a revolutionary nature-knowledge, enabling modern science to stay in the world.[47]

As mentioned at the outset, Eurocentric accounts of the triumph of the West have not only distorted our understanding of the West within global history, they have also tended to obfuscate the role of the Arab-Islamic world in the rise of the West. Several important recent contributions have sought to illuminate this little known dimension of history and to contribute to a more holistic conception of Europe's rise. In *The Eastern Origins of Western Civilisation*, John Hobson vigorously argues that the East played a crucial role in enabling the rise of modern Western civilization.[48] Eurocentric accounts of the rise of the West, he claims, neglect three points: the East pioneered its own rise after 500; the East actively created and maintained its own economy; and the East contributed to the rise of the West through the development and transmission of many 'resource portfolios' to Europe.[49] After 500, the East is believed to have established a global communications network through which its resource portfolios were diffused to, and assimilated by, the West. In addition to this process of 'diffusionism', Europeans appropriated Eastern economic resources following 1492.[50]

The development and expansion of the Eastern economic system is thought to owe much to the Arab-Islamic Empire.[51] This stands in contrast to the Eurocentric assumption that Islam was an inherently regressive religion that blocked the emergence of capitalism. Yet, religion and material life are not contradictory in Islam. The *shari'ah* ('sacred law') outlined provisions for contract law. Moreover, there were signs of greater personal freedoms under Islam than in Europe, and public offices were also determined by 'egalitarian contractualism'.[52] A number of innovations were crucial to the development of Muslim trade: the lateen sail and the astrolabe; breakthroughs in astronomy and mathematics, due in particular to the use of the zero as a result of Al-Khwarizmi's work; paper and textile manufacturing; iron and steel production. Energy was also harnessed through the use of windmills and watermills. Islam also had a comparative advantage over Europe in scientific knowledge and military technologies.[53] The revival and expansion of European trade was, in Hobson's account, due to its integration into an already developed trading system dominated by Eastern powers rather than to Italian pioneers. All the central innovations that lay behind the commercial revolution in Europe are believed to have derived from the East, the Middle East and China in particular. Key financial innovations, such as the *commenda,* as well as the bill of exchange, credit institutions, insurance and banking are often attributed to Italians, but they originated in the Islamic and pre-Islamic Middle East. Europe was not, therefore, the self-contained, regional economic system frequently depicted in Eurocentric accounts of the rise of the West after the year 1000.[54]

The idea of Europe as an autonomous system that pioneered the development and expansion of its own commercial and financial success is problematized by Hobson,[55] who argues that the feudal revolution in Europe is likely to have taken place partly as a result of a global transmission of Eastern technologies that had laid the foundations for the feudal state and economy by the eighth century, notably the stirrup, which enabled the development of the shock cavalry. However, once the situation had settled around 1000, the feudal form of relationship between nobles and peasants had to be legitimized and this need became intertwined with the construction of European identity. There was no intrinsic homogeneity in Europe at that time. Europe, as such, did not exist. Given that there was no Self to speak of, the Self became defined by what it was not. The imaginary Other against which Europe was defined was Islam. Europe came to be known as Christendom because it was constructed as Catholic Christian against Islamic Middle East, celestial hierarchy being transposed onto feudal social hierarchy.[56]

The assumption that the feudal period in Europe followed Antiquity as a transitional phase within a linear progressive trajectory toward modernity, giving Europe the unique path to modernity, itself intimately tied to the construction of European identity, is also re-examined by Jack Goody in *The Theft of History,* in which Goody claims that there was nothing intrinsic in feudalism that led to mercantile capitalism and later industrial capitalism. Some form of feudal social relations are believed to have existed almost everywhere following the Bronze Age.[57] This challenges Eurocentric interpretations of history in which feudalism was associated with a degree of individual freedom, whereas irrigated agriculture in the East was believed to be linked to despotism, together forming the so-called Asiatic mode of production.[58]

The notion that Europe experienced an autonomous rebirth after the intervening darkness of the Middle Ages is highly problematic in Goody's view. Knowledge of Greek had progressively declined in Europe, limiting direct access to ancient Greek texts until the Renaissance. In addition to these linguistic constraints, the growth of Christianity in post-Roman Europe placed greater emphasis on religious rather than non-religious learning. Christians in Europe, in fact, played a minor role in the preservation, let alone expansion, of classical knowledge. The role of Nestorian Christians in the East was far more significant in this respect. They translated some classical texts into Arabic. Indeed, the growth of knowledge during this period was taking place in the East.[59] In Goody's interpretation, the Renaissance was a response in some ways to the 'splendours of the Islamic East that had provided models of luxury and civilization, including deeper knowledge of classical texts. The return to those texts, whether they came through Spain or Constantinople, was at one level an appeal to the past in the face of the Ottoman Empire and Mongol societies that had penetrated Eastern Europe and that were being opposed by the Orthodox and Catholic churches, the churches of the East and West Roman empires, respectively.'[60] The classical revival and the Scientific Revolution owed much to the Arabs and Muslims in general. A great deal of scientific knowledge was transmitted to Europe from the Arab-Islamic Empire, as mentioned earlier. Indeed, the notion that Islam necessarily hindered scientific and rational learning is confounded by historical evidence.[61]

Contact with the Arab-Islamic world also helped to fuel the Renaissance in Europe through the transmission of intellectual knowledge. Toledo in Al-Andalus was a vibrant city where Arabic texts were translated into Latin. It was a major point of transmission of classical, as well as Arabic knowledge to Christian Europe.[62] Philosophy in the West is usually assumed to have an Antiquity-Renaissance trajectory, when, as mentioned, Muslims also looked back to classical learning. The works of Greek philosophers and mathematicians that had been lost to Europe were to be found here. Ibn Rushd's twelfth century critique of Aristotle was central to Europe's classical revival. His summaries and commentaries were translated from Arabic into Latin in the thirteenth century by Michael Scott and Herman the German. Gerard of Cremona translated, among other works, Al-Zahrawi's medical encylopedia, Ibn Haytham's *Book of Optics*, Al-Kindi's treatise on geometrical optics and Al-Razi's *A Study and Classification of Salts and Alums* (sulphates).[63] Ancient science and that of the Arab-Islamic world was often translated by Jewish doctors who had fled Spain.[64] As the case of medicine shows, the West is indebted to the Islamic world for the rebirth of scientific enquiry.[65] Moreover, Muslim scholars were not simply the keepers of Greek knowledge, as is often claimed in Eurocentric accounts of the exchanges between the Arab-Islamic world and the West. Classical texts were not only preserved by the Arab-Islamic world, but also elaborated on by Muslim scholars. As Goody remarks, the Arab-Islamic Empire played a critical mediating role in the rebirth of knowledge associated with the Renaissance, which was also stimulated by the contributions of Arab scholars.[66] The revival of classical knowledge also helped to enable a degree of secularization. In the West, secularism did not replace religion, but restricted religious learning and led to the growth of humanism. Religion was rationalized to some extent in terms of reducing appeals to rituals and mystification – very much in line with Protestant reformism.[67]

Philosophical traditions in Europe did not escape the influence of the Arab-Islamic world. A number of Arab-Islamic philosophers were influential in Europe. Among them was Al-Razi, who was born in 865 CE and wrote philosophical works exploring the relationship between religion and philosophy. He believed that all religious and ethical truth could be attained through rational thought. Ibn Sina, who lived in the tenth century, was also widely known in the West for his theological contributions. A century later, Al-Ghazali made the case for a literal interpretation of the Quran, asserting that the employment of reason alone to attain truth would lead to the destruction of religion and morality. Ibn Rushd was born in the twelfth century and wrote a commentary on Aristotle. When interest in philosophy began to flourish in the twelfth century, Islamic philosophy not only became a source of knowledge in its own right, it also provided a means by which Europeans could become familiar with Greek texts that had become lost to them. As Robert van de Weyer notes, the influence of Muslim philosophers in the long run was to liberate European thought from religious dogma, which, in turn, contributed to the European Renaissance and related developments.[68]

Scientific inquiry also flourished in the so-called golden age of Islam. Muslim scholars made important advances in astronomy, compiling tables that calculated the movements of the sun, the moon and the planets.[69] They not only drew on Greek texts, but also Persian and Indian astronomical knowledge to further their own understanding of the universe, as well as contributing to the development of astrology. They refined the Ptolemaic system.[70] However, these mathematical methods were soon discovered to be inadequate and this resulted in the search for new techniques that led to the development of trigonometry and other mathematical methods.[71] Islamic scholars developed mathematics as an independent science, introducing, above all, a more sophisticated number theory, which made computations much simpler.[72] Knowledge of astronomy and mathematics entered Europe from Spain.[73] While some interest in astronomy can be traced back to the Carolingian period in Europe, later advances were only made based on Arab-Islamic astronomical knowledge. Given the paucity of translations of Greek texts, the major stimulus to the growth of the discipline came through contact with the Arab-Islamic world and Latin translations of Arabic astronomical studies.[74] Prior to the introduction of Arabic numerals, which themselves had Indian origins, Europeans had employed Roman numerals that limited mathematical operations and set back the development of mathematical theory in Europe. The introduction of Arabic numerals into Europe is thought to have occurred in the early thirteenth century through the publication of *Liber abaci* by Leonardo Fibonacci, whose father was in charge of a Pisan trading colony in today's Algeria. In preparation for his dealings in business, Fibonacci's father sent him to learn mathematics with an Arab teacher.[75]

While historians have often traced the development of medicine in Europe back to Antiquity, a very significant contribution was made to this field by Arab-Islamic scholarship. The Arab-Islamic world had preserved the greater part of Galenic medical knowledge. Jewish refugees fleeing repression in reconquered Spanish lands brought medical knowledge from the Arab-Islamic world, stimulating the study of medicine at Lunel, Narbonne and Montpellier in the south of France. The Italian town of Salerno, a medical centre in the Middle Ages, was also influenced by Arab-Islamic medicine.[76] Muslim scholars not only employed Greek texts, but produced their own original works. The study of anatomy was advanced by the tenth century works of Abu Al-Qasim, known in Europe as Abulcasis, who was able to work on humans. Thus, the development of medicine in Salerno and Montpellier were not simply the result of the resurrection of classical learning and a continuation from them. Developments owed much to Arab-Islamic world, which acted both as a medium of transmission of Greek knowledge and as a source of new medical knowledge.[77] The work of Ibn Al-Nafis, who critiqued Galen's work on the human body, laid many of the foundations for the later work of William Harvey.[78] Ibn Sina's book *Kitab al Shifa* [The Book of Healing] introduced the principals of logic and its use in the acquisition of knowledge to Medieval Europe, and his works placed science and religion on an equal footing in terms of comprehension of the world. Other major scholars in the medical field included Al-Razi (Al-Razes) and Ibn Rushd.[79] Europe continued to depend on Arabic medicine until well into the fifteenth and sixteenth centuries.[80]

The diffusion of ideas, techniques and institutions from the Arab-Islamic world to Europe came to be virtually erased from the collective memory of Europeans and Westerners in general. There are many reasons for this. Despite cultural borrowing from the Arab-Islamic world, a negative and menacing image of Islam came to dominate in Europe. Scholarly interest in Islam as a religion is thought to have only begun at the time of the Crusades, though a misunderstanding of Islam generally reigned. While a number of prominent translators demonstrated a deeper knowledge of Islam and translated the Quran in the early twelfth century, the image of Islam that developed in Medieval Europe was one of Islam as a falsehood, a religion of the sword and self-indulgence, and of Mohammed as an antichrist. This was contrasted with a European image of Christianity as true, converting by rational argument and persuasion, and a religion of asceticism.[81] Montgomery Watt was perhaps correct when he said that '[i]n general the feelings of western Europeans over against Islam were not unlike those of an underprivileged class in a great state. Like the underprivileged class they turned to religion in their effort to assert themselves against a privileged group ...'.[82] In this sense, Islam helped to prompt Europe into developing a new self-image.[83] The temporal identity that would gradually replace a predominantly spiritual identity of Christendom was, as discussed, premised on a progressive linear trajectory that left no room for acknowledging outside influence, let alone that from the Arab-Islamic world.

'An ocean model of civilization'

This book aims to recapture this lost dimension of history, and it is my hope that in so doing it will contribute to a better understanding of both the West and the Arab-Islamic world, their exchanges and shared heritage, as well as help to foster more positive present and future relations. East and

West have not, after all, only met in conflict and their common history is not only one of tension and antagonism. Moreover, their positive encounters served to advance our collective knowledge.[84] As I have mentioned in *Sustainable History and the Dignity of Man: A Philosophy of History and Civilisational Triumph*, '[e]ach high point in the history of human civilization has taken place where the conditions were ripe and has borrowed and built upon the achievements of other cultures whose "golden age" may have passed'.[85] Advances in human civilization are cumulative and the fruit of collective achievements. The human story is one story. Rather than conceiving of multiple civilizations, we ought to think in terms of multiple geo-cultural domains that together comprise one human civilization. In *Sustainable History and the Dignity of Man*, I have outlined 'an ocean model of one human civilization' into which flow multiple rivers that each contribute to its character and depth (see Figure 1.1).[86]

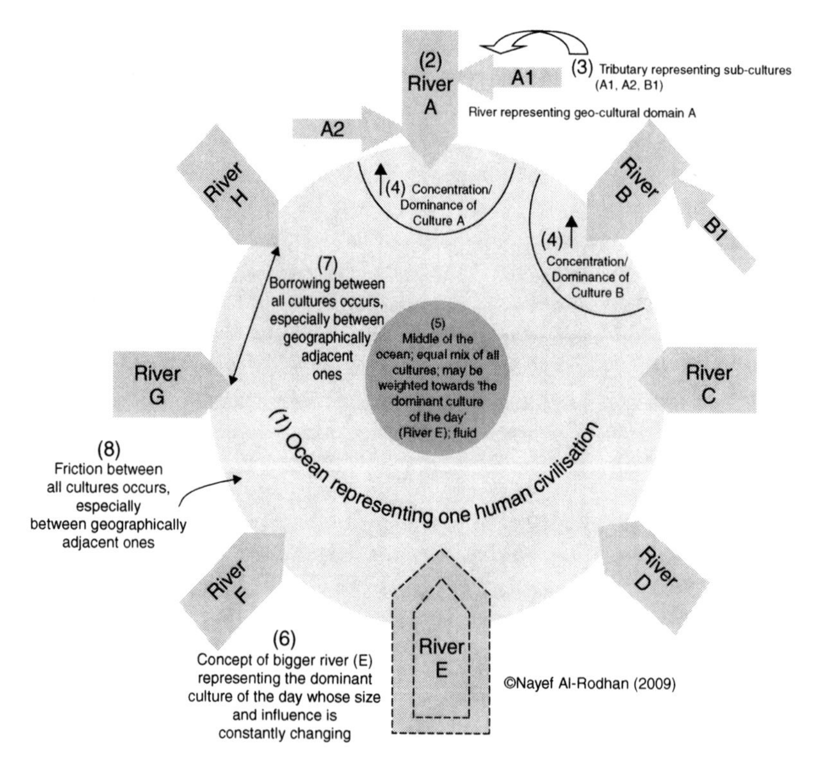

Figure 1.1 The ocean model of one human civilization

Source: N .R. F. Al-Rodhan (2009), *Sustainable History and the Dignity of Man: A Philosophy of History and Civilisational Triumph* (Berlin: LIT), p. 37, reproduced with the permission of LIT.

Advances in knowledge during the golden ages of the Arab-Islamic Empire were themselves influenced by the achievements of earlier contributions to human civilization, such as those of ancient China, India and Greece, and were acknowledged as such.[87] Their debt to scholars from other cultures and earlier epochs were always meticulously acknowledged in their citations. The Hadith authenticity methodology served as a cultural and intellectual framework for citation. Islam's belief system, cultural norms, intellectual codes, moral principles and political regulations are all governed by the Quran and the Hadith. The Hadith are practical dimensions of the Quran's religious instructions demonstrated by the Prophet Mohammed's own life. The Hadith are classified according to their level of authenticity. Al-Bukhari and Muslim collections of Hadith are deemed to have the greatest authenticity. The authenticity of the Hadith are dependent upon those within the chain of people reporting the sayings of the Prophet.[88] The reliability of narrators within this chain was rigorously verified in order to eliminate the possibility of fabrication or inaccuracies. The Hadith methodology may be thought of as providing the basis for the intellectual practice of citation in the Arab-Islamic world that appears to have been missing in Europe.

The debt to Muslim scholars is, for the most part, unacknowledged by European scholars who drew upon their work. Indeed, the work of Arab-Islamic scholars appears, in some instances, to have been copied almost verbatim. For example, the remarkable similarities between Al-Ghazali's work and that of René Descartes have been the subject of much discussion. Both Al-Ghazali and Descartes argued against the infallibility of sense perception. There are also similarities between Al-Ghazali's theory of causation and that of David Hume.[89] The work of St Thomas Aquinas resembles very closely that of Ibn Rushd. Indeed, it is possible that St Thomas Aquinas came into contact with Ibn Rushd's work at the University of Naples, which was founded by Frederick II of Sicily, who was a great admirer of Arabic philosophy.[90] Ibn Al-Haytham's mathematical works are also believed to have influenced those of Roger Bacon, Descartes, Frederick of Fribourg, Kepler and Christiaan Huygens.[91] Da Vinci, John Locke, Voltaire, Descartes, Kant and Rousseau are all believed to have been influenced by Ibn Tufayl's book *Hayy Ibn Yazan*, which tells the story of a child who grew up on a desert island and through the application of reason became enlightened.[92] What seems to be a lack of correct citation in European scholarship, particularly in the Middle Ages, may have been due to different practices within Europe at the time. However, the reigning religious animosity towards Islam and a sense of inferiority in Europe may also have been partly responsible for European reticence in acknowledging their debt to earlier Muslim works. Europe's failure to acknowledge its cultural and intellectual debt to the Arab-Islamic world not only perpetuates the myth of Europe as the birthplace of modernity, but also understandably continues to anger and frustrate Arabs and Muslims today.

Viewing the successes of the West within the broader context of the development of a collective human civilization, helps to break down Eurocentric assumptions about the nature of its rise, as well as the nature of the Arab-Islamic world, and the binary opposition of a superior, progressive West and an inferior, stagnant Near East that have very real socio-cultural and political consequences. As we have seen, the Arab-Islamic Empire played a pivotal role in the rise of the West. Fatalistic assumptions about the Muslim world that have tended to abound in the contemporary era, as the notion of the 'Arab predicament' illustrates, also depend to some extent on the assumption of a stagnant Middle East immune to reason, liberty and democracy.[93] When, as the chapters of this book demonstrate, this is confounded by the historical record. Philosophy as well as scientific inquiry existed alongside Islam in large part due to the belief in the human capacity for reason. Islam and faith in individual judgment were not considered incompatible. Moreover, rationalistic forms of authority and just leadership were at the heart of the triumph of the Arab-Islamic world.

The West as an independent pioneer of its own success is also problematized by this approach that stresses collective human civilization. Not only were advances in European knowledge built upon many contributions from the Arab-Islamic world, but trade and finance also flourished alongside Islam. Even the rationalization of the state so frequently believed to be inherent to the West, largely due to the influence of Weber on sociological thought, is rendered more complex when the role of the Arab-Islamic world in the rise of the West is acknowledged. By the tenth century, a unified body of laws, the *shari'ah,* was established throughout the Arab-Islamic Empire. This system of law has four pillars: divine revelation, the *sunna,* the words and deeds of the Prophet Muhammed, consensus and analogical reasoning. From the establishment of Islamic jurisprudence onwards legal scholars have sought to discern immutable ethical principles in the Quran that form the basis of the *shari'ah,* while allowing the means of applying them to be different according to different circumstances.[94] 'The overriding objectives are generally held to be the promotion of fairness, equality, prosperity, and human dignity, the establishment and maintenance of a government that consults the people, the prevention of injury, the removal of hardship, and moral education.'[95]

While the Arab-Islamic Empire and Christendom coexisted fairly peacefully for many centuries, as we have seen, Islam became Europe's formidable Other. This continued into contemporary times, as the perceived stagnant and despotic Muslim world became juxtaposed with a modern, progressive Europe. In this scheme, the West appeared to be starkly differentiated from the Muslim world. They were conceived as polar opposites, each with their distinct and radically different historical trajectories. This polarization has become largely naturalized and almost commonsensical. While some people may concede that at one time the Arab-Islamic Empire may well have been a beacon that lit up Europe, for the most part they adamantly insist that at some point the Muslim world took a different turn creating stark differences that are insurmountable. This view has gained even more prominence in relation to the rise of political Islam in recent times.

Building bridges is, therefore, essential. Gaining a more nuanced understanding of the Arab-Islamic world's contribution to the rise of the West serves several purposes. First, it helps Westerners to better understand their own position in world history – a history that is not synonymous with that of Europe – and, by so doing, exercising self-reflection. The wealth of exchanges and cultural borrowing that took place with the Arab-Islamic world is not only humbling, but also provides a basis upon which the West may more positively engage with the Muslim world. Knowing our common cultural heritage brings us closer together. We have philosophical, technological, scientific and commercial histories that are intertwined. Once we look back at the richness of our common history, we can see that assumptions made about Islam are also ill-founded. Above all, recognition of the role that the Arab-Islamic Empire played in the rise of the West helps to instil a respect for peoples of the Muslim world that has been sorely lacking. Despite the fact that the Muslim world has fallen on bad times, not in small part due to European colonialism and its aftermath, this does not mean that it is not a viable partner in today's world. The West has tended to view the Arab-Islamic world as peripheral, only gaining importance in relation to geo-strategic and energy concerns. However, as this book demonstrates, there is a much richer and fruitful basis upon which relations between the West and the Arab-Islamic world can and should be based.

Respect for Muslims and a recognition of Europe's debt and connection to the Arab-Islamic world also help to bring communities closer together in today's pluri-cultural societies. Islam in Europe, for example, is at present a controversial topic, raising fears and encouraging polemical discourses designed to play on those fears. The mistrust with which Muslims are often met contributes to their alienation. The lack of knowledge of Islam and Europe's debts to the Arab-Islamic world must seem astounding to Muslim immigrants, though not inexplicable when we consider that Islam has long been Europe's constructed Other. It also has a lot to do with the way that history is taught in schools – largely along Eurocentric lines. All of this, as Jack Goody rightly notes, has led to an 'implicit rejection' of the role of Islam in Europe.[96] As a result, Islam has come to be seen as something wholly Other. However, rather than being Judeo-Christian, Europe has been penetrated by Christianity, Judaism and Islam: 'they are all part of Europe, part of our heritage'.[97] This has a significance for those who seek to minimize the public space for Muslims in Europe as well those who claim that the European Union should be defined as Judeo-Christian and, therefore, exclude Turkey. The sense of rejection may also prompt Muslim immigrants to identify more strongly with Islam, as well as result in the burning of possible bridges. Recognizing the contributions of the Arab-Islamic Empire to the rise of Europe and the long-standing presence of Islam in Europe may assist in the acceptance and recognition of Islam in Europe in the present. As the chapters of this book show, there is a substantial basis upon which dialogue may occur and mutual respect may be enhanced. This is all the more important as the world moves forward with even more connectedness and interdependence than in the past.

Each of the chapters of this book focuses on a dimension of the rise of West. In Chapter 2, Jack Goody discusses the role that the Arab-Islamic world played in laying the foundations of the European Renaissance. The central place that the Arab-Islamic world had in the transmission, critique and elaboration of classical knowledge is highlighted, a body of knowledge that was not frozen but built upon by the Arabs and Muslims, who developed their own intellectual traditions in a myriad of fields. In Chapter 3, Frédérique Guerin then discusses the impact the Arab-Islamic world had on the Reformation in Europe, problematizing the dominant historiography of the sixteenth-century reform movement within European Christendom and arguing for a 're-orienting' of the Reformation that may have been inspired by Islam. In Chapter 4, Lisa Watanabe examines the possible influence of Islamic legal institutions on the emergence of a rule of law in Europe, in particular in medieval England, which themselves contributed to the development of the modern, impersonalized state and capitalist social relations. This is then followed by a chapter by John M. Hobson on commerce and finance in the Arab-Islamic Empire and their influence on the development of commercial and financial institutions in Europe, as well as their critical role in enabling and maintaining an emergent global economy. Samar Attar then discusses the influence of Muslim scholars on the development of European philosophical ideas associated with the Enlightenment and modernity. Focusing in particular on the way in which Ibn Tufayl's thinking influenced what is often thought of as a quintessentially European rationalist philosophy, a dimension of the transition from Classical Antiquity to the Renaissance in Europe that is conventionally overlooked in dominant Western accounts of the European Enlightenment. This is followed by a chapter by Mohammad-Mahmoud Ould Mohamedou on the impact of ideas from the Arab-Islamic Empire on humanism and education in Europe. Finally, Mohammed Abattouy outlines the debt that the West owes to the Arab-Islamic world for the transmission of scientific knowledge in pre-modern Europe and argues that recognition of such a debt is critical to the development of a universal history of science. Each of the above-mentioned authors not only provides a strong critique of Eurocentric interpretations of the rise of the West, recovering the Arab-Islamic world's role in its success, but also reflects on the many ways in which East to West transmission of ideas, techniques and institutions provides the basis for common ground, mutual respect and recognition, and the foundations for cultural dialogue and positive engagement between the West and the Muslim world.

Notes

1. W. Montgomery Watt (1972), *The Influence of Islam on Medieval Europe* (Edinburgh: University of Edinburgh Press), pp. 9–10.
2. N. R. F. Al-Rodhan (2009), *Sustainable History and the Dignity of Man. A Philosophy of History and Civilisational Triumph* (Berlin: LIT), pp. 142–3, 148.
3. De Lacy O'Leary (2003), *Arabic Thought and Its Place in History* (New York: Dover Publications), p. 105.
4. M. Graham (2006), *How Islam Created the Modern World* (Maryland: Amana Publications), p. 159.
5. Al-Rodhan, *Sustainable History and the Dignity of Man*, p. 147.
6. FSTC Limited, 'The Impact of Translations of Muslim Sciences on the West', MuslimHeritage.Com, 4 March 2003.
7. See, for example, J. A. Makdisi (1999), 'The Islamic Origins of the Common Law', *North Carolina Law Review*, Vol. 77, No. 5, pp. 1635–739.

8. See, for example, J. Goody (2009), *The Theft of History* (Cambridge: Cambridge University Press); J. M. Hobson (2004), *The Eastern Origins of Western Civilisation* (Cambridge: Cambridge University Press); J. Goody (2004), *Islam in Europe* (Polity Press); J. Goody (2010), *Renaissances: The One or the Many?* (Cambridge: Cambridge University Press); R. van der Weyer (2002), *The Shared Well: A Concise Guide to Relations between Islam and the West* (Washington: Brassey's Inc.); Watt (1972), *The Influence of Islam on Medieval Europe*; J. Freely (2009), *Aladdin's Lamp: How Greek Science Came to Europe through the Islamic World* (New York: Alfred A. Knopf); M. H. Morgan (2007), *Lost History: The Enduring Legacy of Muslim Scientists, Thinkers, and Artists* (Washington, DC: National Geographic); S. Attar (2007), *The Vital Roots of European Enlightenment: Ibn Tufayl's Influence on Modern Western Thought* (Lanham: Lexington Books); T. Wallace-Murphy (2006), *What Islam Did for Us: Understanding Islam's Contribution to Western Civilization* (London: Watkins Publishing); G. Saliba (2007), *Islamic Science and the Making of the European Renaissance* (Cambridge, Mass.: The MIT Press); M. Graham (2006), *How Islam Created the Modern World* (Beltsville, MD: Amana Publications); B. Bowden (2007), 'The River of Inter-civilisational Relations: The Ebb and Flow of Peoples, Ideas and Innovations', *Third World Quarterly*, Vol. 28, No. 7, pp. 1359–74.
9. Watt, *The Influence of Islam on Medieval Europe*, p. 80.
10. E. W. Said (1979), *Orientalism* (New York: Vintage Books).
11. Goody, *The Theft of History*, p. 26.
12. Ibid., p. 68.
13. B. S. Turner (ed.) (2003), *Islam: Critical Concepts in Sociology* (London: Routledge), p. 3; G. Masur (1962), 'Distinctive Traits of Western Civilization: through the Eyes of Western Historians', *The American Historical Review*, Vol. 67, No. 3, p. 604.
14. M. Weber (1992), *Histoire économique: esquisse d'une histoire universelle de l'économie et de la societé*, translated by C. Bouchindhomme, preface by P. Raynaud (N. R. F. Gallimard), pp. 356–60, 377.
15. M. Weber (2002), *The Protestant Ethic and the 'Spirit' of Capitalism and Other Writings*, edited and translated by P. R. Baehr and G. C. Wells (New York: Penguin Books), pp. 6–7; Weber, *Histoire économique*, pp. 385–6.
16. Goody, *The Theft of History*, p. 84.
17. K. Marx (1853), 'The British Rule in India', *New York Daily Tribune*, 25 June; Andre Gunder Frank (1998), *ReOrient: Global Economy in the Asian Age* (London: University of California Press), p. 14.
18. Gunder Frank, *ReOrient*, pp. 14–15, 17.
19. Masur, 'Distinctive Traits of Western Civilization', p. 604.
20. Ibid., p. 593.
21. Ibid., pp. 604–5.
22. O. Spengler (1991), *The Decline of the West: An Abridged Edition* (Oxford: Oxford University Press), pp. 12–13.
23. Ibid., 410.
24. A. J. Toynbee (1946), *A Study of History: Abridgement of Volumes I-VI* by D. C. Sommervell (New York and Oxford: Oxford University Press).
25. Goody, *The Theft of History*, pp. 191, 194–7, 201; F. Braudel (1995), *A History of Civilizations* (New York: Penguin Books), pp. 50, 64, 316–21, 374, 388.

26. C. M. Cipolla (1993), *Before the Industrial Revolution: European Society and Economy 1000–1700*, 3rd edn (London: Routledge), pp. 117–18.
27. Ibid., pp. 120–2.
28. Ibid., p. 161.
29. Ibid., p. 150.
30. D. S. Landes (1998), *The Wealth and Poverty of Nations: Why Some Are So Rich and Some So Poor* (Little, Brown and Company), p. xxi.
31. Ibid.
32. Ibid.
33. T. E. Huff (2011), *Intellectual Curiosity and the Scientific Revolution: A Global Perspective* (New York: Cambridge University Press).
34. Ibid., p. 7.
35. Ibid., p. 14.
36. Ibid., pp. 299–300.
37. Ibid., p. 8.
38. Gunder Frank, *ReOrient*, pp. 3–5, 19.
39. J. Abu-Lughold, (1989) *Before European Hegemony* (Oxford: Oxford University Press), pp. 4–19.
40. J. M. Blaut (1993), *The Colonizer's Model of the World: Geographical Diffusionism and Eurocentric History* (New York: Guildford Press), p. 51.
41. K. Pommeranz (2001), *The Great Divergence: China, Europe, and the Making of the Modern World Economy* (Princeton: Princeton University Press), pp. 31–47.
42. J. Goldstone (2009), *Why Europe? The Rise of the West in World History, 1500–1850* (New York: McGraw Hill), pp. 166–9.
43. H. F. Cohen (2010), *How Modern Science Came into the World: Four Civilizations, One 17th-Century Breakthrough* (Amsterdam: Amsterdam University Press).
44. Ibid., pp. xiii, xv, xxiv.
45. Ibid., pp. 726–7.
46. W. R. Shea (2011), 'Galileo Then and Now: A Review Essay', *Historically Speaking*, June, p. 26.
47. Cohen, *How Modern Science Came into the World*, p. 732.
48. Hobson, *The Eastern Origins of Western Civilisation.*
49. Ibid., p. 5.
50. Ibid., pp. 2–3.
51. Ibid., p. 34.
52. Ibid., pp. 37–8.
53. Ibid., pp. 43–4; Morgan, *Lost History*, p. 88.
54. Hobson, *The Eastern Origins of Western Civilisation*, pp. 116–21.
55. Ibid., pp. 68–9.
56. Hobson, *The Eastern Origins of Western Civilisation*, pp. 102–7, 113–4.
57. Goody, *The Theft of History*, pp. 68–9.
58. Ibid., p. 97.
59. Ibid., pp. 72–3.
60. Ibid., p. 48.
61. Ibid., p. 58.
62. Goody, *Islam in Europe*, p. 60.
63. Goody, *Renaissances*, pp. 36–7; S. T. S. Al-Hassani, E. Woodcock and R. Saoud (eds) (2007), *1001 Inventions: Muslim Heritage in Our World*, 2nd

edn (Manchester: Foundation for Science Technology and Civilisation), pp. 93–5.
64. Goody, *Renaissances*, p. 46
65. Ibid., p. 56.
66. Ibid., p. 57.
67. Ibid., pp. 62, 87.
68. van der Weyer, *The Shared Well*, pp. 27–41.
69. Ibid., p. 42.
70. R. El Diwani (2005), 'Islamic Contributions to the West', paper presented at Lake Superior State University, p. 9.
71. van der Weyer, *The Shared Well*, p. 45.
72. Diwani, 'Islamic Contributions to the West', p. 9.
73. Watt, *The Influence of Islam on Medieval Europe*, p. 59.
74. Ibid., pp. 64–5.
75. Ibid., pp. 63–4.
76. Goody, *Renaissances*, pp. 44, 47–9, 51.
77. Ibid., pp. 55, 57.
78. Hobson, *The Eastern Origins of Western Civilisation*, p. 179.
79. Diwani, 'Islamic Contributions to the West', p. 11.
80. Watt, *The Influence of Islam on Medieval Europe*, p. 67.
81. Ibid., pp. 73, 77.
82. Ibid., p. 82.
83. Ibid., p. 84.
84. Al-Rodhan, *Sustainable History and the Dignity of Man*, p. 137.
85. Ibid., p. 138.
86. Ibid., p. 36.
87. Ibid., p. 138.
88. I. A. Khan (1992), *Authentification of Hadith: Redefining the Criteria* (Bangalore: Iqra Welfare Trust), pp. XIII–VI.
89. H. N. Rafiabadi (2002), *Emerging from Darkness: Ghazzali's Impact on the Western Philosophers* (New Delhi: Sarup and Sons), p. 3.
90. O'Leary, *Arabic Thought and Its Place in History*, pp. 280, 286.
91. Morgan, *Lost History*, p. 104.
92. S. Hunke, (1997) *Le Soleil d'Allah brille sur l'Occident*, (Paris: Éditions Albin Michel) pp. 23–6.
93. N. R. F. Al-Rodhan, G. P. Herd and L. Watanabe (2011), *Critical Turning Points in the Middle East: 1915–2015* (Basingstoke: Palgrave Macmillan).
94. van der Weyer, *The Shared Well*, pp. 46–7.
95. Ibid., p. 47.
96. Goody, *Islam in Europe*, p. 13.
97. Ibid., p. 14.

2
The Arabs and the Italian Renaissance

Jack Goody

The word Renaissance is taken in the West to mean the Italian Renaissance, the rebirth of classical European culture after a long period dominated by the Christian Church. A church that, in some significant respects, tried to set aside the pagan, non-Christian, heritage of Greece and Rome, doing away with both its gods and its secular tradition of knowledge. Essentially the rebirth was a revival of the classical, largely secular culture, which left room for Christianity and, indeed, promoted it worldwide, at the same time carving out a space for writing about nature, science and natural science, which had taken very much a back-seat in the Middle Ages. For the Bible had said all that was necessary on the subject and further enquiry was not encouraged.

It was not much different with Judaism and Islam, except that in the Near East Abbasid Islam welcomed the classical knowledge that Orthodox Christianity had largely rejected and scholars were sent to centres of learning, including to Byzantium, to collect classical manuscripts and have them translated into Arabic. In this way, important scientific texts were preserved and, subsequently, found their way to the West, stimulating attempts to recover other work in the early Renaissance in Europe. This knowledge was not frozen, but was built on by the Muslim world in various ways and they developed their own traditions in astronomy, medicine, geography and timekeeping, all activities that chimed with the interests of the Islamic world and fed into those of the European Renaissance.

I want to emphasize that there was nothing specifically European about the idea of a Renaissance, a rebirth. It could and did happen in any literate culture, because then one could look back and revive the written past (the word) in a way that is impossible in a purely oral culture. Oral memory works in a different way from archival memory, as psychologists such as Frederic Bartlett and Ulric Neisser have emphasized.[1] You cannot look back on oral culture in the same way, since it is always changing or has disappeared. The idea of a relatively fixed traditional culture works for certain technological features, but not for others.

The essential feature behind the extension of knowledge and the arts in such a Renaissance is the flowering of the economy. That seems to be a *sine qua non* of much secondary activity, by which I refer only to the need for literary or artistic specialists to be supported by the rest of the community. Of course, in many ways, education supports the other secondary activities; and so too do the arts.

The Islamic world comprised not only Arabs, although Arabic was the language of the sacred book, but also Persians, who were speakers of an Indo-European language, as were the northern Indians, as well as some in the Eurasian corridor, all of whom developed literacy and a scientific culture, which then, in turn, fed into the Near East and into the Arabic world.

Most notable were the so-called Arabic numerals (in fact of Indian origin) and the concept of zero, so essential for European mathematics, which Needham saw as critical to the whole enterprise of what he called 'modern science'. Indeed, it is difficult to see how the West could have made progress in this field on the basis of the clumsy Roman numerals that we now use only for gravestones and monuments, that is, for prestige rather than for calculation. The East, from and through Islam, made substantial contributions to mathematics before the Italian Renaissance, the contributions coming from both India and China, written cultures, which had their own Renaissances and assisted in ours.

They did this largely through the intermediacy of Islam, which had been accepted by a huge swathe of peoples, stretching from the Atlantic and southern Spain to the borders of China; indeed, there was a mosque in Beijing and the Three Jewelled Eunuch, who led a famous seafaring expedition to Africa, was himself a Muslim, like many members of his crew. They had much contact with their compatriots at Malacca in present-day Malaysia, a staging post not only for the Portuguese and the Dutch going to the East, especially the East Indies, but long before to the Arabs travelling to Canton shortly after the time of the Prophet himself. He and members of his family were engaged in trade and it was through traders that some important contributions probably came to the West. One thinks particularly of the compass, so useful for travellers by sea, who need to navigate out of sight of land. Because of its lines of communication between China, India, the Near East and Spain, Islam was able to transmit technology and knowledge between the East and the West, giving it an understanding of the terrain involved and producing significant advances in the science of geography in which its scholars were much valued. Islam needed this knowledge not only because of its 'worldwide' trade, but also because Muslims had always to know the direction to Mecca, so they could orient themselves for the daily prayers, as well as to be aware of the route to travel to make the annual pilgrimage, the *Hajj*. Indeed, in West Africa, Muslims often kept an itinerary of the towns they had to pass through in order to make their way to Mecca, a primitive map to indicate one's personal journey.

One major means by which such knowledge was transmitted was on paper. This the West had not enjoyed until it arrived from China through Islam. Before that, Europe had to import Egyptian papyrus, use wax tablets or slates or process parchment out of animal skins. Only with the arrival of paper in the thirteenth century was there material cheap enough to provide an easy material for everyday writing, as well as official record keeping and the production of books. The difference this made to the flow and consideration of information was enormous. At the turn of the first millennium, the largest library in Christian Europe was that of St. Gall in Switzerland, where the monastery had some 800 volumes. The library of Cordoba had some 400,000 (600,000 according to another source), an enormous difference in scale, which also marked the comparative availability of knowledge in the different cultures. Moreover, whereas in Europe the books were held by the monastery, Cordoba was a royal library; there was restricted access in both, but in the second case it was more open and subject to secular rather than religious control. In the duality of religious (monastic) and secular (royal) power, it was the latter that was more open to the growth of knowledge, since it was not usually held back by the limitations of beliefs. However, in Cordoba the difference had more to do with their books being made of cheaper paper, from rags and other fibres, rather than from expensive skins expensively worked; also, the fact that Islam could draw on knowledge extending from Europe to China, long before the trader, Marco Polo, and the occasional Franciscan friar reported on their journeys to the East. That not only widened the scope of their knowledge of the world, including the construction of 'universal' histories like that of Rashid Al-Din in the fourteenth century and of geographical information like that of Al-Idrisi in the twelfth, but also meant that Islam could act as intermediary and transmitter of part of Chinese science and technology, not only of paper, as we have seen, but of Chinese art and even block printing (for banknotes), which it soon rejected. Yet, Persian art was much influenced, despite the Islamic ban on representations.

The information contained in those books in Cordoba related to medicine and to astronomy, as well as to geography and history. Medicine had developed in conjunction with that of the Christians and Jews who depended upon classical medicine, elaborated in the schools and hospitals of Gondeshapur, as well as in Syria; especially in Baghdad in the case of the latter. To this the Muslims added, making use of the Persian knowledge developed from earlier civilizations, as well as the contributions from the Indian tradition through that town and through Persia as a whole. The Muslims brought it all together in their hospitals and passed it on to the West, including the organization of hospitals themselves. They transmitted this knowledge partly through the publication of medical works, which were widely consulted; indeed, many were standard teaching texts in Medieval Europe, especially the many works of Galen and Hippocrates.

The translating into Arabic of classical scientific texts had begun before the Abbasids (750–1258), who wanted a link with the previous pre-Islamic regime, and especially with the Magi (Magians) in Khorasan, an earlier centre of Graeco-Bactrian learning. This continuation was partly due to the exporting trade flowing eastwards, as well as to the encouragement of the scholarship and arts, not only by the Abbasids, but by their viziers, the Barmakids, formerly a Bactrian family of eminent Buddhist priests. The caliph had translated Aristotelian logic, Ptolemy's *Almagest* and Euclid's *Elements*. In fact, almost all classical works on science were translated from the Greek, as well as others from Sanskrit, much being done by the Christian community of Nestorians, who had been excluded from the West and who had earlier translated the works of Galen into Syriac. The translations included Indian texts, which then made their way into the European corpus, including the all-important Arabic (and Indian) numerals.

Knowledge of the human body was restricted, as it was in all the Abrahamic religions and Hinduism, by the ban on dispersing and cutting up the body. Only in Egypt was that knowledge acquired, where dissection was included in the ancient tradition of embalming. Galen's anatomy was based on dissecting monkeys. Yet, work on humans themselves was conducted in the new anatomy theatres of Bologna and Padua, which had links with Salerno, much influenced by Islamic medicine. Abulcassis did make a start. Europe's first theatres were constructed under tiered structures, in which it was the barber/surgeon who had a special dispensation to cut up the bodies, while the professor explained what he was doing.

Astronomy was similarly developed in specialist institutions, like the observatories at Maraghah in western Iran with all their specialist equipment, which again was a model for the West. That too, was knowledge that contributed to the Renaissance. Indeed, it has been claimed that the theories of Galileo and Copernicus, so central to the new learning, were prefigured by Islamic astronomers, especially Ibn Al-Shatir (1304–75) and Nasir Al-Din Al-Tusi (1201–74). Their work was translated by the Byzantines into Greek and, ultimately, reached Copernicus and others, who employed some of its aspects. The clear skies of the East clearly helped in their study, and this interest was embodied in a number of important mechanical devices, like the astrolabe, whose advent was celebrated by Geoffrey Chaucer in the fourteenth century.

By that time, Arabic science had started to flow to the West, partly through the reconquest of Muslim territories in Spain and Sicily. Toledo, becoming Christian with the Reconquista, was the centre of the translation movement in Spain, attracting a flock of Christian scholars to translate various Arabic works, including important contributions from classical Europe preserved through the earlier Abbasid translation movement. Many of these were translated by Gerard of Cremona (1114–87) under the patronage of the bishops after the Reconquista by Alphonso of Castille in 1085, an activity that had some impact on the early Renaissance of the twelfth century in Europe.

The Arabic works of Al-Razi and Ibn Sina were especially important. Many translations were made by Constantine the African, who took up residence in Monte Cassino during the eleventh century. Outside the medical sphere, there were the important translations of Aristotle, whose works became known after the taking of Toledo and advanced the direction of scientific thinking; Adelard of Bath went to the town to translate Euclid's *Elements* and Al-Khwarizmi's tables, leading to a more scientific spurt of enquiry in the work of Roger Bacon and others. Gerard of Cremona translated some 87 works, including Ptolemy's *Almagest* and works of Avicenna, Galen and Hippocrates, Al-Razi and Al-Farabi were credited to him. The work of translators included the very influential Averroës in the twelfth century, who made many commentaries on Aristotle, paraphrased Plato's *Republic*, as well as studying meteorology and medicine, especially important for the history of the West. Also important was the medical work of Abulcassis (Abu Al-Qasim), who produced a medical encyclopaedia in 30 volumes and was the first to use surgery, in cauterization, for example.

Other scholars went to the environs of Barcelona to the north, like Gerbert of Aurillac, later Pope Sylvester II. He had been a pupil in Clermont Ferrand and had taken up residence in a Spanish monastery to become acquainted with Islamic knowledge. In the same way, a teacher of Dante became an envoy to Spain and, thereby, absorbed parts of Arabic culture, which may have influenced his pupil. Nor was this culture all scientific. The courts of Muslim Spain and Christian Europe participated in similar activities. Singers crossed from one court to another, taking songs with them. It was in this way that, in the twelfth century, at a time when Europeans considered they had invented love, songs embodying romantic ideas were sung in both courts, having been influenced by the long Islamic tradition of such sentiments, crystallized in this case in the work of Ibn Hazm (994–1064). This influence revived an interest in the kind of song that had earlier inspired the poetry of Ovid.

This was just one aspect of oriental culture that may have affected the West. It is said that the Crusaders were much impressed by the comparative luxury of the bourgeoisie in the East and that they brought back some aspects to their spartan homes in the West. Contact with the Muslims by the Crusaders and in Spain helped diffuse citrus fruit (in the orangeries of elite houses) and rice, along with culinary practices such as the employment of almond milk, saffron, rosewater and the widespread use of sugar. The Muslim elite were looked upon as more luxurious than that of the West. Fulcher of Chartres, a chronicler of the First Crusade writing after 1100, claimed that the attractions of the East meant that Westerners had become Easterners. This may even have been the case with baths, which had not formed a prominent part of early Christian culture. In these times, the Roman bath at Verulamium, now St. Albans, was left to decay or was actually pulled down, like the theatre, as a sign of Roman paganism. Baths were also associated with the Jewish *mishna*, quite apart from a belief in the harmful effect of too much bathing. Bathing for the nobility returned, but for the rest of the population, public baths were latecomers to the West. Even in the East, they disappeared at Ephesus, only to be reinstated under the Turks as a *hammam*, which provided an occasion for public meetings and discussion.

In some other respects, the East was a source of luxury culture. The gardens of Rome and the flowers in Roman cemeteries had been seen – and would again be seen by the Puritans – as a pagan gesture, worshipping the dead rather than the one and only Abrahamic God. Thus, flowers were not grown for ceremonies, although they later made their way into Catholic rituals. Consequently, gardens were only notional, like the Garden of Eden. Their revival in the West was greatly stimulated by the actual gardens of the Near East that were to be found in Persia and elsewhere.

It could be said that in many ways Islam was equally as puritanical as Christianity, rejecting offerings to the deity in the same monotheistic spirit, as well as prohibiting the representation of God's creation (as in Judaism or early Christianity). However, courts largely escaped these restrictions, encouraging not only poetry, and sometimes singing, but also allowing a limited representation and even the portrait of Mohammad II by Gentile Bellini (in the Venetian fashion), much to the more orthodox disapproval of the former's successor. Other luxury behaviour, such as the use of perfume, only reached the Christian West much later and, again, was often rejected in Puritan circles. In some respects, the Islamic courts were more permissive than those of the West and transmitted their practices to western bourgeoisie.

An aspect of this luxury is seen in the hybrid activities of the Norman court in Palermo, Sicily. Hybrid because the Normans had taken it over from the Muslims and their architecture contributed greatly to the later court. So too did the scholars and scientists who assembled there, some of whom remained after the rulers had left. As in the case of Al-Idrisi, the famous geographer who wrote his great work, *The Book of Roger*, under Norman rule. Michael Scot, the reputed magician, came there to study in 1220. It was the possible birthplace of certain forms of later Italian poetry as well as being an important influence on the practice of medicine at Salerno, reputedly the oldest medical school in Europe. Nearby, the Abbey of Monte Cassino was the home of Constantine the African, who composed or translated a number of medical works, which became so basic in teaching in Europe.

For medical education, Salerno competed with the University of Montpellier in the south of France. Montpellier was a Christian establishment, its degrees approved by the bishop of the town. Yet, its medicine was much influenced by the presence of a number of Jewish doctors at hand in other towns, who were, in their turn, reinforced by the great tradition of Arab-Jewish scholarship that existed in Andalusia and was dispersed in various directions by the Christian Reconquista of the country. Some practitioners and scholars fled to southern France, where they practised medicine (though the Christians were not always welcoming), and they had their own synagogues and schools. There they joined their co-religionists in Lunel and other towns and translated a number of works in Arabic, including Galen and Aristotle, but also Averroës, Al-Razi and Maimonides.

It was not only medical works that circulated. There was little call for the specifically religious in the West, but the work of the alchemists attracted much attention. While there were other traditions, this one gave the field its name. It invoked both the search for wealth and for health, for the secret of changing base metal into gold and the secret of eternal, or at least long, life. This search resulted in many experiments, in the development of laboratory apparatus and some have seen in it the foundation of modern chemistry; indeed, the experimental approach altogether. Alchemy was one of the roots of the empirical procedures attempted by modern science. The German writer, Agricola (Georg Bauer), who wrote extensively on mine production in sixteenth-century Europe was very sceptical about the theories of the alchemists. However, his editor, Henry Hoover, considers him almost one of them. In any case, this work not only had a profound influence on European practitioners, but also the re-emergence of science after the long sleep of natural enquiry in the Middle Ages.

As far as science is concerned, the Abbasid regime in Baghdad took up the translation of Greek and Roman works with enthusiasm, leading scholars to search for manuscripts through the area. In this, they were aided by the fact that Byzantine Christians at times adopted a purist view to their faith, attempting to set aside the works of the classicists in favour of specifically Christian literature. For this search they employed many former Nestorian Christians in the great library of the House of Wisdom in Baghdad, like Hunayn (809–73), who could put the texts into Arabic. In this way, almost every classical text of this kind was preserved so that versions translated into a western European language could be available at the Italian Renaissance. Yet, this was already an Islamic Renaissance, because Arabic-Islamic literacy permitted the 'resurrection' of 'dead' works, and they led to the continuation of enquiry, especially in the fields that particularly interested Islam, namely medicine, astronomy/astrology and the study of space. The results were largely disseminated in regal libraries, for which they could be copied onto the paper now being produced so widely in the Near East. Paper-making spread through Islamic countries to Spain and then to Italy, where its manufacture benefited from the use of non-human energy in the shape of ample water power, which was rare in the Near East, but plentiful in northern Europe, where the industry was newly developed.

It was this adaptation of many Near Eastern industries to the new and cheaper production techniques of the north that spurred on development in that area. The Near East had experienced its own Renaissance and advancement of learning under the Abbasids, perhaps its own Reformation under the Sunnis, which certainly brought in a more orthodox element, partly leading to a brake upon new knowledge. Yet, it eventually produced an economic revolution, if not an industrial one.

Even when links with Europe had diminished, the Near East maintained communication with India and beyond. Indeed, Islam itself had spread into north India, which developed ties with Persia and with that branch of Muslim learning. Islam even reached the gates of China and penetrated the interior. Indeed, there were mosques in Guangzhou (Canton), for the Muslim sailors and merchants, and in Beijing. Arab and Islamic traders continued to exchange both with India and with China, and, although it could send very little to Europe, it could consume more itself. Trade and industry flourished under the Abbasids, and permitted the Islamic Renaissance of the translation movement and beyond. Later, in Egypt under the Mamluks, trade was again a substantial activity that led to the growth of the bourgeoisie.

The historian of the Near Eastern economy, Eliyahu Ashtor, writes of that growth in Syria. They employed *condottieri*, and had a life and polity comparable to their counterparts in the Italian city states.[2] Indeed, at one point, they took over the government of their towns. There is plenty of evidence that a substantial bourgeoisie existed in the Near East (and elsewhere), not solely in the 'capitalist' West. The historian, Shelomo Dov Goitein, speaks in these terms of the Jewish communities in Cairo in the context of the Geniza documents, which show the constant trade with India at the time.[3] Some of this trade was in the hands of Karimi merchants, originally protectors of caravans, later traders themselves. These traders built large houses and contributed to public monuments, like mosques, behaving in many ways like the bourgeoisie in European towns proceeding by, what he calls, 'rational accounting' methods. They exploited not only trading but banking and manufacturing as well, although that activity was also carried out by royal workshops, as was the case elsewhere, in France, Germany and even Britain. That 'rational accounting' was an inheritance from the Roman and Ancient Near Eastern writers, including versions of the *commenda* and joint trading voyages. Equally, some industrial activities were organized on a considerable scale as in the royal factories in *tiraz* ('a type of embroidery'). Yet, although they reached a high level of commercial and industrial activity, it was insufficient to rival the success of Europe, though it did stimulate it. Europe had the natural resources, which the Near East lacked, in particular the metals and the coal to smelt them. Nor did it have the water power to drive the host of mills of all sorts that appeared in Europe. Gradually, the products in which the Near East had specialized were taken over and produced more cheaply: paper, which was now made there (and exported); and the production of silk and cotton. In many ways, their importation from the Near East and the automated production of textiles that followed, was the focal point of the so-called Industrial Revolution. Although the Near East and India had developed these materials it was the energy and the machines that enabled Europe to take over their production and make cheaper goods using the cheaper, non-human, energy, which was found in profusion along with the iron needed for the machines. European advantage was quite specific, not the result of a particular form of ethics nor of an inevitable progression towards capitalism. The Islamic world also had its quota of traders, bankers and manufacturers. It also had a manufacturing industry, in the form of textiles of linen, cotton, silk and wool, as well as soap and glass. All these industries were taken over by the West and helped to finance their own Renaissance out of the profits, both through the exchange and manufacture of goods and through trade with the East, partly for the spices, cloths and perfumes, This trade later became a target of 'import substitution' and the manufacture of goods was practised by mechanised methods. The Near East had its own advances in the manufacturing industry, as Ashtor points out, putting them on the road to 'capitalism'.[4] However, they could not keep up with the metal-based, factory production of Europe.

One of the contributions of Islam and the Near East to this flourishing of the Renaissance in Europe was its early demand for European products, especially for metals. Despite inaugurating the Bronze Age the Ancient Near East had few metals, either precious or everyday ones, so these had to be imported, especially from the West. This later remained true for the Arabs who could not develop their manufacturing industry because of this shortage, unlike 'barbarian' Europe, which was conveniently well provided with the metals that were essential for 'modernity'.[5]

They utilized a variety of sources. One important one was Venice, which drew upon the resources of the Tyrol, Southern Germany and Austria. These metals consisted of silver, as well as non-precious ores. Gold came from the West African mines and made its way directly to Cairo. It was this trade, together with its counterpart in spices, silk and perfume, that fed the trade with Venice, which was so important that it even had an inn (*Fondaco dei Tedeschi*) for the German merchants coming from the North, as well as a *Fondaco dei Turchi* for those coming from the East. The latter had a *hammam*, as well as a mosque, and gave hospitality to the Muslim traders. Dürer went there in Muslim garb. The commerce was very profitable for the Venetians, who monopolized the Mediterranean trade with their armed fleet built in their industrialized arsenal, guarded against pirates of all nationalities and engaged in the well-paid transport of pilgrims. Venice was the essential intermediary in all this exchange, re-introducing and developing a banking system at the Champagne fairs and then on the Rialto to finance the trade on behalf of its rich merchants (also patrons of its luxury art), stimulating the Italian Renaissance in numerous ways – including providing double-entry book-keeping, so prominent in the eyes of European historians as a model of rational procedures. Certainly the influence of secular life was prominent in Venice with its close contacts with the East, this so concerned the Vatican that, at one time, it led to its temporary exclusion from the Christian community.

At the Renaissance, Florence also got rich on its treatment and export of wool. The Near East had produced wool and woollen goods from earlier times; this had formed the basis of the Assyrian exports to Kanesh for Anatolian metals. However, the wool in tropical countries was far less rich than in the North, especially that of Britain from where the most prized material came, to be washed and treated in the river flowing through Prato, next to Florence. This highly-valued product was the foundation of the Medici wealth, as well as that of the merchant of Prato himself. They exported many woollen products to the East, in return for the much-valued spices, as well as some textiles from the Orient, especially silk, until that was eventually copied in the West, including the process of growing the mulberry and breeding the silkworm. Carpets remained an esteemed import and frequently appear in Renaissance paintings as the symbol of eastern luxury, as was the case with the spices, which were shipped through Arab lands and were a major reason for Europe's trade with that area. Nor was this trade simply a matter of material goods as we have seen. In the case of Florence, it led to contacts with the Muslim world, as well as with the eastern Christians of Constantinople, and it was from there, as it was being surrounded by Turkish Muslim forces, that scholars brought additions to Greek learning. The Medicis called them to the West and, as a result, a number of Greek scholars, such as Argyropoulus came to teach at the Platonic academy. The necessary texts had been faithfully preserved in Byzantium, despite the burning of the books and the closure of colleges as the result of the Iconoclastic movement of the eighth century, which would have been an even worse disaster had so much of the knowledge not been preserved in Arabic translation. This was an important connection that stimulated the Italian Renaissance. Yet, above all, it was the trade with the East that brought wealth to the Italian city states and encouraged them to patronize that movement and to steer it towards a degree of secularism, or at least to breaking the hold of the church on art and learning.

This is something that the Arabs certainly contributed to the Italian Renaissance. Not only did they have their own revival, not so much of their own earlier achievement, but of the science of Greece and Rome, preserving part of that achievement to be later resurrected, but there was its own not inconsiderable achievements in astronomy, in some ways preceding Copernicus, the focus of the new science, in formulating a heliocentric theory, as well as in medicine, helping to restart surgery and anticipating William Harvey's theory of the circulation of the blood, as well as advancing on a number of other fronts, including medical training and hospital organization. The pulmonary circulation had already been described by Ibn Al-Nafis, who may have influenced the theologian-doctor, Michael Servetus, whom Calvin had burnt at the stake. There was certainly a drop in activity from the twelfth century. Yet, this did not imply a total drying up of scholars there or of research.

One area on which Islam had little influence in the Italian Renaissance was that of the pictorial arts. The obvious reason was that Islam followed the Abrahamic prohibition on figurative representation, although it did develop some in Persia, stimulated by China. However, abstract art was cultivated in Islam and had widespread repercussions, especially on Venetian metalwork. Italian painting and even the centres of troubadour song may have been similarly influenced. Yet, the important achievement, apart from philosophy and religious thought largely prohibited in the medieval West, except in the form of saints' tales (which were meant to be true). Islam was almost as restrictive, except for the Indian influence. However, it was largely in terms of scientific works, rather than the more frivolous arts (except for the art of bourgeois living) that Islam made its extensive contribution to the Italian Renaissance.

Recognition of the contribution of the Arab and Islamic world to the European Renaissance encourages a different way of conceiving of the rise of Europe and more generally the West, in which the Italian Renaissance was critical, that calls into question the popularly accepted idea that Europe made phenomenal strides towards modernity in a completely autonomous manner. In fact, Europe is indebted to the Arab and Islamic world, as the latter was to ancient Indian and Chinese civilizations. The intertwined histories of the West and the Near East have a richness with very contemporary relevance. Not only does it help to break down stereotypes about the Islamic world, which had its own flowering of knowledge and Renaissance, but also prompts a better understanding of that of the West and its historical trajectory. That trajectory was tied up with the fact that the Bronze Age, which established urban culture and writing in the Ancient Near East had no metals in the river valleys and had to seek these from the 'barbarians' in the hills. When metals became intrinsic to developing industrial manufacture and new weaponry the 'barbarians' took over and the Near East could not then keep up. Oil has tended to compensate for that lack, but any later intellectual advantage of the West has to be seen in this context.

Notes

1. F. C. Bartlett (1932), *Remembering: A Study in Experimental and Social Psychology* (Cambridge: Cambridge University Press); U. Neisser (1982), *Memory Observed: Remembering in Natural Contexts* (New York: Freeman).
2. E. Ashtor (1976), *A Social and Economic History of the Near East in the Middle Ages* (London: Collins).
3. S. D. Goitein (1967), *A Mediterranean Society: The Jewish Communities of the Arab World as Portrayed in the Documents of the Cairo Geniza. Volume One: Economic Foundations* (Berkeley: University of California Press).
4. Ashtor, *A Social and Economic History.*
5. J. Goody (forthcoming) *The Pursuit of Metals* (Cambridge: Cambridge University Press).

3

Re-orienting the Reformation? Prolegomena to a History of the Reformation's Connection with the Islamic World

Frédérique Guerin

There is arguably no more Western historical event than the sixteenth-century reform movement within European Christendom that later became known as the Reformation. Traditionally defined as 'the rise of an evangelical Christianity that could not accommodate itself to the old theology and ecclesiastical institutions'[1] and limited to the years 1500–1650, the Reformation is considered by mainstream historiography as a development that was instrumental in the advent of Western modernity. The Protestant Reformation is believed to have contributed to the emergence of the nation state in Europe through the process of confessionalization, to have freed European political and social institutions from an ecclesiastic grip, to have introduced the principles of religious tolerance and liberty of conscience resulting in a new emphasis on individualism, and, ultimately, to have created a new work ethic, which enabled the rise of modern capitalism.[2] To Western historians, the Protestant Reformation is, therefore, much more than a theological reform of medieval Christianity. The forces unleashed by the confessional battles are assumed to have contributed to shaping the identity of continental Europe as a political and cultural entity,[3] endowing Western civilization with a new value system that accounted for the rise of the West and its eventual supremacy over other civilizations.

Recent scholarship has revealed the limitations of the historiography of the Reformation as developed by European scholars since the sixteenth century.[4] Reformation studies have been carried out mostly by insiders (Protestant theology scholars, later joined by Catholic scholars), governed by religious bias and an eschatological dimension that prevented them from accessing mainstream history.[5] The study of the Reformation has also been influenced by the role it has been assigned in the writing of modern national historiographies, especially in Germany, The Netherlands, Scandinavian countries and England. In recent decades, a new emphasis on the social history and regional specificities of the Reformation has led to a proliferation of research in local studies, looking specifically at the development of the Reformation in particular localities.[6] From the sacred to the national and the local, the historiography of the Reformation has been considered in an exclusively Eurocentric manner. It has been more often the object of celebration as decisive in the rise of the West than as an object of critical historical scrutiny.

The field of Reformation studies has remained immune to the major epistemological challenges brought about by postmodern theories of historical knowledge, which have significantly unsettled traditional methodological assumptions and discredited most of the grand historical narratives. Comparatively, many aspects of the European Renaissance are being reconsidered under the light of what has been termed a '"new globalism" in early modern studies... which is concerned with larger, systemic changes in cultures and economies and with the interlocking and interactive aspects of cross-cultural encounters in world history'.[7] This new emphasis on extra-European influences, which has revealed how inputs from the Muslim world have been critical to the rise of modern culture in Western Europe,[8] has regrettably hardly affected the historical narrative of the Reformation. Although Reformation scholars readily acknowledged that the Reformation was a global phenomenon, they have been more concerned with assessing its global impact than with exploring extra-European influences on this historical event. Yet, given the intensity of intercultural exchange between Christian Europe and the peoples of the Mediterranean and south-eastern Europe throughout the Middle Ages, it is hardly conceivable that the Protestant Reformation took place in isolation. Given the prominent position of Muslim empires in Reformation Europe, it is indeed surprising that so little attention has been paid to the role played by Muslim civilization in the unfolding of the European Reformation. It might be argued that the essence of the phenomena itself – a movement that called for a return to the gospels and the eradication all heresies – makes it inconceivable that it might have been inspired by Islam, one of the most abhorred forms of heresy in Christendom. Yet, if one considers the history of the Reformation outside the theological impasse, where it has been for so long, and dismantles the mental walls historians have built around Europe, not to say on the river Elbe, then a more complete narrative can emerge that reveals just how intertwined the history of the European Reformation and the contemporary Muslim world really are.

This chapter does not claim to make an original contribution to the study of the Reformation's engagement with the world of Islam, nor does it aim to be an exhaustive review of scholarship supporting this perspective. Rather it is an effort to raise awareness and a call for further research. It aims to reveal the current state of our knowledge (or lack thereof) of the Reformation's connections with the Muslim world and argue for a 're-orienting' of our perspectives on the Reformation in order to further our scientific understanding of this major historical phenomenon and, more broadly, to reassess the dynamic of transcultural relations in the early modern period, which have been so critical in establishing our modern world views.[9]

The advent of Islam: an early call for Christian reform

The dramatic rise of Islam in the seventh century was a major occurrence in the history of Christendom that constituted an enduring and evolving source of questioning for Christian theologians. The advent of a religion that claimed to supersede the Bible and that was so successful in gaining new followers and in establishing thriving political and cultural systems, was both a spiritual and temporal challenge. Islam was never considered, either by the Prophet Mohammed or by his followers, as a new religion. The Quran revealed to Mohammed was conceived as a sacred text aimed at restoring the true teaching of God, which had been corrupted by those very men who claimed leadership over the flocks. It was considered as God's most perfect teaching to humankind, the final law that superseded previous revelations. Given the position claimed by Islam in the history of monotheism, Islam can be thought of as an earlier reform of Christianity and Mohammed as anticipating the reformers in several ways.[10] He was against a structured and hierarchical clergy and distrusted intercession between Man and God. He proclaimed the message of predestination and a divine ruling of human affairs.[11] He challenged the monarchical tendency of the Catholic Church, which he attributed to the deification of Jesus and, on this last point, he went further than the reformers and introduced a lasting point of opposition between Islam and Christendom.

Acknowledging that forms of reasoning similar to the Protestant movement did exist in Islam does not mean that Islam has been a source of inspiration for Christian reformers. Indeed, as Norman Daniel argued long ago in his seminal study *Islam and the West*, European representations of Islam have long remained based on ignorance, prejudice and misrepresentation.[12] Christian theologians were not interested in obtaining a proper knowledge of Islam. They considered Mohammed's Quran a diabolically perverted derivative of their own faith, a human-made heresy of no theological value. However, they had to account for Muslims' conspicuous successes which, according to traditional patristic thought, could be identified with religious truth. Until the Reformation, the Church's response to the challenge of Islam comprised, for the most part, polemical treatises that presented Islam as the arch-enemy of Christianity and explained the growth of that religion in terms of biblical eschatological prophecy. Medieval writers were mobilized to disseminate a distorted vision of Islam, depicting Muslim civilization with the most despicable and horrifying traits.

With the increase of travel to Muslim lands, there were also some voices to account for the splendour of the East, a growing curiosity about the customs and beliefs of the Muslims, and some serious, if limited, attempts to gain more accurate knowledge of Islam.[13] In time, Islam became, in the eyes of critics of the Christian Church, a contrasting image with which to denounce the spiritual and political corruption of Christian societies and ecclesiastical institutions, as well as a call for a reform of Christianity. John Wycliffe (c. 1328–84), traditionally considered the 'morning star of the Reformation' by Protestant historians, was the first theological scholar to compare Islam and Christianity in order to criticize the latter.[14] He explained the success of Islam by the degeneration of the European Christian Church (the growth of greed, pride, violence, materialism and the lust for power), which appeared to him far worse than the misguided faith of Mohammedans. Although he retained the old medieval prejudices against Islam, he denounced European arrogance and predicted that Islam would continue growing until Christians returned to the real spirit of the Gospels.

On the eve of Luther's posting of the *Ninety-Five Theses*, the spiritual and political challenge that Islam represented to Christianity was even more acute. The fall of the Byzantine capital to the Turks in 1453 constituted a tremendous blow to the long-held assumption about the triumph of Christian civilization while fulfilling an old Islamic aspiration articulated by the Prophet Mohammed himself. The Ottoman Empire emerged as a great Muslim empire whose provinces reached into

Asia and Europe. Islam was not a remote cultural or religious phenomenon. It was a European one, which played a notable part in the emergence and spread of the ideas of the Reformation.

Islam, a European phenomenon in the reformation era

The way Ottoman power is commonly portrayed in sixteenth-century European writings and in modern Western historiography traditionally features the Turks' 'ruthless dedication to conquest and predation'[15] and uncivilized savagery. As a matter of fact, the war against the Turks – the generic term then used for Muslims – constitutes the prevailing background of the Reformation. In the 1520s, the advance of the Ottomans in Central Europe, which climaxed with the Siege of Vienna in 1529, spread panic across Central Europe. In the beginning of a century saturated with apocalyptic expectations, both in Christendom and in the Muslim world,[16] the confrontation between the Holy Roman Empire and the Ottoman Empire was elevated to a soteriological battle articulated in messianic terms around competing universalist imperial ideologies.[17] However, the intensity and fierceness of political and religious disputes in the sixteenth century proved to be greater within each Empire. Much of Charles V's reign was devoted to the Italian Wars against France, and then to directly opposing the Protestant rebellions. In the same way, the Shi'a-Sunni controversy and the war against the Safavid Empire constituted the essential feature of the Ottoman Empire's historical experience during the sixteenth century; by comparison the collision between the empires remained marginal.[18] The messianic rhetoric used by the Emperors was, therefore, mostly targeting a domestic audience in a context of intra-faith fragmentation.

Indeed, the centuries old trend of ever-increasing cross-cultural exchange between Christian Europe and Muslim powers remained largely unaffected by political and ideological hostility in the early modern period.[19] From the mid-fifteenth century up to the seventeenth, the Islamic and Christian lands had become so intimately connected as to form what Daniel Goffman has called a 'greater Western world', with Constantinople as its centre of gravity. While contact between the Christian and Muslim cultures in the Middle Ages has been rather well documented, the more intensive cross-cultural exchanges during the Reformation remain largely unexplored. Early modern Muslim history has been somehow ignored by European historians of Islamic civilizations because it falls between the glory days of Islamic power and knowledge, which supposedly ended in 1258, and the troubled times of European imperialism, two periods that have traditionally monopolized attention.[20] Besides, European scholars of Islamic studies have long retained an Arabist view of Muslim history, full of prejudice against the Turks, because of the legacy of the fear of the conquering Turk and a liberal view of history that focused on the national struggles within the Ottoman Empire.[21] Yet the Ottoman Empire was not merely the bloodthirsty, fanatic and oppressive entity that was portrayed in early modern *Türkenbüchlein*[22] and later Western historiography.[23] It was a much more progressive actor in early modern Europe, which has influenced reformers' world vision, courses of action and systems of thought in several ways.

Recent scholarship on the history of the Ottoman Empire has aptly challenged the idea that the Ottomans survived and evolved purely through military might and religious zeal, and revealed instead that Ottoman resilience was as much the result of great flexibility and the power of attraction as of military force.[24] Expanding rapidly and continuously over vast territories, it had to find innovative mechanisms to cope with a multi-ethnic, multi-cultural and multi-confessional population. In order to accommodate its substantial non-Muslim population,[25] the Ottoman state established a system of government based on the *dhimma* principle, a legal system of religious tolerance and community autonomy that was established in the very beginnings of Islam. According to this principle, *dhimmis* (the Peoples of the Book, such as Christians and Jews) had the freedom to pursue their own religious beliefs and practices provided they paid the *jizya*. This special tax imposed on *dhimmis* has often been considered a discriminatory measure, while it was in fact a replacement for the *zakat*, a religious tax imposed on Muslims and therefore not applicable to non-Muslims. The genuine nature and degree of tolerance granted by the *dhimmi* status has been the object of various kinds of questioning which cannot be addressed within the scope of this chapter.[26] What is important to note here is that the Ottoman *dhimma* system did grant some tangible spiritual freedom to its Christian subjects and, as such, it contrasted with the missionary passion and sectarian intolerance of contemporary Europe. Many persecuted religious individuals and movements, such as Huguenots, Anglicans, Quakers, Anabaptists or even Jesuits or Capuchins, found refuge in Ottoman territories where they were given right of residence and worship. Ottoman rule in Europe was also often reported to be more benevolent than Christian feudality in terms of governance and social justice, notably in terms of distribution of land tenure.[27] As a result, the Turks were frequently welcomed as liberators by peasants from the Balkans and Central Europe and were rallied by many Christians in their fight against the Habsburg.[28] The *dhimma* system was also appreciated for the economic opportunities it offered non-Muslims, opportunities which were unmatched in Christendom. European visitors to the East regularly brought back tales of their compatriots living and prospering in Ottoman lands. The development of trade, commerce and financial exchanges between European and Muslim societies was accompanied by the intensification of political and diplomatic relations. Both led to a great movement of people between the Christian and Muslim worlds during the early modern period. As Renaissance historian Jerry Brotton underlines, 'there were no clear geographical or political barriers between east and west in the Renaissance. It is a much later, nineteenth-century belief in the absolute cultural and political separation of the Islamic east and Christian west that has obscured the easy exchange of trade, art and ideas between these two cultures.'[29]

The concept of Christendom was becoming increasingly empty, and even embarrassing as integration with the Ottoman Empire encouraged commercial ties, political alliances and cultural exchanges.[30] This phenomenon is well illustrated by the largely unilateral flow of converts to Islam in the Reformation era,[31] an uncomfortable fact which has long remained unacknowledged in Western historiography. Recent studies have demonstrated how the power of attraction of Islam, which drove hundreds of thousands of European Christians into apostasy, was critical to the emergence of early modern European and confessional identities.[32] Historians do not agree on whether conversions were mostly forced or voluntary. However, it is widely acknowledged that apostasy was taking place in the absence of any active policy of proselytism, if one excludes the forced conversions taking place in the framework of Ottoman *devşirme*.[33] Scholars like Nabil Matar or Bartolomé and Lucile Bennassar have unearthed sources that show that conversion was often considered an opportunity for social, economic and sometimes political advancement for poor Europeans and was often the result of a voluntary choice rarely questioned over time.[34] Numerous European slaves captured during wars or commercial incursions and enrolled in the service of the Sultan, often found their lives less arduous than they had previously been in Christian territories, and many of them converted without any physical or psychological pressure.[35] Ottomanist historian Paul Coles argues that widespread Sufi orders within Ottoman society that 'taught that all organized religion – Christianity and Islam alike – represented an imperfect approximation to the truth, which lay in mystic personal communion with God' may have somewhat facilitated Christian conversions.[36] In embracing Islam Christians may have felt that they were merely repudiating the bigotry of their earlier parochial experience, in much the same way as Christians turning to Protestantism would later feel.

Whatever the motives, Christian conversion to Islam was clearly recognized and understood in Reformation Europe. The figure of the Christian 'turned Turk' was a popular icon of early modern literature, which generated both fear and fascination.[37] This phenomenon was one of the most pressing issues for Christian theologians in the early sixteenth century. Luther himself was painfully aware of the power of attraction of Islam[38] and was deeply concerned with the prospect of Christians making contact with Muslims. He believed that if the Turks made their way further into Europe, Christians would convert *en masse* to Islam. The phenomenon of conversions to Islam was a major manifestation of the crisis of European Christendom. As Nabil Matar writes:

> converts to Islam both embarrassed and provoked some of the most important writers and theologians of the European Renaissance. While the 'direct encounter' with Islam affected the 'small men' of Christendom – sailors, fishermen, merchants and soldiers – the intellectual and religious impact of that encounter challenged men whose writings and influence have been instrumental in defining early modern European culture: from Pope Pius to Martin Luther and John Locke, from John Calvin to Christopher Marlowe, from John Foxe to George Fox, from Cervantes to Shakespeare, Massinger and Dryden – all reflected to varying degrees in their writings, on the interaction between Christendom and Islam. Furthermore, all recognized that Christians were converting to Islam more often than Muslims were to Christianity and that the 'infidels' challenged Europe not only by their sword but also by their religious allure.[39]

A Protestant tradition of engagement with Islam

Given the place of Islam in the centre of European consciousness, it is not surprising to find references to the Turks in the writings of almost all reformers. Historians of the Reformation have commonly attributed the reformers' contemplation of Islam to the contemporary military pressure of the Ottomans more than to any other factor. They have dismissed their engagement with Islam as mostly geopolitical or strategic. It is, indeed, a widely acknowledged fact that the Reformation's political successes throughout Europe were made possible to a great extent thanks to the assistance provided by the Ottomans to the Protestant movements.[40] Romanian historian Stephen Fisher-Galati long ago revealed how Lutheranism benefited from Ottoman imperialism in south-eastern Europe in consolidating its position and obtaining legal recognition in Germany.[41] In the Low Countries, the Dutch Calvinists diffused Habsburg military pressure and, ultimately, won their independence in 1609 largely thanks to the military support and commercial advantages (capitulations) granted by Istanbul. During their revolt against Spanish-Catholic rule, Dutch Calvinists also used ideological symbols that referred to the famous Ottoman religious tolerance; such as silver medallions in form of the Islamic crescent moon on which the slogan *Liever Turks dan Paaps* ('Rather Turkish than Papist') was engraved. Elizabethan England also entered into a strategic alliance with the Ottoman Empire and the Barbary States to protect the country's territorial security and new confessional identity against the threat of conquest by Spain and the reestablishment of Catholicism. In the seventeenth century, while state relations with the Habsburgs had normalized, English and Dutch Protestants continued to oppose Catholic states through a piratical collaboration with Muslim privateers against Catholic shipping. The spread and maturation of Calvinism and various forms of radical Protestantism in southern Hungary and eastern Transylvania was a direct consequence of the Ottoman policy of protecting Protestant movements in Europe.[42] Protestant émigrés and local communities in Hungary felt they were safer under Turkish than Habsburg rule, and allied themselves with the Ottomans in order to drive the Austrian army out.[43] This multifaceted rapprochement between the Protestant Reformation and Muslim powers, referred to as turco-calvinism or calvino-turcism by Catholic powers, was one of the main factors that contributed to the ultimate success of the Reformation movements. The rationale for what might seem an unnatural alliance was to a great extent purely strategic, stemming from the convergence of the interests of the Ottoman Empire and the Protestant movements in opposing the Habsburg Catholics. However, new scholarly works have suggested that there were more than just reasons of state or sectarianism in the Protestant-Islamic entente.[44]

It has been long noted that in addition to opposing the same enemy, Protestants and Muslims had common doctrinal affinities, which arouse feelings of congeniality. Both religions prohibited icons in places of worship, did not treat marriage as a sacrament and rejected monastic orders.[45] Strategic alliances were accompanied by diplomatic exchanges in which the similarities between Protestantism and Islam were noted and discussed.[46] In the 1550s, Suleiman the Magnificent pledged support to Lutheran princes on the grounds that they were closer in religious terms to Islamic monotheism than were Catholics. This idea was further developed in an epistolary exchange between Queen Elizabeth I (1533–1603) and Sultan Murad III (1546–95). This diplomatic correspondence, traditionally considered mere rhetoric by European historians, deserves more attention as a cultural–philosophical exchange of ideas between East and West, as Ottoman historian Kemal Karpat had already noted in 1974,[47] and should be weighed against wider views and debates taking place among Protestant reformers. In fact, references to Islam were ubiquitous in Protestant religious treatises, sermons and polemics. Islam was the object of a violent diatribe in these documents. Yet it also played an important, if subtle, role in Protestant theological development. Indeed, the reformers undertook a remarkable intellectual engagement with Islam, and this deserves more attention.

Luther's interest in Islam has been the object of a great number of scholarly studies.[48] They reveal his lifetime commitment to obtaining objective knowledge of Islam and shed light on his pioneering eschatological interpretation of the Muslim faith. The meaning of Luther's approach to Islam has been the object of many interpretations, most of them seeing in it a cynical instrumentalization of Islam aimed at depreciating the papacy. However, recent analyses have uncovered greater subtleties in the Wittenberg Reformer's approach to Islam.[49] Adam Francisco recently published a monograph in which he studies some aspects of Luther's attitude towards Islam that have been traditionally overlooked by other scholars. He emphasizes that Luther had a quite substantial knowledge of the Muslim religion and culture, given the standards of his time, and was well aware of the allure of Islam, as demonstrated in the following excerpt from his preface to the 1530 Latin edition of Georgius of Hungaria's *Libellus de ritu et moribus Turcorum*:

> From this book [the Quran], accordingly, we see that the religion of the Turks or Muhammad is far more splendid in ceremonies – and I might almost say, in customs – than ours, even including that of the religious or all the clerics. The modesty and simplicity of their food, clothing, dwellings, and everything else, as well as the fasts, prayers, and common gatherings of the people that this book reveals are nowhere seen among us... Our religious are mere shadows when compared to them, and our people clearly profane when compared to theirs.... This is the reason why many persons so easily depart from

> faith in Christ for Muhammadanism and adhere to it so tenaciously. I sincerely believe that no papist, monk, cleric, or their equal in faith would be able to remain in their faith if they should spend three days among the Turks.[50]

Francisco argues that Luther's attitude towards Islam was more than mere propaganda and had important theological implications for his theology. More recently, Ian Almond has delivered a compelling analysis of Luther's Islam, revealing the ambiguities of Luther's approach and highlighting their role in the development of his theology. Almond notes how seriously Luther viewed Islam as a living, dynamic and vibrant faith, which aroused feeling of inferiority in Christendom. His sincere desire to obtain a reliable translation of the Quran placed the infidel text in the same position as the Holy Scriptures. The recognition of Islam's worldly superiority profoundly unsettled the theologian. Luther was perpetually torn between demonizing the Turks' religion as a monstrous perversion, and the followers of the Muslim faith as Satan's army, and lauding them as a Christian schoolmaster or equating them with the instrument of divine punishment which would help restore the sacred on earth. Aware of the existence of ideas similar to his own in Muslim theology, Luther chose a strategy of polarization: he distinguished Christian predestination from its flawed Muslim equivalent by drawing on two familiar features of medieval representations of Islam, pride and fanaticism; he grudgingly acknowledged the validity of Islam's position on the question of image but denounced the Turks' excessive, anarchic and destructive approach to iconoclasm; finally, he attributed Islam's acceptance of the four gospels to a diabolical inspiration. Luther's 'othering' of Islam also implied a racial and geographical understanding of Islam. Overall, Almond concludes, 'what the fundamental ambiguity of Luther's destructive/restorative Turk reveals, more than anything else, is the ambiguity of hatred itself; the fact that hatred, like love, is a relationship of intimacy, an act of negative devotion. Hatred, like love, requires attention and energy; it brings the object of hatred into the world of the hater, accords it a privileged place, imbues it with an incontestable (if unenviable) significance.'[51]

Luther's interest in Islam was more than a personal undertaking. Many of his followers demonstrated an equally profound interest in Islam and a commitment to increasing and disseminating reliable information about the Muslim religion. German Lutherans translated Ottoman chronicles and dispatched envoys such as Simon Schweiggle or Stefan Gerlach[52] to Istanbul to collect information about Islam.[53] The reformers' knowledge of Islam was enriched by personal contacts within the Muslim world, with orthodox authorities in Constantinople[54] or reformed churches in Ottoman territories.[55] A similar stance existed among the Swiss Reformers.[56] Zurich theologian Theodor Bibliander produced a massive anthology on Islam[57] and managed to get a Latin edition of the Quran into print for the very first time in history.[58] His translation of the Quran was widely read among Lutheran circles, not so much for traditional missionary or controversialist purposes as for theological purposes. As Reformation historian Susan Boettcher notes, Lutheran authors read Bibliander's translation in conjunction with Revelations as a way of understanding their own age.[59] The Reformers' varied and nuanced approach to Islam remains an almost unexplored field of study, which could open fresh perspectives on the role that Islam played in the development of Protestantism. Thus far, only the instrumentalization of Islam in the Catholic–Protestant dispute is widely known, if not yet thoroughly studied. Protestant writers either pointed at resemblances in perversion between Catholicism and Islam to discredit the former or compared tropes of Muslim religious practices to Catholic forms of worship to disparage the latter. As Catholic polemicists were using the same arguments about Protestants, references to Islam appeared to many Reformation scholars a rather insignificant tool in the service of more fundamental intra-Christian theological debates. As Zurich professor of Church history Emidio Campi remarks, 'it is important...to place their [the Reformers'] writings and statements [about Islam] in their historical context. While many aspects of their thinking were products of the age in which they lived and are therefore only of historical interest to us now, the deeper one ventures into the whole body of their works, the more one is struck by just how rich in fundamental theological insights they are. And having been left by and large untouched for centuries, these nuggets are now just waiting to be unearthed.'[60]

Recent scholarship has started looking at the significant role that Islam played in the very definition of the new theology and confessional identities fostered by the Reformation movements. In her study on English Reformation literature,[61] Jennie M. Stevenson argues that reference to Islam was a dynamic force in the intra-Christian struggle that did more than simply discredit one's opponents. It was an essential element in the definition and codification of Protestantism. Stevenson recalls that British reformers were tasked with establishing a unique brand of Protestantism in a period where cross-cultural contact with diverse faiths was increasing. With Islam occupying an overwhelming position in the early modern Western world, Reformers were called upon to distinguish their new faith not only from Catholicism but also from Islam. Comparisons with Islamic doctrine and practices served to provide answers to the pervasive Reformation questions about how Protestantism should differ from Catholicism, for example on issues related to idolatry or ceremonial reform. Stevenson also demonstrates that the reformers used the trope of conversions to Islam and applied it to a doctrinal shift within Christianity to reify Protestantism as an independent doctrine from Catholicism and justify the need to convert from Catholicism to Protestantism. Reformation historian Susanne Boettcher also pointed to the use of Islam in the process of Protestant confessionalization – the process by which Lutherans and other reformed movements consolidated and extended their belief system and religious culture in competition with other confessions in the later sixteenth century.[62] She asserts that the image of the Turk as the enemy served to construct a geography of contemporary religion and as such became an integral component of the delimitation of European identity. German historian Felix Konrad similarly notes in his contribution to the online scholarly project of European trans-cultural history-writing, that the religious-theological discourses of alterity that turned Muslims into the antithesis of European Christianity was used in the Reformation to build and strengthen the identity of one's own denominational group.[63]

The Muslim world has also been part of several developments often linked or attributed to the Reformation. The establishment of universities in Medieval Europe on the model of Islamic institutions of learning and the use of paper and block printing are two imports from the East that contributed directly to the spread of Reformation ideas.[64] Arabic translations of classical and religious sources were widely used by the reformers in their exegetical efforts to define Protestant theology.[65] Arabic philology therefore became a key element of Protestant theological training.[66] It is, indeed, significant that the rise of Arabic and Islamic studies in the seventeenth century took place not in those European countries that had been in close contacts with the Muslim world, but in Protestant countries such as England and Germany.[67] The Islamic-Protestant entente played an important role in the genesis of European capitalism. It led to great movements of people and increased commerce between the Protestant powers and the Muslim world. Protestant traders had critical trading advantages over their Catholic counterparts that were granted by Istanbul in the framework of specific agreements. Elizabethan England, for example, enjoyed a quasi monopoly in the trade of weapons with Muslim powers because it did not feel constrained by the papal ban on a trade in metals with the infidels. Protestant countries also benefited from the Protestant-Muslim anti-Catholic piracy in the Mediterranean Sea. Overall, as Jack Goody notes in *Islam in Europe*, part of the success of the Protestant countries in penetrating foreign markets lay precisely in their being freer to establish commercial and other relationships with Muslim regimes.[68]

The idea of religious toleration is another key development commonly attributed to the European Reformation and with universal dimensions that has been revisited as a phenomenon directly inspired by Islamic influences.[69] To John M. Headley, a world history scholar rather protective of the uniqueness of European values and intellectual legacy, the Dutch slogan *Eher Türkisch als Päpstisch* ('Better Turkish than Papist') was more than simply a rhetorical gambit.[70] Muslim religious toleration preceded the Reformation and addressed deep-seated, early modern European needs that were to be heightened by the Reformation. Religious refugees and Protestant communities in Ottoman-ruled Europe directly experienced the permissiveness of Ottoman administrative practice regarding local customs and religions. Protestant travellers and preachers in Ottoman lands brought back accounts of the Turks' tolerance that were used by Western European reformers in their struggle to obtain freedom of conscience.[71] It is not insignificant that the 1557 *Edict of Torda*, a document which historians have celebrated as the first European text articulating expansive religious toleration, was adopted in Transylvania in the sixteenth century under Ottoman protection. To Unitarian scholar Susan Ritchie, this document was the result of the direct influence of Islamic Ottoman theological commitment to religious toleration and of the profound cultural enmeshment between Muslims and some forms of radical Protestantism, which have been almost erased from mainstream European historiography.[72] It is ironic, Ritchie notes, that historians have commonly celebrated the progressive, diversity-promoting character of the earliest European statements of religious toleration in ways that obliterate Islamic influences.[73] And, it is all the more ironic, as Headley again highlights, that Muslim religious toleration outlasted the Reformation.[74] Luther and the reformers, who had been fighting to obtain freedom of conscience, retained the medieval principle of a single religion per state and adopted a hard line on rigorous orthodoxy when toleration appeared to play in favour of their opponents, whether Protestant radicals or non-Christians.[75]

The history of the Reformation in Ottoman-ruled Europe and Transylvania is a period of European cultural and religious history that has a great deal to reveal about the role of Islam in the development of early modern Europe. This history is practically unknown in the English-speaking world, while existing studies by local historians have been reluctant to consider any connections between local reformers and Islam.[76] The first comprehensive English-language study of Calvinism in Hungary and Transylvania by British scholar Graeme Murdock offers a few clues to the social interactions between Christians and Muslims, but these only scratch the surface of a buried story still waiting to be told.[77] The specific encounter between Muslims and the radical Reformation, which has been alluded to by Professor Ritchie, is another promising field of research. French scholar of Protestant sectarianism, Jacques Tual, and Gül A. Russell, a scientist specializing in the rise of empiricism and cultural transmission of scientific ideas during the Renaissance, have both argued that the British seventeenth-century Puritans not only demonstrated empathy for the Islamic faith, but that their theology was directly inspired by Muslim scriptures and philosophy.[78] They both reveal that the Quaker authoritative theological summa *An Apology for the True Christian Divinity*, developed by Robert Barclay in 1678, contained explicit references to Ibn Tufayl's *Hayy Ibn Yaqzan* to support three key propositions: (1) the universalism of divine Truth and Redemption; (2) the 'sufficiency of inner light', that allows access to knowledge of the 'Truth' without using external rituals; and (3) the universality of individual spiritual revelation.[79] Here again, Islamic influences were erased from historical records when the reference to Ibn Tufayl's book were removed from the post-eighteenth century editions of Barclay's *Apology*.

Finally, I would like to note that the notion of confessionalization as a specifically European phenomenon has been also convincingly called into question. The Muslim world at the time of the Reformation was subject to an analogous intra-confessional strife generated by the rise of the Safavid Twelver Shi'ite dogma diametrically opposed to the Ottoman Islamic orthodoxy.[80] Ottoman Sultans had to defend Islamic orthodoxy and fight against heresy in ways that were not dissimilar to the Catholic powers at the time. Tijana Krstić, a historian of the early modern Ottoman Empire, has taken these reflections further in a fascinating survey of conversion narratives in the Ottoman Empire from the fifteenth to the seventeenth centuries, in which she argues that the process of confessionalization encompassed the Muslim world.[81] Based on mostly unknown sources, she demonstrates that Ottoman Muslims were engaged in debates on questions of religious reforms usually considered germane only to post-Reformation Christianity.

The principle of *cuis region, eius religio* was upheld in the Ottoman and Safavid Empires as well, while debates on spiritual authority in the Muslim community or correct rituals, were conducted in a language reminiscent of the Catholic–Protestant dispute. Krstić further argues that the formation of Ottoman and Safavid imperial identities and religious orthodoxies ran parallel and at a similar pace to the confessionalization process in the Habsburg territories, and gave rise to the formation of the Sunni and Shi'a Muslim confessional and territorial blocks that still exist today.

Conclusion

As new scholarship in early modern European history and in Ottoman studies increasingly reveals how integrated the Christian European and Muslim Ottoman worlds were in the sixteenth century, a reassessment of the role played by Islam in the intellectual turmoil that shook Europe during that century is in order. While the state of research remains sketchy in this field, recent scholarly works are increasingly revealing that Islam was an important and dynamic factor in the intellectual debates and political affairs of Reformation Europe. Or, as historian Daniel Goffman highlights, 'Islam and Judaism were acknowledged (if not accepted) as part of the re-evaluation of the relationship between religion and society that accompanied the early modern collapse of the Catholic ecumene. Even ideologically, then, differences receded and the two societies more and more resembled each other. An examination of this state of affairs opens for the historian a new world of research and interpretation.'[82]

Due to their almost exclusive focus on the textual record of religious controversies, Reformation historians have failed to account for the influence of trans-cultural encounters on early modern Christendom. Unravelling complicated chains of causation in diffuse and ill-documented cross-cultural exchanges is difficult and poses genuine methodological challenges. First among them is to find innovative scholarly methods of inquiry, given that contacts during this period were not primarily textual but rather cultural and socio-political.[83] Reformation historians, therefore, need to diversify their traditional sources and go beyond the conventional textual approach. This implies gathering inter-disciplinary scientific teams, because of the wide array of linguistic, methodological and field-specific skills required for further research into connected histories between the Muslim and Christian worlds in the Reformation era.

This undertaking is important for our understanding of the Reformation and for contemporary relations between the Arab-Islamic world and the West. Integrating elements of cross-cultural history in Reformation studies will contribute to refining our understanding of some of the subtleties of the Reformation's theological debates. Overall, it will enable the writing of a more complete Reformation narrative, and will undoubtedly uncover fascinating aspects of the engagement of the radical Protestant movements with Islam. Adopting a globalist perspective, notably by incorporating new scholarship on Christian converts into the study of the Reformation, will also shed new light on the social dynamics that accompanied the sixteenth century confessionalization process.

Understanding the reformers' engagement with Islam also has potential implications for contemporary endeavours to alleviate tensions between the Muslim world and the West. The traditional Eurocentric historiography of the Reformation is a key component of the way Europe has understood itself ever since the sixteenth century, as a unique and self-sufficient model of civilization that reached modernity and supremacy following a linear path of development and progress that should be replicated in other parts of the world. Revisiting the Eurocentric narrative of the Reformation is not intended to contest the European specificity of the sixteenth-century Reformation, but to demonstrate that even such a uniquely European phenomenon has been shaped by a dialectical relation with a non-European alterity. Unveiling how Muslim and Christian societies were intertwined in the Reformation era will help to disclose that, beyond the discourse of hatred, religious histories have evolved in a dynamic, interactive way, characterized by hostility as much as by intellectual exchange, human encounters and mutual assistance. Disclosing such interaction also promises to contribute to the deconstruction of persistent Eurocentric prejudices against Islam, which have been shaped to a considerable extent by those very Protestant othering discourses discussed earlier.[84] Orientalizing the Reformation might then enable a de-christianizing of current calls for a reform of Muslim societies, and allow for a more constructive and dispassionate exchange within this field.

Notes

1. H. J. Grimm (1958), *The Reformation Era, 1500–1650* (New York: Macmillan), p. 2.
2. M. Weber (1998), *L'éthique protestante et l'esprit du capitalisme*, 2nd edn (Paris: Pocket).

3. G. F. Elton (1999), *Reformation Europe, 1517–1559*, 3rd edn (Oxford: Blackwell Publishers).
4. A. J. Hillerbrand (2003), 'Was There a Reformation in the Sixteenth Century?' *Church History*, Vol. 72, No. 3, pp. 525–52; A. Pettegree (ed.) (2000), *The Reformation World* (London: Routledge); C. Lindberg (2010), *The European Reformations* (Sussex: Wiley-Blackwell).
5. Lindberg, *The European Reformations* p. 4.
6. Pettegree, *The Reformation World*, p. 2.
7. D. Viktus (2002), 'Introduction: Toward a New Globalism in Early Modern Studies', *Journal of Early Modern Cultural Studies*, Vol. 2, No. 1, pp. v–viii.
8. G. Sarton (1927–31), *Introduction to the History of Science*, Vol. I–IV (Baltimore: Carnegie Institution of Washington); W. Montgomery Watt (1972), *The Influence of Islam on Medieval Europe* (Edinburgh: Edinburgh University Press); M. Graham (2006), *How Islam Created the Modern World* (Beltsville, MD: Amana Publications); M. H. Morgan (2007), *Lost History: The Enduring Legacy of Muslim Scientists, Thinkers, and Artists* (Washington, DC: National Geographic); J. Goody (2010), *Renaissances. The One or the Many?* (Cambridge: Cambridge University Press); G. Makdisi (1990), *The Rise of Humanism in Classical Islam and the Christian West: With Special Reference to Scholasticism* (Edinburgh: Edinburgh University Press).
9. This call echoes similar and promising endeavours being undertaken in the field of Renaissance studies. See G. MacLean (ed.) (2005), *Re-orienting the Renaissance: Cultural Exchanges with the East* (Basingstoke: Palgrave Macmillan).
10. M. Nafissi (2005), 'Reformation, Islam, and Democracy: Evolutionary and Antievolutionary Reform in Abrahamic Religions', *Comparative Studies of South Asia, Africa and the Middle East*, Vol. 25, No. 2, pp. 407–37; A. A. Mazrui (1990), *Cultural Forces in World Politics* (London: J. Currey; Nairobi: Heinemann Kenya [etc.]), pp. 73–6; J. Goody and S. Fennell (2010), 'Rebirth in Islam' in Goody, *Renaissances. The One or the Many?* p. 98.
11. Mazrui, *Cultural Forces in World Politics*, p. 73.
12. N. Daniel (1960), *Islam and the West. The Making of an Image* (Edinburgh: Edinburgh University Press).
13. A remarkable attempt to reappraise the relations between Christianity and Islam was undertaken by Peter the Venerable (c. 1092–1156), the reform-minded Abbot of Cluny, who collected and translated a host of sources on, and writings about, Islam, including the Quran, later known as the *Cluniac Corpus* or *Corpus Toletanum*. This early effort was not taken further seriously until the Protestant Reformation, despite several noteworthy individual attempts to bring first-hand information about Islam to the European audience. Among them, the writings of George of Hungary, a captive of the Turks for 20 years, and Riccoldo da Monte Croce, an Italian Dominican monk who travelled extensively in Muslim lands, were considered as the only reliable sources on Islam by Luther. On the medieval literary corpus of Islam and its transmission to the Reformers, see V. Segesvary (1978), *L'Islam et la Réforme: étude sur l'attitude des réformateurs zurichois envers l'Islam (1510–1550)* (Lausanne: Edition l'Age d'Homme), pp. 39–101.

14. Segesvary, *L'Islam et la Réforme*, p. 56.
15. P. Coles (1968), *The Ottoman Impact on Europe* (New York: Harcourt, Brace & World, Inc. Publishers), p. 77.
16. The phenomenal progress of the Muslims was interpreted in line with biblical eschatological prophecy as the rise of the Antichrist in Christian Europe. Millenarian prophecies and apocalyptic expectations were also widespread in the early sixteenth-century Muslim world as it entered the last century of the Islamic millennium, which started in 1495 CE (901 H). T. Krstić (2009), 'Illuminated by the Light of Islam and the Glory of the Ottoman Sultanate: Self-Narratives of Conversion to Islam in the Age of Confessionalization', *Comparative Studies in Society and History*, Vol. 51, No. 1, p. 39.
17. In 1519, the newly-crowned Holy Roman Emperor Charles V assumed the mythical role of the 'Last World Emperor' and proclaimed a grandiose policy aimed at recapturing Constantinople and Jerusalem and establishing a 'universal Christian monarchy'. This monarchical ideology directly clashed with the imperialism of Ottoman Sultan Süleiman I, who had officially claimed Caliphal authority over the Muslim world after having defeated the Mamluk Sultanate in the Near East, and incorporated the holy cities of Mecca and Medina in 1517. G. Ágoston (2007), 'Information, Ideology, and Limits of Imperial Policy: Ottoman Grand Strategy in the Context of Ottoman-Habsburg Rivalry', in V. H. Aksan and D. Goffman (eds) *The Early Modern Ottomans: Remapping the Empire* (Cambridge, New York: Cambridge University Press), pp. 75–103.
18. Coles, *The Ottoman Impact on Europe*, p. 74.
19. J. Brotton (2002), *The Renaissance Bazaar: From the Silk Road to Michelangelo* (New York: Oxford University Press), p. 53.
20. N. Matar (2009), *Europe through Arab's Eyes* (New York: Columbia University Press), p. 4.
21. W. H. McNeill (1974), 'The Ottoman Empire in World History', in K. H. Karpat (ed.), *The Ottoman State and Its Place in World History* (Leiden: E. J. Brill), pp. 34–5; B. Lewis (1951), 'Europe and the Turks: The Civilization of the Ottoman Empire', *History Today*, pre-1980 Vol. 1, No. 10, http://www.historytoday.com/bernard-lewis/europe-and-turks-civilization-ottoman-empire.
22. *Türkenbüchlein* or *Turcica* were anti-Turkish pamphlets typical of the sixteenth-century that were widely circulated through the new technology of the printing press.
23. E. Gibbon (1855), *History of the Decline and Fall of the Roman Empire*, Vol. 7 (London: John Murray).
24. See, for example, C. Finkel (2005), *Osman's Dream: The Story of the Ottoman Empire 1300–1923* (London: John Murray); G. Ágoston (2003), 'A Flexible Empire: Authority and Its Limits on the Ottoman Frontiers', *The International Journal of Turkish Studies*, Vol. 9, Nos 1–2, pp. 15–31, reprinted in K. Karpat and R. W. Zens (eds) (2003), *Ottoman Borderlands: Issues, Personalities and Political Changes* (Madison, Wisc: The University of Wisconsin Press); D. Goffman (2002), *The Ottoman Empire and Early Modern Europe* (Cambridge: Cambridge University Press).
25. Non-muslims were predominant in the Ottoman Empire until the conquests of Selim I (1512–20) in the Levant and the Arabian peninsula.

26. G. Veinstein (1998), 'Retour sur la question de la tolérance ottomane au XVIe siècle', in *Chrétiens et Musulmans à la Renaissance*, actes du 37e colloque international du CESR, sous la direction de Bartolomé Bennassar et Robert Sauzet (Paris: Honoré Champion Editeur), pp. 161–75.
27. C. D. Rouillard (1940), *The Turks in French History, Thought and Literature* (Paris: Boivin).
28. Coles, *The Ottoman Impact on Europe*, pp. 112–13; I. Almond (2009), *Two Faiths, One Banner: When Muslims Marched with Christians across Europe's Battlegrounds* (Cambridge, Mass.: Harvard University Press), pp. 139–80.
29. J. Brotton (2006), *The Renaissance: A Very Short Introduction* (New York: Oxford University Press), p. 33.
30. Coles, *The Ottoman Impact on Europe*, pp. 147–8.
31. W. Monter (2006–7), 'Religion and Cultural Exchange, 1400–1700', in H. Schilling and I. G. Tóth (eds) *Cultural Exchange in Early Modern Europe*, Vol. 1 (Cambridge: Cambridge University Press), p. 16.
32. N. Matar (1998), *Islam in Britain 1558–1685* (Cambridge: Cambridge University Press); B. Bennassar and L. Bennassar (1989), *Les chrétiens d'Allah: l'histoire extraordinaire des renégats, XVIe et XVIIe siècles* (Paris: Perrin); L. Colley (2002), *Captives* (New York: Pantheon Books).
33. The *devşirme* was a system of child tribute exacted on Christian peoples in the Empire's European margins. It was instituted in the fifteenth century to contribute to the modernization of the Empire. The youngsters levied in the framework of the *devşirme* were offered brilliant prospects within imperial institutions. As a result, even the fate of those Christians who were forced to convert did not serve as a repellent. The remarkable social mobility of these slave converts actually impressed many contemporary European observers who (mistakenly) considered it to be the hallmark of the Ottoman system. M. A. Zilfi (2009), 'Slavery', in G. Ágoston and B. Masters (eds) *Encyclopedia of the Ottoman Empire* (New York: Infobase Publishing), p. 352.
34. According to Bennassar, between 1560 and 1650, more than half the population of Algiers was composed of renegades, who constituted the elite of the city. B. Bennassar and L. Bennassar, *Les chrétiens d'Allah*. See also Colley, *Captives*, pp. 117–19.
35. Coles, *The Ottoman Impact on Europe*, p. 54.
36. Ibid.
37. D. Vitkus (2003), *Turning Turk: English Theatre and the Multicultural Mediterranean 1570–1630* (New York: Palgrave Macmillan); M. Dimmock (2005), *New Turkes: Dramatizing Islam and the Ottomans in Early Modern England* (Aldershot; Burlington, VT: Ashgate).
38. In *Heerpredigt*, Luther notes how he heard and read that Christians in Muslim lands commit 'apostasy and willingly and without force believe the faith of the Turks or Muhammad for the sake of the great external appearances that they have in their faith'. M. Luther, *Heepredigt*, WA 30/2: 185, pp. 25–8, quoted in A. S. Francisco (2007), *Martin Luther and Islam. A Study in Sixteenth-century Polemics and Apologetics* (Leiden, Boston: E. J. Brill), p. 88.
39. Matar, *Islam in Britain 1558–1685*, p. 19.
40. D. Vaughan (1954), *Europe and the Turks: A Pattern of Alliance. 1350–1700* (Liverpool: University of Liverpool Press); K. M. Setton (1962), 'Lutheranism and the Turkish Peril', *Balkan Studies*, Vol. 3, pp. 133–68; G. W. Forell

(1945), 'Luther and the War against the Turks', *Church History,* Vol. 14, No. 4, pp. 256–71; M. Iyigun (2007), 'Luther and Suleyman', *Quarterly Journal of Economics,* Vol. 123, No. 4, pp. 1465–94.

41. S. A. Fischer-Galati (1959), *Ottoman Imperialism and German Protestantism: 1521–1555* (Cambridge, MA.: Harvard University Press).
42. C. M. Kortepeter (1972), *Ottoman Imperialism during the Reformation: Europe and the Caucasus* (New York: New York University Press); B. K. Király (1975), 'The Sublime Porte, Vienna, Transylvania and the Dissemination of Protestant Reformation in Royal Hungary', in B. K. Király (ed.) *Tolerance and Movement of Religious Dissent in Eastern Europe* (New York: Columbia University Press), pp. 199–221.
43. Kortepeter, *Ottoman Imperialism during the Reformation*, pp. 197–8; Almond, 'Muslims, Protestants and Peasants', pp. 139–80.
44. Colley, *Captives*, p. 122.
45. J. Goody (2004), *Islam in Europe* (Cambridge [etc.]: Polity), p. 42.
46. A. C. Hess (1968), 'The Moriscos: An Ottoman Fifth Column', *The American Historical Review*, Vol. 74, No. 1, p. 19; Goody, *Islam in Europe*, pp. 42, 150; G. MacLean (2007), *Looking East. English Writing and the Ottoman Empire before 1800* (Hampshire: Palgrave Macmillan), p. 46; H. Inalcik (1974), 'The Turkish Impact on the Development of Modern Europe', in K. H. Karpat (ed.) *The Ottoman State and Its Place in World History* (Leiden: E. J. Brill), p. 53.
47. Karpat, *The Ottoman State and Its Place in World History*, p. 8.
48. H. Buchanan (1956), 'Luther and the Turks, 1519–1529', *Archiv Für Reformationsgeschichte*, No. 47, pp. 145–59; C. U. Wolf (1941), 'Luther and Mohammedanism', *The Moslem World*, Vol. 31, No. 2, pp. 161–77; G. Miller (2000), 'Luther on the Turks and Islam', *The Lutheran Quarterly*, Vol. 14, pp. 79–97; G. Simon (1931), 'Luther's Attitude toward Islam', *The Muslim World*, Vol. 21, No. 3, pp. 257–62; H. P. Smith (1923), 'Luther and Islam', *The American Journal of Semitic Languages and Literatures*, Vol. 39, No. 3, pp. 218–20; G. H. Williams (1969), 'Erasmus and the Reformers on Non-Christian Religions and Salus Extra Ecclesiam', in T. K. Rabb and J. E. Seigel (eds) *Action and Conviction in Early Modern Europe* (Princeton: Princeton University Press), pp. 319–37.
49. Francisco, *Martin Luther and Islam. A Study in Sixteenth-century Polemics and Apologetics*; I. Almond (2010), *Representations of Islam in Western Thought* (Sarajevo: Center for Advanced Studies Publications), pp. 19–65.
50. M. Luther [1530], *Vorwort zu dem Libellus de ritu et moribus Turcorum* (*Preface to Libellus de ritu etmoribus Turcorum*), translated by J. L. Boyce and S. Henrich (1996) 'Martin Luther–Translations of Two Prefaces on Islam: Preface to the *Libellus de ritu et moribus Turcorum* (1530), and Preface to Bibliander's Edition of the Qur'an (1543)', *Word & World*, Vol. XVI, No. 2, p. 29.
51. Almond, 'Deconstructing Luther's Islam', p. 60.
52. Lutheran chaplain, Stephan Gerlach stayed in Constantinople from 1573 to 1578 to organize an ecumenical correspondence between the Greek Patriarch and two prominent Lutherans from Wittenberg, Jakob Andreae (1528–90) and Martin Crusius (1526–1607).
53. K. Karpat (2002), *Studies on Ottoman Social and Political History* (Leiden: E. J. Brill), p. 488.

54. Melanchton was directly in touch with orthodox authorities in the Ottoman Empire, including the Patriarch of Constantinople, who was in effect an official of the Sultan. Melanchthon provided hospitality to Demetrios Mysos, a Serbian deacon sent by the Patriarch of Constantinople to find out about the new religious movement in Germany.
55. There was a close correspondence between the reformers at Wittenberg and scholars in Hungary. G. Murdock (2000), *Calvinism on the Frontier 1600–1660. International Calvinism and the Reformed Church in Hungary and Transylvania* (Oxford: Oxford University Press).
56. Segesvary, *L'Islam et la Réforme*; E. Campi (2010), 'Early Reformed Attitudes towards Islam', *Theological Review of the Near East School of Theology,* No. 31, pp. 131–51; K. Vehlow (1995), 'The Swiss Reformers Zwingli, Bullinger and Bibliander and Their Attitude to Islam (1520–1560)', *Islam and Christian-Muslim Relations*, Vol. 6, No. 2, pp. 229–54.
57. T. Bibliander (1543), *Machumetis Saracenorum principis vita ac doctrina omnis, quae & Ismahelitarum lex, & Alcoranum discitur.*
58. T. Bibliander (1543), translated, annotated and introduced by H. Lamarque (2007), *Le Coran à la Renaissance: plaidoyer pour une traduction* (Toulouse: Presses universitaires du Mirail).
59. S. R. Boettcher (2004), 'German Orientalism in the Age of Confessional Consolidation: Jacob Andreae's *Thirteen Sermons on the Turk,* 1568', *Comparative Studies of South Asia, Africa and the Middle East,* Vol. 24, No. 2, p. 104.
60. Campi, 'Early Reformed Attitudes towards Islam', p. 150.
61. J. M. Evenson (2005), *Judaism, Islam and English Reformation Literature*, PhD dissertation (English Language and Literature), University of Michigan, unpublished.
62. Boettcher, 'German Orientalism in the Age of Confessional Consolidation', pp. 105, 108.
63. F. Konrad (2011), 'From the "Turkish Menace" to Exoticism and Orientalism: Islam as Antithesis of Europe (1453–1914)?' in *European History Online* (EGO), published by the Institute of European History (IEG), Mainz 14 March 2011, http://www.ieg-ego.eu/konradf-2010-en.
64. On the influence of Islamic scholarly institutions on the rise of universities in Europe, see G. Makdisi (1981), *The Rise of Colleges: Institutions of Learning in Islam and the West* (Edinburgh: Edinburgh University Press). On the role of the press in the Protestant Reformation, see R. G. Cole (1984), 'Reformation Printers: Unsung Heroes', *Sixteenth Century Journal*, Vol. 15, No. 3, pp. 327–39; M. U. Edwards (2004), *Printing, Propaganda and Martin Luther* (Minneapolis, MN: Fortress Press).
65. G. H. Williams (cop. 1992), *The Radical Reformation* (Kirksville/Missouri: Sixteenth Century Journal Publishers), pp. 27–8.
66. G. A. Russell (1994), 'Introduction: The Seventeenth Century: The Age of "Arabick"', in G. A. Russell (ed.) *The 'Arabick' Interest of the Natural Philosophers in Seventeenth-century England* (Leiden; New York [etc.]: E. J. Brill), pp. 3–5.
67. Segesvary, *L'Islam et la Réforme*, p. 58.
68. Goody, *Islam in Europe*, p. 49.
69. S. Ritchie (2004), 'The Islamic Ottoman Influence on the Development of Religious Toleration in Reformation Transylvania', *Seasons*, pp. 59–70;

J. Headley (1987), '"Ehe Türckisch als Bäpstisch": Lutheran Reflections on the Problem of Empire, 1623–28', *Central European History*, Vol. 20, No. 1, pp. 22–3; A. H. Compier (2010), 'Let the Muslim Be My Master in outward Things'. References to Islam in the Promotion of Religious Tolerance in Christian Europe, *Al-Islam eGazette*, p. 7, https://eric.exeter.ac.uk/repository/bitstream/handle/10036/90953/Islam-in-Christian-tolerance-201001.pdf?sequence=2.

70. Headley, 'Ehe Türckisch als Bäpstisch', pp. 22–3.
71. Compier, 'Let the Muslim Be My Master in Outward Things', p. 7.
72. Ritchie, 'The Islamic Ottoman Influence', p. 61.
73. Ibid., p. 69.
74. Headley, 'Ehe Türckisch als Bäpstisch', p. 21.
75. Segesvary, *L'Islam et la Réforme*, pp. 263–4.
76. See, for example, A. S. Unghváry (1989), *The Hungarian Protestant Reformation in the Sixteenth Century under the Ottoman Impact: Essays and Profiles* (Lewiston: Edwin Mellen Press).
77. G. Murdock (2000), *Calvinism on the Frontier 1600–1660. International Calvinism and the Reformed Church in Hungary and Transylvania* (Oxford: Oxford University Press).
78. G. A. Russell (1994), 'The Impact of *The Philosophus Autodidactus*: Pocockes, John Locke, and the Society of Friends', in G. A. Russell (ed.) *The 'Arabick' Interest of the Natural Philosophers in Seventeenth-century England* (Leiden; New York [etc.]: E. J. Brill); J. Tual, 'La Réception du Hay Ibn Yakdan en Angleterre du 17ème siècle : Islam et quakerisme', *Civilisations et littératures du monde anglophone*, Centre de Recherches Littéraires et Historiques de l'Océan Indien, http://crlhoi.univ-reunion.fr/litrun/index.php/articles/civilisations-et-litteratures-du-monde-anglophone/103-la-reception-du-hay-ibn-yakdan-en-angleterre-au-17eme-siecle-lislam-et-la-lumiere-interieure-des, accessed 11 April 2011.
79. References are to be found in the Fifth and Sixth Propositions of Barclay's *Apology: Concerning the Universal Redemption by Christ*, and *Saving and Spiritual Light Wherewith Every Man Is Enlightened*.
80. Karpat, *The Ottoman State and Its Place in World History*, pp. 8–9.
81. T. Krstić (2011), *Contested Conversions to Islam: Narratives of Religious Change in the Early Modern Ottoman Empire* (Stanford: Stanford University Press).
82. Goffman, *The Ottoman Empire and Early Modern Europe*, p. 20.
83. Ritchie, 'The Islamic Ottoman Influence', p. 60.
84. S. Khalaf (1997), 'Protestant Images of Islam: Disparaging Stereotypes Reconfirmed', *Islam and Christian-Muslim Relations*, Vol. 8, No. 2, pp. 211–29; S. Foley (2009), 'Muslims and Social Change in the Atlantic Basin', *Journal of World History*, Vol. 2, No. 3, pp. 377–98.

Roman law were lost to Europe during the early Middle Ages, although remnants of Roman law remained. Large areas of Europe were influenced by Germanic law, in particular England, France and Spain, due to the spread and settling of German tribes. The majority of medieval law was customary, unwritten law.[2] Justice in the West was believed to be decided largely by God through trial by ordeal, which included burning people with red-hot irons or boiling water, submerging them in cold water, or trial by duel.[3] The philosophy behind this method of proof was that God, or nature in the case of cold water (water being a 'pure element' that would not receive those stained with crime), would shield the innocent from injury and reveal the guilty. The law was, thus, believed to be determined by divine authority or by nature, and could not be altered by human agency, even if it could be interpreted by human beings in novel circumstances.[4]

However, at the close of the eleventh century, economic, social and cultural changes sweeping through Europe would transform European laws and legal practices over the following century and a half. The social and commercial expansion of the time required, among other things, a means of dealing with contracts, credit, banking and transferring property. In Bologna, specialized schools devoted to Roman civil law began to appear from 1100 onward. The church's canon law began to distinguish itself from theology during the twelfth century. Changes in the field of law impacted the lives of everyone in what has become known among Medievalists as the Renaissance of the twelfth century.[5] The emergence of a rule of law had tremendous social, political and economic implications. It implied that individuals were free to sell and transfer property without being constrained by rules established by kinship, religious authorities or the state. It also meant that people could enter freely into contracts, and that those contracts could be enforced, thus providing for predictability in trading relations.[6] Moreover, the establishment of permanent, impersonal institutions, agreement on the need for an authority capable of giving final judgments and an acceptance that loyalty to the state should be the ultimate loyalty, represented a keystone in medieval state formation.[7]

The systematization of a set of legal rules that stood above social groups, the state and the church is often assumed to be among the many characteristics that distinguished Europe from the rest of the world, enabling its inexorable rise, in no small part due to Max Weber's influential thought. Older forms of justice had originated in conflict resolution between kinship groups. Weber considered this 'primitive' form of justice 'irrational' in the sense that it was not derived from a systematized body of rules, which meant that there was no generalized way of arriving at decisions or discerning how decisions were arrived at after the fact.[8] The rationalization of law occurred as irrational procedures were gradually eliminated and substantive law was systematized. Integral to Weber's process of rationalization was the secularization of law and the development of formal juridical thought.[9] In Weber's view, '[j]uridical formalism enables the legal system to operate like a technically rational machine. Thus, it guarantees to individuals and groups within the system a relative maximum of freedom, and greatly increases for them the possibility of predicting the legal consequences of their actions. Procedure becomes a specific type of pacified contest, bound to fixed and inviolable "rules of the game".'[10] Under rational systems, facts are established by rational procedure, notably through the examination of witnesses.

While Weber recognized that all organized societies possessed law, European legal systems were considered distinct. Only European law was believed to be suited to the needs of capitalism. European law was, thus, deemed to have played an important role in the emergence of capitalism in Europe. The European legal system was viewed as unique among civilizations in its formal and structural nature. Weber emphasized the significance of two elements of law for the development of capitalism: one was calculability; and the other its ability to create the conditions for a market system, most notably freedom of contract.[11] England was somewhat of an anomaly in that industrial capitalism is believed to have developed there first, even though its legal system was not fully formally rationalized. Weber attempted to account for this apparent discrepancy by emphasizing that capitalists were favoured by the courts and that the rules of due process provided a degree of rationality and, as a result, calculability.[12] Europe's formally rational legal systems were believed to stand in contrast to those in other parts of the world, including the Islamic world. Weber argues that the systematization of Islamic law was impossible, because innovations could be brought about by *fatwa* or through disputations between the various schools of law, and because of the inadequacy of the rationality of juridical thought. Officially licensed individuals (*muftis*) could be called upon by religious–juridical officials (*qadis*) to give a legal opinion, but that opinion would vary from person to person. This, according to Weber, increased the irrationality of sacred law. Moreover, Islamic law only applied to Muslims and not to subject peoples that belonged to other confessions, leading to 'legal particularism'.[13]

Weber's schema finds echoes in more recent scholarship on the emergence of the rule of law in Europe. Francis Fukuyama, for example, has argued that Western Europe was unique insofar as law was institutionalized earlier and to a much greater degree than elsewhere. The systematization of canon law in the eleventh century, he argues, contrasts with the Eastern Church or Hindu and Muslim traditions, the latter of which were not codified until the encroachment of Western influence in the nineteenth century. This new body of codified law, in his view based on Roman law, was at first the domain of the church, but was gradually taken over by legal specialists trained in canon and civil law. Fukuyama rightly notes that in this regard law became entrusted to legal specialists in both Christian and Muslim as well as Hindu lands. Yet, like Weber, Fukuyama emphasizes that what separated Hindu and Muslim systems from that of Christian Europe was the lack of a fully systematized or codified legal system, and neither *brahmin* nor *ulama* formed a unified and powerful hierarchy. Both *panditas* (religious jurist) and *qadis* applied existing precedents to new cases as they arose.[14] Similarly, in his study of the Scientific Revolution in Europe from a comparative perspective, Toby Huff has recently argued that Chinese, Indian and Islamic civilizations 'lagged with respect to legal innovation' when 'the extraordinary fusion of Greek philosophy, Roman law, and Christian theology gave Europe a new and powerful civilizational coherence'.[15]

Given that a rational, as opposed to divine, character of the justice system and the separation of temporal and divine power are also understood to be major factors distinguishing Europe in particular, and the West in general, from the Muslim world, and for the emergence of capitalism and Europe's rise, it might seem odd to look for possible similarities between Islamic and European legal systems. At first glance, the religious character of Islamic law and rationally constructed Western jurisprudence appear to have very little in common. Yet, as Fukuyama himself points out, while it is often assumed that the West and Muslim lands differed in the relationship between spiritual and temporal authorities, in fact, there is a greater similarity than is often assumed. What is different, he argues, is the degree of separation. While religious and temporal authority was often fused in European sovereigns, the jurisdictions of caliphs and sultans frequently became separated and the *ulama* had their own standards and acted as checks on temporal power.[16] Moreover, the rationalization of law and the state, which led to the separation of the church and the state, may not have occurred in Europe as autonomously as many people have become accustomed to thinking, and the dissimilarity of modern European institutions from those of Islamic lands may not be as great as first imagined. Indeed, Islamic societies were based on the rule of law long before those of the West.[17] It would not be surprising, then, if Europeans who came into contact with the more advanced legal institutions of the Arab and Islamic world applied them to their own societies.

Indeed, a number of scholars, most notably John Makdisi, George Makdisi,[18] as well as Marcel A. Boisard, Gamal Mousr Badr and P. J. Hamilton, have undertaken fascinating studies on the possible influence of Arab–Islamic legal institutions on those of the West. They suggest a plausible influence of Islamic legal institutions on the development of common law in England, as well as some aspects of the Spanish and French legal systems. It is not surprising that similarities may be found between some legal institutions in Spain and England and those of the Islamic world; the reconquest of Spain by Spanish Catholics and of Sicily by the Normans (who were simultaneously in England), brought Islamic and European legal traditions into direct and, in the case of England, indirect contact. The Crusades, that were well underway by the twelfth century, also provided a conduit to the countries engaged in them, such as France, although the similarities and opportunities for transmission of Islamic legal institutions to Europe can only be suggested. A more far-reaching study would require an examination of documents related to Spain following the Reconquest, Norman Sicily, Norman England, the Crusades, as well as the records of the military-religious orders that were present in the Holy Land and Europe. Moreover, it must be pointed out that similarities and opportunities for the borrowing of ideas do not amount to proof of transmission. Nevertheless, the hypothesis of a possible influence of Islamic legal institutions on those of early Medieval Europe does merit investigation and is most marked in the case of England. Indeed, the most substantial research on the contribution of the Arab and Islamic world to European legal institutions has focused on England. Since England is attributed a central role in the rise of the West, I focus in particular on the possible contribution that Islamic legal institutions may have had on the institutional changes that took place in that country as part of the emergence of a rule of law and the formation of the modern state – developments that were essential for the transformation of social relations involved in the transition from feudalism to capitalism. I do, nevertheless, suggest how the legal institutions of other European countries may have been influenced by those of Islamic lands.

The emergence of a rule of law and the development of an impersonal state in England

By far the most documented case of the possible transmission of Islamic legal institutions to Europe is that in England. Notions of power and government in the twelfth century were very different from today's. Developments that took place then were highly significant to the transformation of 'political society' in Europe. Law, legal systems and the growth of governance linked to increasingly sophisticated administrative structures were particularly important in bringing about this wide-ranging change. In England, the introduction of a new body of legal practices and concepts had a profound impact on the evolution of law, governance and politics in that country. Legal pronouncements by the king were statements of policy regarding the relationship of English law to the church's international canon law on the one hand, and the evolution of the royal system of jurisprudence on the other. Law and legal argument played an important role in stimulating notions of state. Under King Henry II (1154–89), royal courts were made the final courts of appeal against decisions made by lords in manor courts. They also offered procedures by writ in order to recover debts and settle disputes over land and inheritance. The growing sophistication of legal procedures generated a greater need for people with specialized legal knowledge, such as judges and lawyers. As their numbers increased, dedicated schools would be required to train them. Attitudes to the concept of proof were also changing during this period. Trial by jury began to replace trial by ordeal. During this transition, justice became associated with the temporal as opposed to the spiritual realm, although trial by battle continued for some time but increasingly became an anachronism outside of the chivalric domain. These legal innovations would have an important impact on the idea of politics, which was associated largely with lordship until the twelfth century. The notion that part of a ruler's responsibility was to ensure justice for the people of the land would take hold thereafter.[19]

The major features emerging in English common law were contract law, property law and trial by jury. To take the first, the writ of debt in the twelfth century was the earliest, most commonly used, royal writ issued to recover contract debts. It compelled buyers and sellers in the sale of goods to honour their obligations. This contrasted with Anglo-Saxon contracts in which obligations were established through a formality, such as a handshake, and depended on the morality of the contracting parties. After making the promise, the seller had an obligation to deliver the property that was his/her own to the buyer and the buyer to pay the agreed price for whatever was being sold. The obligation was based on the notion of debt initiated by entering into a contract.[20]

In the same century, the notion of ownership was advanced within emergent property law. Henry II ordered his judges to protect those in possession of land, referred to as *seisin*, against eviction in the absence of legal process. The grand assize (or grand jury), which traces its origin to the Assize of Clarendon enacted by Henry II in 1166, enabled any defendant whose title to land was challenged to demand a hearing at the royal court. Instead of a judgment decided by trial by battle, judgment was made by sworn jury. Through petty assizes of *novel disseisin* – *disseisin* being the act of dispossessing someone of their land – and *mort d'ancestor*, an actual occupant or the heir of a deceased occupant, if evicted without trial, could ask for a royal writ for a hearing by a jury in the king's court.[21] While dispossessing someone of their land may seem necessarily wrong, before these institutional changes were made, custom allowed it as a form of coercion if a tenant, for example, failed to render services to his lord. Seeking justice through the courts was not the only means through which people sought to right wrongs, in some instances this was only the last resort. Indeed, customary law was not necessarily opposed to forcibly depriving someone of his land, as long as the defendant had right on his side.[22] The assize of *novel disseisin* revolutionized the means of protecting land ownership in England. By order of a writ purchased in the king's court, twelve jurors would inspect the property and aspects of the specific case. These jurors would then state the facts in the king's court, which would then decide whether the plaintiff had been removed from the land unjustly. This process was more rational than an action brought by writ of right, which took place in a lord's court and required that proof of ownership be provided by either the plaintiff or the defendant. This could end in trial by battle should the evidence not be strong enough to constitute proof of ownership. The assize of *mort d'ancestor* provided a way of deciding between rival claimants, one of whom would have been in possession of the land in question.[23]

The method of proof also underwent change. While trial by oath had been in practice in England, alongside trial by ordeal, trial by jury became predominant. The grand assize called for inquiry to be made into those suspected of robbery, murder or theft, or of harbouring those guilty of such crimes,[24] and called for four knights to choose twelve knights to reach a verdict; for the criminal assizes, the sheriff chose twelve freeholders from each hundred (a county sub-division) and four men from each village; for petty assizes, twelve men were selected by the sheriff. Title to property was now decided by jurors and not by battle. The success of the system was partly due to its similarity to ancient custom, by which villagers would give judgment and village tithings would present the guilty.[25]

The implications of the legal innovations of the twelfth century had profound social and political ramifications. Feudal relations comprised mutual obligations via the grant of land. The lord committed himself to protecting and maintaining his tenant. In return, his tenant undertook to protect his lord's honour, which included rendering knightly and other services. Upon the tenant's death, the lord would become his heir's guardian and would choose the heir's spouse. While feudal relations entailed the subordination of the tenant to the lord, they were not governed by any definitive notion of rights and obligations. Moreover, feudal courts were not strictly regulated by a higher authority. Were the lord's tenant to die, his heir and widow could remain on the land only as part of the lord's obligation to the deceased not because of any kind of property right. The lord could, however, disinherit a tenant for disloyalty or incompetence. Property rights meant that a person's claim to land was no longer dependent on a personal relationship, but was protected by a bureaucratic authority and set rules,[26] '[l]and left the sphere of personal relationships and became property.'[27] Tenants were now protected from abuses by lords in that they could seek justice by appealing to the King.

The effect of the new legal procedures introduced during the reign of Henry II was to reduce the authority of lordship. These changes would help pave the way for a transformation of societal relations through the concept of ownership. The assize of *novel disseisin* protected landowners usurped of their land under the king's law and, thus, property rights.[28] Power was in the process of being rationalized as well as centralized. Indeed, common law contributed to the growth of the state in England. The gradual transfer of authority from manorial courts to a uniform national common law administered by the royal courts was central to the formation of the modern state, marking a shift in the balance of baronial and royal power. Henry II consolidated royal authority through the advances made in the establishment of common law under his reign. At the same time, the forfeitures of the convicted contributed to a growth in the royal coffers. Henry II's successor, King Edward I, further strengthened the authority of the royal courts. The royal writs marked the end of feudal justice in the manorial courts.[29] The predominance of trial by jury as opposed to trial by ordeal signified a transition from transcendental to temporal appeals for justice and, as a result, a greater emphasis on temporal rather than spiritual power.

Enforcing the provisions of the assizes necessitated full-time justices. As they grew in number, justices came to resemble a bureaucracy.[30] The most advanced apprentices of law formed permanent societies that were similar to guilds (Inns of Court), where teaching could take place and apprentices could be selected by the more senior members to be licensed as advocates to assist the judges in the king's courts.[31] This practice differed from much of the European Continent, where law was taught in universities. Indeed, the University of Bologna, as mentioned earlier, specialized in legal studies. The English Inns of Court were attached to places of worship. In London, the inns emerged during the reigns of King Stephen (1135–54) and his successor Henry II. One was attached to the Church of St. Paul, St. George's Inn was attached to the Church of the Sepulchre and Thavie's Inn attached to St. Andrew's. By the thirteenth century these early law schools, or church inns, were secularized by apprentices-at-law, who then became subordinate to them. Four such Inns of Court exist today: the Inner Temple, the Middle Temple, Lincoln's Inn and Gray's Inn.[32] Unlike today, the students and lawyers of the Inns of earlier times did not go home at night. The Inns were closed communities and their members observed their customs, owed them their loyalty and, indeed, lived their lives within them. The Inns had humble beginnings, functioning as seminaries and hostels. Yet, they were to become organized institutions, with recognized authority. Even in present-day England, no one may practice at the Bar without being a member of one of the Inns of Court.[33] The Inns of Court themselves were created through the use of another legal innovation, the trust, or the use as it was also known. The use was an arrangement in which the owner of the property, the *foeffor*, granted legal estate to a *foeffee to uses*, who was given the full rights of ownership of the *foeffor*. The *foeffee* had, however, to use these rights of ownership for the benefit of another person. To this day, the Inns of Court are unincorporated guilds that fit within the trust tradition.[34]

The origins of English common law: a possible connection with the Arab and Islamic worlds?

The origins of these institutional changes that together formed a significant part of common law have been much debated. The most important influences are often thought to be Roman civil law and canon law.[35] However, another possible source of influence has been advanced. As John Makdisi notes, 'the legal institutions of the common law fit within a structural and functional pattern that is unique among western legal systems and certainly different from that of the civil law'.[36] Makdisi suggests that the origins of common law may be found in Islamic law. He argues that the institutions that together helped to form common law by introducing the concepts of contract law, property rights and trial by jury may have their origins in three analogous institutions in Islamic law, the *'aqd*, the *istihqaq* and the *lafif*.[37]

The action of debt, so important for contract law, is most frequently attributed to Roman law. Yet, under Roman law, while the buyer had an obligation to pay the agreed price to the seller and the seller to deliver the goods to the buyer, ownership was not transferred at the point of entering into a contract. While there was a notion of being owed under Roman law, the common law writ of debt implied ownership and, hence, property rights, even before delivery of the goods. A possible source of influence for the idea of property as ownership transferred upon agreement, Makdisi argued, may be found in the Islamic *'aqd* or law of contract, which predated the frequent use of the royal writ of debt in England. There is a possibility, then, that the notion of property as ownership passed at the time of agreement to a contract in English common law could have been influenced by the already existing Islamic law of contract.[38]

Like the notion of debt as ownership in English contract law, the origin of the assize of *novel disseisin* has never been determined. The assize does not seem to have come from Normandy or been derived from Anglo-Saxon law. Some similarity does, however, exist between the assize of *novel disseisin* and canon and Roman law. Consequently, the origin of the assize has been frequently attributed to canon as well as Roman law. Yet, despite similarities with the Roman interdict *unde vi* that enabled the recovery of possession of property, the Roman interdict protected possession rather than ownership. This same distinction existed between canon law and the assize. Yet the Islamic *istihqaq*, which constituted an action for recovery of land in case of usurpation, was also based on the presumption of ownership. In addition, the assize of *novel disseissin* and the *istihqaq* shared a number of similarities, including a jury of twelve witnesses charged with providing the facts of the matter. Moreover, the existence of these shared features in Islamic law predated their emergence in English law, making it possible that the origins of the assize of *novel disseisin* were influenced by Islamic law.[39]

As mentioned, trial by jury as a procedure for providing proof differed remarkably from what went before. Anglo-Saxon or Norman origins of the jury have been identified by some scholars.[40] Others argue that it is most likely the result of a gradual development of ancient customs, introduced into England by its earliest invaders, which then came under Norman influence and, thereafter, evolved with the growth of an increasingly complex society.[41] The Frankish inquisition of the

Normans used members of the community to swear on the truth of a matter. Yet it was used as an administrative rather than a judicial procedure. The closest Anglo-Saxon tradition that approximates to a jury is the custom of using a group of neighbours to resolve conflicts through their own verdicts. However, the tradition of 'recognition' took place with the agreement of the parties or by preference of the court, and not as a matter of right.[42] Moreover, the witnesses were possibly only employed prior to a trial to establish whether a case could go to trial. In this sense, they were witnesses upon which the plaintiff could make his case.[43] The Islamic *lafif* appears to more closely approximate the English jury than any Anglo-Saxon and Norman antecedents.[44] The principal method of proof under Islamic law was the testimony of witnesses. The characteristics of these witnesses closely resembled those of the jury of the English assizes. They came from the neighbourhood and were generally twelve in number. As under English common law, judges were bound by the verdict of the *lafif* or jury.[45]

Gamal Moursi Badr notes that a parallel also exists between common law and Islamic law in relation to the institution of agency, which was unknown to Roman law. Under Roman law, an individual could act as an agent and conclude a contract on behalf of another individual. Moreover, unlike modern civil law, common law like Islamic law recognizes the institution of the undisclosed principal. An agent could conclude a contract without the other contracting party knowing of a principal's existence or their identity. Yet, once the principal's identity or existence became known to the contracting party a link between the two, nevertheless, was made. While this was unknown under civil law, it existed within Islamic law before its appearance in English common law.[46] Yet, as Moursi Badr is eager to point out, these parallels do not amount to proof of diffusion from one system to the other.

The origins of the legal profession in England are often thought of as somewhat obscure. In addition to parallels related to the legal institutions discussed, the first law schools in both England and Islamic lands were church inns and mosque inns, respectively. In London, the Inns were attached to churches, whereas in the Muslim world, they were attached to mosques. In Islam, Islamic guilds of the legal profession, *madhhabs*, existed from the late ninth century onward. *Madhhab* meaning that which is followed or the opinion that one adopts. While higher education of all kinds took place in mosques, *madhhabs* were attached to mosques because of the long years of study and concentration required by those studying law. Law students were unable to lodge in the mosques and, therefore, there was a need for separate lodgings.

In both cases, as George Makdisi and John Makdisi point out, church inns and mosque inns were created as unincorporated guilds. While early colleges in England also started this way then later became incorporated, Inns of Court remained unincorporated. Moreover, the method of teaching, based on lectures and disputations also resembled that of mosque inns. Like the *madhhabs* that were autonomous from the state and legitimate representatives of the *Umma*, the Inns of Court also enjoyed autonomy as the representatives of the community of lawyers and had a monopoly on legal affairs.[47]

Inns of Court were created within the tradition of the English trust, as mentioned, whose origins have been the subject of much debate. The trust provides an additional example of the apparent transmission of Islamic legal institutions to England. It has been suggested that the origin of the trust in England may be found in the Islamic *waqf*. Western scholars have explored the possibility of Germanic or Roman influence, or indeed both.[48] However, more recently, it has been suggested that the trust may have its origins in the Islamic *waqf*. The Islamic legal institution thought to have been the source of inspiration for the trust was developed sometime during the first three centuries of Islam. The *waqf* was an unincorporated charitable trust. An endowment of this sort had either a religious or a public nature. The *waqf* was generally used to endow hospitals, colleges and, mosques.[49] While the *wqaf* is not mentioned in the Quran, there are references to it in the Hadith. The Prophet Mohammed's sayings recount instances where people gave away land, for instance, for charitable purposes. One hadith tells of how Caliph Omar wished to give away land as *sadaqa* (charity), but was told by the Prophet to retain the land itself and devote its fruits to virtuous ends.[50] Monica Gaudiosi argues that the trust resembles the *waqf* more closely than it does either the *fideicommissum* in Roman law or the *Salmannus* of the Salic law of the Franks/Normans, believed to have been introduced to England at the Norman Conquest. Both the trust and the *waqf* have a *waqif* or settler, a *mutawalli* or trustee and beneficiaries.[51] While stressing that similarities between legal institutions do not necessarily imply that one influenced the other, Avisheh Avini concurs that if the trust originated from elsewhere, the Islamic *waqf* is the most likely source of inspiration.[52]

Quite apart from the remarkable similarities between English and Islamic legal institutions, the opportunity for transmission of institutions from Arab–Islamic lands to England during the reign of Henry II – when the major dimensions of common law came into being – existed principally via Norman controlled Sicily, which had not long before been part of the Islamic Empire. As John Makdisi points out, the Islamic legal institutions that so closely resembled those that emerged in England following the Norman Conquest belonged primarily to the Maliki school of Islamic law, which predominated in North Africa and Al-Andalus (Muslim Spain) during the medieval period. The Maliki legal tradition was particularly entrenched in Ifriqiya (now Tunisia) and Sicily. There was, thus, an opportunity for the transmission of elements of the Maliki doctrine to Europe, and to England in particular, through Sicily.[53] Sicily had strong ties with Ifriqiya and with its capital Qayrawān in particular, making the Maliki legal school predominant in Sicily. The Sidi Ukbah bin Nafi in Qayrawān played a significant role in the dissemination of the Maliki school of law across the western part of the Islamic Empire. Qayrawān was an influential centre of learning and culture, and a number of mosque schools were to be found first in urban centres and later in rural areas. They drew renowned scholars from the eastern part of the Islamic Empire and, in time, encouraged the indigenous North African population to embrace Islam. The ruling dynasty of Ifriqiya, the Aghlabids, sent judges trained in Maliki law to Sicily during their conquest of the Island. Within legal studies, the *madhhab* of Maliki law was dominant in Islamic Sicily.[54]

Ifriqiya and Sicily were part of the Islamic Empire from the ninth to the twelfth century. Significantly, when the Normans conquered Sicily, they did not seek to replace Islamic institutions and Muslim culture with their own, rather, they integrated them. Muslims were able to practice their own religion and were subject to their own laws. Norman administration integrated aspects of the existing government and administration, especially in the area of bureaucracy and finance. Moreover, Sicily maintained close links with Ifriqiya, King Roger II of Sicily (1095–1154) even occupied Ifriqiya.[55] Conversion to christianity was not a precondition for political positions within the kingdom. Many Muslim leaders continued to occupy their previous posts even after the Norman Conquest of Sicily. Indeed, conversion seems to have been discouraged under Count Roger I, who had conquered the Island between 1061 and 1072. There is also evidence that the Muslims of Sicily continued to use Shari'ah law for judgments related to custom and civil disputes.[56]

Roger II had grown up in Norman Sicily, where Norman and Muslim cultures merged. He was known to have remained close to his Muslim subjects, as his father had done before him, and integrated Islamic traditions into his government, over which he presided from 1112–54.[57] He had, nevertheless, maintained ties to the Norman kingdom of England. Robert of Selby, Roger II's chancellor and trusted aid was an Englishman.[58] The reign of Henry II began in England the year of Roger II's death. Sicily under Roger II's reign from 1130 to 1154 and England under Henry II, whose reign lasted from 1154 to 1189, shared a number of similar features, including the treasuries, high courts and chanceries charged with administering and coordinating other departments of state. Sicily was a key point on the journey between northern Europe and the Holy Land for crusaders, as well as for trade between Europe and Islamic lands. A continual movement of personnel between England and Sicily also took place.[59] The Knights Templar handled a great deal of the capital of Western Europe for more than a century. They became experts in financial and commercial methods that revolutionized trade and finance. The relations between the Templars and the English Crown may have contributed to the development of the fiscal system in England in the thirteenth century. They became the king's bankers. Indeed, Eleanor Ferris writes that the Templars had worked out a system of bills of exchange to transfer money to the Continent without the actual transfer of money.[60]

During the Crusades, Henry II's son, Richard the Lionheart, passed through Sicily on his way to Palestine; Henry II's daughter, Joan of Plantagenet, married King William of Sicily in 1177;[61] Peter of Blois, William II of Sicily's tutor and friend, and a friend of Henry II, also moved between the two Norman kingdoms.[62] Another such example was Henry II's special advisor, Master Thomas Brown, born in England around 1120, he was also present in Sicily around 1137 and is believed to have been the protégé of Chancellor Robert of Selby, who had also come to Sicily from England. In 1149, Brown became known as Kaid Brun in the fiscal department of the Sicilian government, the *diwan*. Significantly, the *diwan* dealt with bought and sold land, recovered the king's property and held court to decide land disputes, as well as fiscal matters. Brown was compelled to leave Sicily and return to England in 1154 – the year that Henry II came to the throne – where he held an important position at the Exchequer under Henry II. John Makdisi surmises that Henry II would have had an opportunity to learn about the *istihqaq*, the Islamic legal method for recovering land, as well as the Islamic *lafif* or jury. Indeed, only eight years after Thomas Brown returned to England, the assize of *novel disseisin* and the English jury came into existence.[63] This may, of course, have been pure coincidence. However, the similarities between the emergence of these more rational legal mechanisms and those that already existed in Islamic law, given the opportunity for their transmission, suggests that there may be reason to believe that the action of debt, the assize of *novel disseisin* and the notion of ownership, and trial by jury, that together formed a major part of the emergent common law in England, could have at least some Islamic origins. At the very least, they deserve to be noted and further explored.

The etymology of the word assize is itself unclear. It was thought to derive from the old French *assise*, which denoted the act of sitting or settlement, referring to a legislative sitting of the king. Yet another possible origin has been identified. John Makdisi speculates that the term may have derived from *siyaasah*, denoting the sovereign's administrative authority to dispense justice in the name of Islam. Some of the earliest assizes took place in Jerusalem in 1099 during the First Crusade, in Scotland at the beginning of the twelfth century and in Sicily in 1140 during Roger II's reign.[64] Given the movement of people between England and the Holy Land, sometimes via Sicily, transmission of ideas and institutions, such as the assize, would have been probable, particularly given the more advanced nature of Islamic institutions of governance at that time.

With regards to the Inns of Court and their possible Islamic origin, the early history of the Temple Inns of Court in London is also believed by George Makdisi to have been connected to the Knights Templar and the Knights Hospitaller.[65] The connection with lawyers would come later.[66] The Temple grounds, for example, were once occupied by the Knights Templar until the king sequestered its funds, threw the Master of the Temple into the Tower of London, and treated the Temple grounds as those of the Crown. The sites of the two Inns were settled by the two orders previously.[67] The Order of the Knights Templar itself was established in Jerusalem in the early period of the Crusades in the first half of the eleventh century. King Baldwin II of Jerusalem (an Italian Norman), gave them lodgings in his palace next to the Al-Aqsa Mosque and the Temple of Solomon. The knights were present in the Levant until the thirteenth century. The Order of the Knights Hospitaller was also created in Jerusalem. Its origins were an eleventh-century hospital near the Church of St. John the Baptist. At this time, schools of law in Islam had already existed for quite some time and were in Palestine, Syria and Egypt at the time of the Crusades. It is certainly possible, as George Makdisi notes, that crusaders, pilgrims, merchants and scholars became familiar with their form and function.[68] Indeed, there is also evidence of military cooperation and political interdependence between Latin and Muslim communities in the Levant during the early phase of Frankish settlement.[69] The inns were not only historically linked to London, but also Paris, which was also connected to Jerusalem.

The first inn was founded in Paris in 1180 by John of London, following his return from a pilgrimage to Jerusalem.[70]

The use of trusts in England coincided with increased contacts and exchanges between Europe and the Arab–Islamic world. The Franciscan Friars, who are thought to have introduced the use of the trust to England,[71] were also present in the Middle East. Pilgrimages, as well as the Crusades, would have propelled many Europeans to the Holy Land from the eleventh century. As noted, the Orders of the Templars and the Hospitallers were also present in Jerusalem between the twelfth and thirteenth centuries. The principal house of the Templars was established in London in 1128. It was used as a safe deposit for wealth as well as for banking operations undertaken for the king.[72] Moreover, from the mid-twelfth century, the Templars sometimes acted as trustees for funds that were deposited with them to be used for specific projects.[73] The founder of Merton College in Oxford, Walter de Merton, a clergyman and a civil servant during the thirteenth century, used the New Temple in London to carry out business transactions and as a place to deposit his wealth. The establishment of the college is believed to illustrate the possible Islamic origins of the trust in England. Walter de Merton would have come into contact with people who had been in the Middle East in his function as chancellor. The endowment was initially an unincorporated charitable trust (like a *waqf*) when established in 1264, but became incorporated a decade later.[74] This was thought to mark the beginning of the college system in England.[75]

Beyond England to the European Continent

Much less research has been carried out on the possible influence of Islamic legal institutions on continental European legal systems than on English systems. Yet, some possible elements of transmission may be suggested. Saint Louis IX (1214–70), King of France, was known for his reforms. He appointed royal inquirers, instituted testimonial truth and the right to make a plea to the king.[76] Jean de Joinville was a soldier who accompanied the King on his crusades and wrote what would today be considered a biography of Saint Louis. Louis IX set off on his first crusade in 1248 and returned to France five years later. He was the first French monarch to issue legislation covering the entire realm. He legislated against the practice of trial by battle. As in England, the issue being addressed was how the truth was to be determined in legal cases. The established way was by ordeal, but this was a last resort. Before reaching this stage, the accused could counter the accusation under oath and call what were essentially character witnesses. It was only when an impasse had been arrived at, after both accused and accuser had sworn oaths and secured the necessary character witnesses, that the truth was to be determined by ordeal.[77] As in the case of trial by jury under English common law, it is conceivable that this change in relation to the method of determining the truth took place in France in the thirteenth century was inspired by the same Islamic legal institution, the *lafif.* It is also possible that King Louis IX came into contact with Islamic legal institutions when he was in Palestine. Indeed, the major legal reforms that he instituted were made on his return from Palestine.[78]

As mentioned, the transfer of debt that was not permitted under Roman law was common in Medieval Europe, particularly in relation to commercial transactions. The *aval* in medieval French law is believed by some to have been modelled on the *hawala* in Islamic law. Indeed, according to Moursi Badr, 'the case for the reception by medieval French law of the transferability of debts from Islamic law appears to be stronger than the case for the trust/*waqf* connection. In fact, the word *aval* in French is admittedly a loan word from the Italian *avallo,* and we all know the extent of the trade conducted by the Italian cities with the Muslim world in the Middle Ages.'[79] Indeed, Subhi Mahmasani argues that 'the Muslim jurists of all schools sanctioned it and carried it to Europe through Spain and also Sicily during the Crusades of the twelfth century AD'.[80]

By the time of Philippe II of France, the Templars also acted as the royal treasury. Members of the order were involved in the King's restructuring of Capetian finances. Some members of the Templar Order were even of Syrian origin. At the time of the Second Crusades, crusaders based in the East had adopted local customs. Indeed, the lands that were in Christian hands had majority Muslim populations. As long as they paid their taxes, they were allowed to maintain their own leaders. Temple Masters always had a Saracen secretary and often learnt Arabic.[81] It is, therefore, possible that the Templars provided a means of transmission of some Islamic legal institutions to France.

Yet, as noted, one of the principal points of exchange between the Islamic world and Medieval Europe was Spain. While Spanish law is primarily derived from Roman and Germanic custom, it has been argued that a number of Spanish legal institutions were influenced by Islamic law. From 711, Spain fell under Arab–Islamic rule for approximately 800 years.[82] Spain shared with Sicily the coexistence, at least for a time, of Christian and Muslim populations following the Reconquest of Spain. Alphonse IX (1171–1230), the 'Wise One' was steeped in Muslim culture. Perhaps significantly, he initiated the first codified set of laws in Europe, which was a combination of civil, public and ecclesiastic laws. It was part of a broader effort to unify the country and strengthen royal authority, as was the case in England.[83]

In early Islam, the principal representatives of the legal profession were the *qadis*, who were government employees and administrators, although they had no formal legal training.[84] In Al-Andalus, as it was known during that time, the *qadi* held the highest legal office, with a number of lesser officials working for him. In local *feuro*, the word survived, although was transformed. *Alcadi* came to refer to the judge of a *fuero*. However, it later lost its judicial meaning and became used as *alcade*, referring to the major or chief officer of a community. During Muslim rule, the vizier or *alguacer* was traditionally the person occupying the office next to the sultan. As Spain became more and more decentralized, in places such as Seville, Toledo and Murcia, the title was sometimes used to refer to officers of the cadi's court and it was in this sense that the title was maintained by Spaniards. *Alguacil* is now a part of Spanish jurisprudence and corresponds to constable or sheriff. Curiously, there is room for judicial initiative in the Spanish code of law, as is the case in English common law, which is unusual for civil law that leaves nothing to judicial initiative.[85] Within Islamic jurisprudence the law, of course, evolves through the use of precedent.

Thus, even outside England, in continental Europe, indications of the possible transmission of Islamic legal institutions to Medieval Europe may be found. The extent to which Islamic law and legal institutions may have influenced the emergence of a rule of law and the development of a rational or impersonal state is, however, far from clear. A great deal of further investigation is required to determine whether the impact on continental European legal systems of Islamic legal institutions was, at least at some time, as great as it may have been in England and what remnants of that influence remain today.

Conclusion

Not only did the legal revolution of the twelfth century contribute to the development of a centralized and impersonal state, as well as a separation of temporal and spiritual power, it also acted as a social force for change in the early Middle Ages, altering social relationships that would enable the rise of capitalism. The emergence of a rule of law reduced the power of lords and not only strengthened the power of kings but also gave serfs rights of ownership with regards to the land,

and was therefore critical to the emergence of capitalist social relations. Also essential to the emergence of capitalism was the predictability that contract law provided. The expansion of overseas trade was also greatly facilitated by the notion of partnerships. These are just some of the legal foundations that helped to forge the social and political (not to mention economic) foundations of modern Europe and enable its rise. Yet, as I have suggested, the establishment of a rule of law, so often identified as a critical foundation for the emergence of the modern West may, as we have seen, have been inspired by some Islamic legal institutions, such as the *'aqd*, the *istihqaq* and the *lafif*. The case for the possible influence of Islamic legal institutions on those of the West is strongest in relation to England, the oft-identified birthplace of capitalism, although there are some indications that such transmission also took place elsewhere in Europe, in Spain, France and, of course, Sicily. This would seem logical given the numerous exchanges of people and goods between these European territories and Islamic lands. However, similarities and possibilities of transmission do not amount to proof that some European legal institutions have Islamic origins. Indeed, much work still remains to be carried out on the historiography of relations between the Arab and Islamic world and the West, not least in the area of law, which is still greatly underexplored. Yet, the potential influence of Islamic legal institutions on those of Europe merits thorough examination; not only because it may shed light on origins that are still being debated today but also because such an exercise may provide a better understanding of the historical development of the West within a global context. This seems to be necessary in order to understand what developments were unique to the West and what were shared with others.

Notes

1. See, for example, M. H. Morgan (2007), *Lost History: The Enduring Legacy of Muslim Scientists, Thinkers, and Artists* (Washington: National Geographic); W. M. Watt (1972), *The Influence of Islam on Medieval Europe* (Edinburgh: University of Edinburgh Press); M. Graham (2006), *How Islam Created the Modern World* (Maryland: Amana Publications); J. Goody (2009), *The Theft of History* (Cambridge: Cambridge University Press); J. M. Hobson (2004), *The Eastern Origins of Western Civilisation* (Cambridge: Cambridge University Press); J. Goody (2004), *Islam in Europe* (Cambridge: Polity Press); J. Goody (2010), *Renaissances: The One or the Many?* (Cambridge: Cambridge University Press); R. van der Weyer (2002), *The Shared Well: A Concise Guide to Relations between Islam and the West* (Washington: Brassey's Inc.); J. Freely (2009), *Aladdin's Lamp: How Greek Science Came to Europe through the Islamic World* (New York: Alfred A. Knopf); S. Attar (2007), *The Vital Roots of European*

Enlightenment: Ibn Tufayl's Influence on Modern Western Thought (Lanham: Lexington Books); T. Wallace-Murphy (2006), *What Islam Did for Us: Understanding Islam's Contribution to Western Civilization* (London: Watkins Publishing); G. Saliba (2007), *Islamic Science and the Making of the European Renaissance* (Cambridge, Mass.: The MIT Press); M. Graham (2006), *How Islam Created the Modern World* (Beltsville, Maryland: Amana Publications).

2. B. Tamanaha (2004), *On the Rule of Law. History, Politics, Theory* (New York and Cambridge: Cambridge University Press), pp. 17–18, 23.
3. G. Burton Adams (1924), 'The Origins of the Common Law', *The Yale Law Journal*, Vol. 34, No. 2, pp. 117–18; R. von Moschzisker (1922), 'The Historic Origin of Trial by Jury II', *University of Pennsylvania Law Review and American Law Register*, Vol. 70, No. 2, pp. 83–4.
4. F. Fukuyama (2010), 'Transitions to the Rule of Law', *Journal of Democracy*, Vol. 21, No. 1, p. 34; von Moschzisker, 'The Historic Origin of Trial by Jury II', p. 84.
5. J. A. Brundage (2008), *The Medieval Origins of the Legal Profession: Canonists, Civilians and Courts* (Chicago: Chicago University Press), pp. 75–7.
6. Fukuyama, 'Transitions to the Rule of Law', p. 34.
7. J. Strayer (1973), *On the Medieval Origins of the Modern State* (Princeton: Princeton University Press), pp. 7, 10.
8. J. S. Sterling and W. E. Moore (1987), 'Weber's Analysis of Legal Rationalization: A Critique and Constructive Modification', *Sociological Forum*, Vol. 2, No. 1, p. 73.
9. M. Weber (1978), Economy and Society: An Outline of Interpretive Sociology, edited by G. Roth and C. Wittich (Berkeley: University of California Press, pp. 809–10.
10. Ibid., p. 811.
11. D. M. Trubek (1972), 'Max Weber on Law and Rise of Capitalism,' *Wisconsin Law Review*, Vol. 720, No. 3, pp. 723–4, 740.
12. Sterling and Moore, 'Weber's Analysis of Legal Rationalization, p. 78.
13. Weber, *Economy and Society*, pp. 821, 845.
14. Fukuyama, 'Transitions to the Rule of Law', pp. 36–9.
15. T. E. Huff (2011), *Intellectual Curiosity and the Scientific Revolution: A Global Perspective* (New York: Cambridge University Press), p. 147.
16. Fukuyama, 'Transitions to the Rule of Law', p. 39.
17. G. Mousri Badr (1978), 'Islamic Law: Its Relation to Other Legal Systems', *The American Journal of Comparative Law*, Vol. 26, No. 2, p. 190.
18. See, for example, J. Makdisi (1998–9), 'The Islamic Origins of the Common Law', *North Carolina Law Review*, Vol. 77; J. Makdisi (1990), 'An Inquiry into Islamic Influences during the Formative Period of Common Law', in Nicholas Heer (ed.) *Islamic Law and Jurisprudence* (Seattle and London: University of Washington); G. Makdisi (1985–6), 'Guilds of Law in Medieval Legal History: An Inquiry into the Origins of the Inns of Court', *Cleveland State Law Review*, Vol. 34, pp. 97–112; M. A. Boisard (1980), 'On the Probable Influence of Islam on Western Public and International Law', *International Journal of Middle Eastern Studies*, Vol. 11, No. 4; also see Mousri Badr, 'Islamic Law'; P. J. Hamilton (1917), 'Germanic and Moorish Elements of Spanish Civil Law', *Harvard Law Review*, Vol. XXX, No. 4, pp. 303–18.

19. R. N. Swanson (1999), *The Twelfth-century Renaissance* (Manchester: Manchester University Press), pp. 66, 79–82.
20. Makdisi, 'The Islamic Origins of the Common Law', pp. 1641–2.
21. K. Feiling (1966), *A History of England* (London: Palgrave Macmillan), p. 143.
22. W. L. Warren (1973), *Henry II* (London: Methuen), p. 336.
23. Ibid., p. 46.
24. R. H. Helmholz (1983), 'The Early History of the Grand Jury and the Canon Law', *University of Chicago Law Review*, Vol. 50, p. 613.
25. Feiling, *A History of England*, pp. 143–4.
26. R. C. Palmer (1985), 'The Origins of Property in England', *Law and History Review*, Vol. 3, No. 1, pp. 4–7.
27. Ibid., p. 24.
28. Makdisi, 'An Inquiry into Islamic Influences', p. 136.
29. M. A. Senn (2003–4), 'English Life and Law in the Time of the Black Death', *Real Property, Probate and Trust Journal*, Vol. 38, pp. 536, 538–9.
30. Palmer, 'The Origins of Property in England', p. 18.
31. F. Pollock (1932), 'The Origins of the Inns of Court', *The Law Quarterly Review*, Vol. 48, p. 165.
32. Makdisi, 'Guilds of Law in Medieval Legal History', pp. 3–4, 12.
33. D. Maxwell-Fyfe (1950), 'The Inns of Court and the Impact on the Legal Profession in England', *Southwestern Law Journal*, Vol. 4, pp. 391–2.
34. M. M. Gaudiosi (1988), 'The Influence of the Islamic Law of Waqf on the Development of the Trust in England: The Case of Merton College', *University of Pennsylvania Law Review*, Vol. 136, No. 4, pp. 1240–1, 1250.
35. See, for example, H. J. Berman and W. R. Greiner (1980), *The Nature and Functions of Law*, 4th edn (Mineola, NY: Foundation Press), pp. 572, 578–9.
36. Makdisi, 'The Islamic Origins of the Common Law', p. 1638.
37. Ibid., pp. 1638–9.
38. Ibid., pp. 1647–8, 1650, 1658.
39. Ibid., pp. 1658–61, 1663–7, 1676, 1679–81.
40. See, for example, von Moschzisker, 'The Historic Origin of Trial by Jury II'; C. T. Coleman (1919), 'Origin and Development of Trial by Jury', *Virginia Law Review*, Vol. 6, No. 2, pp. 77–86.
41. R. von Moschzisker (1921), 'The Historic Origin of Trial by Jury', *University of Pennsylvania Law Review and American Law Register*, Vol. 70, No. 1, p. 5.
42. Makdisi, 'The Islamic Origins of the Common Law', pp. 1679–81.
43. Von Moschzisker (1922), 'The Historic Origin of Trial by Jury II', p. 78 .
44. Makdisi, 'The Islamic Origins of the Common Law', pp. 1679–81.
45. Ibid., pp. 1688, 1690, 1692.
46. Mousri Badr, 'Islamic Law', p. 197.
47. Makdisi, 'Guilds of Law in Medieval Legal History', pp. 11, 17–8; Makdisi, 'The Islamic Origins of the Common Law', p. 1712.
48. Until the nineteenth century the origin of the trust in England was believed to be Roman by scholars such as Lord Chief Baron Sir Geoffrey Gilbert, Francis Williams Sanders, Sir William Blackstone, George Spence and Sir Kenelm Edward Digby. During the nineteenth century its origin was believed to be Germanic. However, the belief in the trust's Roman origin was rekindled in the twentieth century. See also, A. Avini (1995–6), 'The

Origins of the Modern English Trust Revisited', *Tulane Law Review*, Vol. 70 for a discussion of the Roman and Germanic theories of the origin of the trust. Frederick Pollock and Frederick W. Maitland argued that the English trust had both Germanic and Roman origins. See, F. Pollock and F. W. Maitland (1898 rpt. 1968), *The History of English Law before the Time of Edward I*, 2nd edn (Cambridge: Cambridge University Press).

49. Gaudiosi, 'The Influence of the Islamic Law of Waqf', p. 1233.
50. Avini, 'The Origins of the Modern English Trust Revisited', pp. 1155–6.
51. Gaudiosi, 'The Influence of the Islamic Law of Waqf', p. 1246.
52. Avini, 'The Origins of the Modern English Trust Revisited', p. 1142.
53. Makdisi, 'The Islamic Origins of the Common Law', p. 1717.
54. W. Granara (2004), 'Islamic Education and the Transmission of Knowledge in Muslim Sicily', in J. E. Lowry, D. Stewart and S. M. Toorawa (eds) (2004), *Law and Education in Medieval Islam* (Chippenham: E. J. W. Memorial Trust), pp. 151–2, 156, 166.
55. Makdisi, 'The Islamic Origins of the Common Law', pp. 1718, 1720–1.
56. A. Metcalfe (2003), *Muslims and Christians in Norman Sicily: Arabic Speakers and the End of Islam* (London and New York: RoutledgeCurzon), pp. 33, 37.
57. Makdisi, 'An Inquiry into Islamic Influences', pp. 143–4.
58. C. H. Haskins (1911), 'England and Sicily in Twelfth Century', *The English Historical Review*, Vol. 26, No. 103, p. 437.
59. Makdisi, 'The Islamic Origins of the Common Law', pp. 1727–30.
60. E. Ferris (1902), 'The Financial Relations of the Knights Templars to the English Crown', *American Historical Review*, Vol. VIII, No. 1, pp. 1, 12.
61. M. Lima (2008), 'English Common Law and Islam: A Sicilian Connection', *Best of Sicily Magazine*, http://www.bestofsicily.com/mag/art283.htm.
62. Makdisi, 'An Inquiry into Islamic Influences', p. 144.
63. Makdisi, 'The Islamic Origins of the Common Law', pp. 1729–30.
64. Makdisi, 'An Inquiry into Islamic Influences', p. 140.
65. Makdisi, 'Guilds of Law in Medieval Legal History', p. 12.
66. P. Infield (1989), 'A Short History of the Inner Temple', *Bracton Law Journal*, Vol. 21, p. 70.
67. Ibid., pp. 69–70.
68. Makdisi, 'Guilds of Law in Medieval Legal History', pp. 13–14.
69. T. S. Asbridge (1999), 'The Crusader Community at Antioch: The Impact of Interaction with Byzantium and Islam', *Transactions of the Royal Historical Society*, sixth series, Vol. 9, p. 324.
70. Makdisi, 'Guilds of Law in Medieval Legal History', pp. 14–15.
71. Avini, 'The Origins of the Modern English Trust Revisited', p. 1159; H. Cattan (1955), 'Law of the Waqf', in Majid Khadduri and H. H. Liebesny (eds) *Law in the Middle East* (Washington, DC: Middle East Institute); Gaudiosi, 'The Influence of the Islamic Law of Waqf', p. 1244.
72. Gaudiosi, 'The Influence of the Islamic Law of Waqf', pp. 1244–5; Ferris, 'The Financial Relations of the Knights Templars to the English Crown', p. 2.
73. Ferris, 'The Financial Relations of the Knights Templars to the English Crown', p. 7.
74. Gaudiosi, 'The Influence of the Islamic Law of Waqf', pp. 1248–50.

75. S. A. Arjomand (1999), 'The Law, Agency and Policy in Medieval Islamic Society: Development of the Institutions of Learning from the Tenth to the Fifteenth Century', *Comparative Studies in History and Society*, Vol. 41, No. 2, p. 263.
76. M. A. Boisard (1980), 'On the Probable Influence of Islam on Western Public and International Law', *International Journal of Middle Eastern Studies*, Vol. 11, No. 4, p. 440.
77. J. A. McCallin (1968–9), 'St Louis IX and the Administration of Justice', *Saint Louis University Law Journal*, Vol. 13, pp. 411, 414, 430–1.
78. Boisard, 'On the Probable Influence of Islam', p. 440.
79. Mousri Badr, 'Islamic Law', p. 196.
80. S. Mahmasani (2008), 'Transactions in the Sharī'a', in M. Khadduri and H. J. Liebesny (eds) *Law in the Middle East: The Origin and Development of Islamic Law*, Vol. I (Clark, NJ: The Law Book Exchange, Ltd.), p. 202.
81. S. Martin (2009), *The Knights Templar: The History and Myths of the Legendary Military Order* (Harpenden: Pocket Essentials), pp. 44, 50, 54.
82. Hamilton, 'Germanic and Moorish Elements of Spanish Civil Law', p. 310.
83. Boisard, 'On the Probable Influence of Islam', p. 435.
84. W. B. Hallaq (2005), *The Origins and Evolution of Islamic Law* (Cambridge: Cambridge University Press), p. 178.
85. Hamilton, 'Germanic and Moorish Elements of Spanish Civil Law', pp. 312, 317.

5

Islamic Commerce and Finance in the Rise of the West

John M. Hobson

> The worst thing ethically and politically is to let [Eurocentric] separatism simply go on, without understanding the opposite of separatism, which is connectedness.... What I am interested in is how all these things work together. That seems to me to be the great task – to connect them all together – to understand wholes rather than bits of wholes.... In a wonderful phrase, Disraeli asks, 'Arabs, what are they?' and answers: 'they're just Jews on horseback'. So underlying this separation is also an amalgamation of some kind. (Viswanathan 2004: 260–1, 424)[1]

Under the influence of the dominant discourse of the West – otherwise known as Eurocentrism – we have long been accustomed to thinking about the worlds of Islam and the West as antithetical entities. Positioned within an imaginary binary Islam occupies a space that stands on 'the wrong side of progressive history'. While Islam might have had some kind of golden age, it was all for nothing given that it was brought to an end by the exogenous impact of the Mongol conquest of Baghdad in 1258, as well as the endogenous impact of regressive religious diktat. Thus, while the fires of commercial trade and development raged across Europe (known at that time as Christendom), they were unable to reach across into the Middle East given that its political and religious structure acted, in effect, as a kind of asbestos barrier. In short, if anything promising had emerged in early Islam it was but an abortive revolution, with the regressive and repressive Muslim religious authorities snuffing out any such progressive light, with the rest of progressive world history being Western.

In this chapter, I provide an alternative reading of the world of Islam and its contribution to global and European progress. I argue that Islam was a crucial force in setting up and maintaining a nascent global economy in general, as well as nurturing European commerce and the rise of Europe in particular throughout its long period of ascendancy. I divide the chapter into several periods or phases of Afro-Eurasian commercial development. In the first section I look at the Islamic contribution in the context of Afro-Eurasian regionalization in its two principal phases, c. 650 to 1000 and 1000 to 1492. The second section then carries the story forward by looking at the role of Islam in contributing to European commercial development in the period of Oriental globalization (c. 1517–1800). It is also important to note that Middle Eastern Islam, in conjunction with Al-Andalus (Islamic Spain) and Islamic Egypt, constituted the Islamic Bridge of the World, serving to relay vital Eastern resource portfolios (ideas, inventions, technologies and institutions) from the East (including India and China), to Europe, many of which were pioneered in the Islamic Middle East and North Africa. Critically, I argue that these Eastern resource portfolios were vital in enabling the rise of Europe,[2] with those that are directly relevant to the development of commerce being woven into the narrative where appropriate.

The Afro-Asian age of discovery and the Islamic origins of Afro-Eurasian regionalization, c. 650 to 1492

While I characterize the era between c. 650 to 1492 as the era of Afro-Eurasian regionalization, I shall subdivide it into two periods. The first period (c. 650–1000) was crucial in establishing a nascent regionalization process, while the second period saw this process intensify, which in turn enabled a smooth transition into Oriental globalization that cut in after 1492.

Islam and the first phase of Afro-Eurasian regionalization, c. 650 to 1000

Although the advent of Islam was vital in cementing in place an emergent Afro-Eurasian regionalization, it is noteworthy that the Muslims built upon the earlier Sassanid Persian achievements, which stemmed back to the third and certainly the fourth century.[3] As I note later, the Sassanids also began developing some of the financial institutions that were advanced much further by the Muslims before they were borrowed and later assimilated by the Italians. Islam was important insofar as it not only united a previously fragmented West Asian region, but also extended its commercial tentacles far and wide, thereby helping to unify much of the Afro-Eurasian ecumene. Eurocentric world history pays no attention to this achievement, losing it in the long dark shadows that were cast by Europe's brilliant light of pioneering commercial progressivity. In the Eurocentric imaginary, while commercial prosperity became a fact at the turn of the second millennium within Europe, its extensity reached only as far as the Middle East, given that Islam acted as a kind of commercial/capitalist firewall, snuffing out the fires of commercialism that threatened to penetrate the agrarian citadel. However, this is problematic for at least four main reasons, all of which reveal that European commerce post-dated that of Islam and that without Islam there might never have been a Venetian trading hub at the centre of European commerce.

First, Islam had a high propensity for commercial trade and capitalist activity. Here it is salutary to note that Mohammed had been a *commenda* (*qirād*) trader. And, in his twenties he married a rich *Qurayshi* woman (the *Quraysh* had grown rich from the caravan trade as well as banking). Interestingly the Meccans (the tribe of *Quraysh*) caused their capital to fructify through trade and loans at interest in a way that Max Weber would call rational. The merchants of the Muslim Empire conformed perfectly to Weber's criteria for capitalist activity. They seized every and any opportunity for profit and calculated their outlays, their encashments and their profits in money terms.[4]

Second, and no less importantly, many linkages between Islam and capitalism can be found in the Quran. Thus, the Quran, '[d]oes not merely say that one must not forget one's portion of the world, it also says that it is proper to combine the practice of religion and material life, carrying on trade even during pilgrimages and goes so far as to maintain commercial profit under the name of "God's Bounty"'.[5] Islam prescribed that businessmen could more effectively conduct a pilgrimage than those who did only physical labour. Indeed, the Quran states that

> If thou profit by doing what is permitted, thy deed is a djihād.... And if thou invest it for thy family and kindred, this will be a Sadaqa [that is, a pious work of charity]; and truly, a dhiram [drachma, silver coin] lawfully gained from trade is worth more than ten dhirams gained in any other way.[6]

Mohammed's saying that 'Poverty is almost like an apostasy', implies that the true servant of God should be affluent or at least economically independent. The booths of the money changers in the great mosque of the camp town Kufa possibly illustrate the fact that there was no necessary conflict between business and religion in Islam.[7]

It is also significant to note that the Quran stipulates the importance of investment. While many in the West associate the *Shari'ah* (the Islamic sacred law) with despotism and economic backwardness, it was, in fact, created as a means to prevent the abuse of the rulers' or caliphs' power and, moreover, it set out clear provisions for contract law. Not surprisingly, there was a rational reason why the Islamic merchants were strong supporters of the *Shari'ah*. Furthermore, there were clear signs of greater personal freedom within Islam than that found within Medieval Europe. Offices were determined on the basis of 'egalitarian contractual responsibilities', which entailed notions of rationality that were, according to Marshall Hodgson, closer to the modern notion of *geselleschaft* than to traditional notions of *gemeinschaft* that characterized medieval Christendom.[8]

Third, the picture of a dense Islamic urban trading network counters the traditional Eurocentric vision of Islam as a desert populated by nomads. As Marshall Hodgson put it, Islam was 'no "monotheism of the desert", born of the Bedouins' awed wonder at the vast openness of sky and land... Islam grew out of a long tradition of urban religion and it was as city-oriented as any variant of that tradition'.[9] Maxime Rodinson reinforces the general claim being made here:

> [T]he density of commercial relations within the Muslim world constituted a sort of world market... of unprecedented dimensions. The development of exchange had made possible regional specialisation in industry and agriculture.... Not only did the Muslim world know a capitalistic sector, but this sector was apparently the most extensive and highly developed in history before the [modern period].[10]

Significantly, Islam forbade tall multi-storey houses, because to reach up towards God was deemed to be arrogant. In general, for Islam, it was morally reprehensible to conquer vertical space. Thus, the most pious sign would be to lower oneself in the eyes of God, to prostrate oneself and to lower one's head to the ground in the face of God's greatness. Similarly, we are told in *The Arabian Nights*, that to show respect for the sovereign is to 'kiss the earth between one's hands'. In short, the notion of *Jihad* (*djihād*) preached that Muslims should conquer not vertical, but horizontal or extensive space through both religion and trade. Accordingly, towns sprang up throughout the Middle East and rapidly formed the major sinews of the Afro-Eurasian trading network.

This naturally flows into the fourth counterpoint to the Eurocentric vision of Islam: that ultimately Islam's comparative advantage lay in its considerable extensive power. That is, Islam was able to conquer horizontal space, realized most fully in its ability to spread and diffuse across large parts of the globe, of which the expansion of commercial capitalism was but a symptom. The centre of Islam, Mecca, was, in turn, one of the centres of the global trading network. Islam's power spread rapidly after the seventh century so that the Mediterranean became in effect a Muslim Lake, and Western Europe a tiny promontory lying on the far western tip of a vast Afro-Asian economy. Islam spread not only westwards into Christendom – most especially into Spain (Al-Andalus) – but also eastwards right across to India, Southeast Asia and China, as well as southwards into Africa through either religious or commercial influence and often both. Its economic reach was so extraordinary that 'the self-evident fact must be accepted that they [the Muslims] were among the pioneers of commerce in those faraway countries and that perhaps, as Tibbets suggests, they acted as middlemen in the trade between China and South-east Asia'.[11] Certainly by the ninth century – as various contemporary documents confirm – there was one long, continuous line of transcontinental trade pioneered by Islamic merchants, reaching from China to the Mediterranean.[12]

The Middle Eastern Ummayads (661–750), Abbasids (750–1258) and North African Fatimids (909–1171) were especially important, serving to unite various arteries of long-distance trade known in antiquity between the Indian Ocean and the Mediterranean. These included the Red Sea and Persian Gulf routes. The Abbasid capital, Baghdad, was linked to the Persian Gulf route, which, in turn, fanned out through the Indian Ocean and beyond into the South China Sea, as well as the East China Sea. As Hourani notes, the contemporary, Al-Ya'qūbi (c. 875), described Baghdad as the 'water-front to the world', while Al-Mansūr proclaimed that 'there is no obstacle to us and China; everything on the sea can come to us on it'.[13] Other Islamic ports were also important, especially Sīrāf on the Persian Gulf (on the coast of Iran south of Shīrāz), which was the major terminus for goods from China and Southeast Asia. The Red Sea route (guarded over by Egypt) was also of special importance. In addition to the sea routes, perhaps the most famous was the overland route to China, along which caravans passed through the Iranian cities of Tabriz, Hamadan and Nishapur to Bukhara and Samarkand in Transoxiana, and then on to either China or India. Marco Polo (the Ibn Battūta of Europe?) was particularly impressed by Tabriz:

> The people of Tabriz live by trade and industry.... The city is so favorably situated that it is a market for merchandise from India and

> Baghdad, from Mosul and Hormuz, and from many other places; and many Latin merchants come here to buy the merchandise imported from foreign lands. It is also a market for precious stones, which are found here in great abundance. It is a city where good profits are made by travelling merchants.[14]

The Muslims were particularly dependent on trade with many parts of Africa (not just North Africa). This was so for a number of reasons including, first, that Egypt presided over one of the vital trade routes that linked the Far East and West (see next section); and, second, African markets constituted probably the most profitable branch of Islam's foreign trade. Islamic cargo boats plied the route down the East African coast as far south as Sufālah in Mozambique and Qanbalu (Madagascar). Gold was mined in various places including Ethiopia and Zimbabwe, while Kilwa (present day southern Tanzania) was the principal entrepôt. The Africans imported beads, cowries, copper and copper goods, grain, fruit and raisins, wheat and, later on, textiles (almost all of which were mass-based goods, not luxuries). The most intense commercial relations experienced by the East African ports were with Aden, Suhār and Sīrāf. This long-distance trade also helped stimulate trade into the African hinterland. Indeed, it would be wrong to assume that West Africa was commercially isolated from the east coast and was brought to life by the Europeans after 1492.[15] For it was the much earlier Islamic arrival at western entrepôts, such as Sijilmassa (in Morocco) and Awdaghast, that enabled the interlinking of the eastern and western coasts both in the northern and sub-Saharan regions.[16]

All in all, even before the turn of the second millennium, on the very eve of the European commercial revolution the Muslims in particular had woven together vast swathes of Afro-Asia into an increasingly singular economic unit. It was into this wider circuit of trade that Europe became inserted, albeit indirectly, when it turned to commerce.

Islam and Europe, c. 1000 to 1517: commerce, finance and the transmission of Eastern resource portfolios via the Islamic Bridge of the World

Eurocentric world history, as already noted, assumes that the rise of commerce was given its decisive thrust by the Europeans, most especially the Italians, after about 1000. This date, of course, conventionally signifies the end of the Dark Ages, which supposedly characterizes the period of world history between c. 476 to 1000. In point of fact, though, while Europe might have regressed into the Dark Ages following the end of the Roman Empire, this period has been characterized more recently as the Eastern Bright Ages.[17] While Afro-Asian trade accelerated after about 1000 this owes its primary thrust to the growing interconnections between the Islamic Middle East and Africa in the west, as well as India, Southeast Asia and especially China in the east. As noted above, it was into this vast system of commerce that the Europeans inserted themselves. Before I describe this wider system, it is necessary to begin this discussion by considering how Europe in general, and Italy in particular, benefited from the growing Eastern trade in general and the role of Islamic West Asia in particular.

Eurocentric historians typically view the rise of Europe after 1000 in terms of a self-contained or autonomous regional economy. Towns in particular were deemed to be autocephalous. Thus, from Max Weber to Henri Pirenne and from Immanuel Wallerstein and Fernand Braudel to Robert Brenner, the consensus is that 'it was the medieval city...which, like the yeast in a mighty dough, brought about the rise of Europe'.[18] In the conventional account, the proliferation of towns is granted almost magic-like qualities, for it is assumed that with the end of the internal disruptions that had ravaged Europe between 370 and 1000, the ensuing internal order inevitably ensured the development of towns and commerce. Underlying such a claim is the assumption that European man was inherently economically rational, and that under the right conditions (peace and minimalist, laissez-faire governments, for example), he would naturally get on and do what he does best, 'truck, barter and exchange'.[19] Here then, is one of the classic Eurocentric assumptions: that Western freedom enabled capitalist or commercial development, no better signified than in the common medieval phrase *stadtluft macht frei* ('town air makes you free'), or *Westen stadtluft macht frei* ('Western town air makes you free').

What is immediately puzzling, though, is the way that the phrase long-distance trade is deployed within Eurocentric narratives. For while it is clear that Europe lay at one end of this nexus, it is not clear what lay at the other. What has been generally missed is that it was the East that not only lay at the other end but also played a crucial role in the rise of European trade. For the fact is that European trade was ultimately made possible only by the flow of Eastern goods, which entered Europe mainly via Italy. Nevertheless, this is not to say that Italy was unimportant to the fortunes of European commerce, finance and production. For it was in fact pivotal, constituting the heart of European trade, thereby pumping goods all round the continent and feeding them into the many intra-regional trading systems (such as the Hanse and the

French Champagne Fairs). However, it was only able to play this central role because Italy was one of the major conduits through which Eastern resources (not just trade) entered and reshaped Europe. As I shall explain below, the vast majority of this trade entered Italy courtesy of the North African Muslims in Egypt, who were supplied by the Southern trade route (based in the Red Sea).[20]

Because of the importance that Italy is accorded to the European commercial revolution a few points are noteworthy in order to reveal the role of Islam in all of this. In fact, as early as the late-eighth century Italy was linked into various sub-systems of the Afro-Eurasian economy, straddling Europe, Africa and Asia. Indeed, it was Italy's direct entry point into this wider and lucrative economy that secured her destiny. As Abu-Lughod notes

> This direct entrée to the riches of the East changed the role of the Italian merchant mariner cities from passive to active. The revival of the Champagne Fairs in the twelfth century can be explained convincingly by both the enhanced demand for Eastern goods stimulated by the crusades and, because of the strategic position of the Italians in coastal enclaves of the Levant, the increased supplies of such goods they could now deliver.[21]

Venice ultimately prevailed over her rival Genoa not because of her so-called ingenuity but because of her lucrative access to the East via Egypt and the Middle East. Braudel supports this through a rhetorical question:

> Can [Venice's lead within Europe] be explained by her preferred (and traditional) links with the Orient, whereas the other Italian cities were more concerned with the Western world, then slowly taking shape? ... The lifeblood of Venetian trade was the Levant connection. So if Venice appears to be a special case, is it because her entire commercial activity from A to Z was dictated by the Levant?[22]

In short, while the Italians played a vitally important role in spreading commercialization throughout Christendom, they were not the great commercial pioneers portrayed by Eurocentrism. Indeed, the Italians were at all times dependent upon the terms and conditions laid down by Middle Eastern and North African Muslims. However, in the end, the most important function of Italy's trading links with the Middle East and later Egypt lay in the fact that these commercial routes constituted important avenues along which many of the vital Eastern resource portfolios diffused across to fertilize the backward West. These resource portfolios enabled the various Italian commercial, financial and navigational revolutions for which they have become unjustifiably famous.

It is generally assumed that a whole series of financial institutions were pioneered by the Italians. The most important innovation we are told was the *commenda* (or *collegantia*), that the Italians allegedly invented around the eleventh century.[23] This was a contractual agreement in which an investor financed the trip of a merchant. Not only did it support international trade through the bringing together of capital and trading labour, but it had similar effects to a stock exchange in that it provided a market for savings which thereby fanned the flames of economic development. The problem, though, is that the *commenda* was invented in the Middle East. Although its roots stem back to pre-Islamic times,[24] it was developed furthest by the early Islamic merchants. Indeed, as Abraham Udovitch notes, 'it is the Islamic form of this contract (*qirād, muqārada, mudāraba*) which is the earliest example of a commercial arrangement identical with that economic and legal institution which [much later] became known in Europe as the *commenda*'.[25] Nevertheless, this should hardly be a revelation given that Mohammed himself had been a *commenda* merchant. Nor should it be altogether surprising that the Italians came to use this institution given that Italy was directly linked into the Islamic trading system. It is also noteworthy that from the eighth century the *qirād* was applied in Islam to credit and manufacturing, not just to trade.[26]

The Italians are also wrongly accredited with the discovery of a range of other financial institutions including the bill of exchange, credit institutions, insurance and banking. For the fact is that all these institutions were derived from either the Islamic Middle East, or the pre-Islamic Middle East, given that 'many of the business techniques had been firmly established before the Qu'rān had codified them'.[27] The Sumerians and Sassanids were using banks, bills of exchange and checks before the advent of Islam. Nevertheless, it was the Muslims who took these early beginnings furthest. Ironically, one reason for this lay with the need for Islamic capitalists to circumvent the ban on usury. For example, payment was often delayed by up to two months or more so as to conceal usury by paying a higher price, thereby requiring such institutions.[28] Such a point can hardly be understated given that one of the principal Eurocentric denuciations of Islam was its supposed usury laws and aversion to lending. Critically, Islamic bankers were common, as were international currency changers, and the banks themselves entered into *commenda* agreements for advancing money or credit in return for profits. The banks were a vital conduit for international trade, transferring funds from one place to another. The Islamic bankers issued notes: the 'demand note' or bill of exchange at a distant location (*suftaja*); and the 'order to pay' (*hawāla*), which was identical to a modern cheque. As Abu-Lughod notes of the *hawāla*: 'At the upper left corner was the amount to be paid (in numbers), and in the lower left corner was the date and then the name of the payer'.[29] As she points out on the same page, the demand note was in fact of Persian origin and preceded its use in Europe by many centuries.

In addition, the Italians are usually attributed with the discovery of advanced accounting systems. But various Eastern accounting systems were also well developed, especially in the Middle East, India and most notably in China. Indeed some of these were probably as efficient as Weber's celebrated Occidental double-entry method. It is true that the Pisan, Leonardo Fibonacci, living in Tunis, was an important figure within Europe who advanced the Italian accounting system. Yet, as I explain below, he was so only because he had learned of the Eastern knowledge while living in Tunis. This, in turn, brings up the role that Islam played in stimulating the Italian Renaissance, to a brief consideration of which I now turn.

That Eurocentric world history sees in this epistemic revolution a necessary prerequisite for the economic development of Europe seems an entirely reasonable proposition. Far less reasonable, however, is the bald assumption that the Renaissance was a purely autonomous European creation. For a number of scholars have argued that the Renaissance owes a huge debt to the Middle Eastern and North African Muslims.[30] There are several aspects that are relevant in terms of stimulating European trade – especially that which followed in the wake of the so-called European Age of Discovery. These comprised principally mathematics, astronomy and geography. I shall deal briefly with each in turn.

It is notable that Ancient Iraqi schools (in Mesopotamia) taught algebra and geometry, knew of the theorem now called after Pythagoras as early as 1700 BCE, and knew the value of Pi. They also developed the sexagesimal system in which the circle is divided into 360 degrees, the hour into 60 minutes, the minute into 60 seconds, and the day into 24 hours. Following on from ancient Iraq through ancient Egypt and thence ancient Greece (the latter benefiting from its proximity to these earlier developers), the next major developmental phase was initiated by the Muslims after about 800, who took these early developments much further. The pioneering mathematician, Muhammad Ibn Musa Al-Khwārizmi (780–847) produced the highly influential book, *On Calculation with Hindu Numerals* (c. 825). This book was largely responsible for the diffusion of the Indian numerical system into Islam and the West. Interestingly, it was the Middle Eastern Phœnicians[31] who first introduced numerals. Nevertheless, the vital breakthrough was made by the Indians, who had developed nine numbers and the zero (*Śūnya*) in decimal place value.[32] This was subsequently adopted around 760 by Arab scholars.[33] In turn, Al-Khwārizmi's work was taken further by a number of tenth century Islamic scholars, including Al-Uqlidisi, Abu'l-Wafā Al-Buzajānī, Al-Māhānī, Al-Kindī and Kushyar Ibn Labban.[34] Having spread throughout the Middle East such ideas diffused principally to Islamic Spain by the end of the tenth century, whence the backward Europeans gained access (especially via Córdoba and in the aftermath of the Fall of Toledo in 1085 and the capture of Saragossa by the Aragonese in 1118).

Despite this access to Islamic knowledge of mathematics, the Europeans were slow to catch on preferring to retain the old system based on the abacus. And, while the Pisan merchant Leonardo Fibonacci was an important figure within Europe, his innovations were, nevertheless, based on the new Eastern concepts. Indeed, he wrote a book rejecting the old abacus system in favour of the new Hindu-Arabic system, which influenced the emergence of the mathematical system within the Italian merchant communes. It is hardly controversial to note, as Charles Singer puts it, that the European adoption of this Eastern numerical system 'was a major factor in the rise of [Western] science, and was not without effect in determining the relations of science and technology in the sixteenth and seventeenth centuries'.[35]

Al-Khwārizmi's work on algebra was equally as important and was translated into Latin in 1145 by the Englishman Robert of Ketton as well as the Italian, Gerard of Cremona. Ketton's translation of Al-Khwārizmi's name was Algorithmi (hence the term algorithm). The term algebra came from the title of one of Al-Khwārizmi's books, *al-jebr w'almuqalah* (given that *al-jebr* was translated as algebra). Moreover, his book remained the major text in Europe right down to the sixteenth century. This was complemented by various Islamic breakthroughs that went beyond the theory of Ptolemy. Ptolemy used chords which were based on a very clumsy theory. Al-Battānī substituted the sine for the chord. Moreover, spherical trigonometry was advanced by Abu'l-Wafā Al-Buzajānī's theory of the tangent, Abū Nasr's theorem of the sines and Ibn Al-Haytham's theorem of cotangents. It is no less noteworthy that by the beginning of the tenth century all six of the classical trigonometric functions had been defined and tabulated by Muslim mathematicians.[36] Nasīr Al-Dīn Al-Tūsī's text on plane trigonometry in the mid-to-late thirteenth century was not matched by any European mathematician until 1533.[37]

Islamic breakthroughs in astronomy were no less influential. In the fourteenth century, Ibn Al-Shātir of the Maragha School, developed a series of mathematical models which were almost exactly the same as those developed about 150 years later by Copernicus in his heliocentric theory. That these models were so similar led Noel Swerdlow to suggest that it 'seems too remarkable a series of coincidences to admit the possibility of independent discovery [on the part of Copernicus]'.[38] Other experts have also argued that Copernicus borrowed Al-Shātir's models.[39] Fittingly, Copernicus has been described as 'the most noted follower of the Maragha School'.[40] Also noteworthy was Al-Khwārizmi's earlier work on astronomy. Not only did he improve on Ptolemy's text, *Geography*, but he also produced various maps that included the positions of many of the stars. These maps would prove important in enabling Oceanic commercial trade. He also calculated the circumference of the Earth to within a margin of error of less than 0.04 per cent (for example, only 41 metres out). His work was taken further by both Al-Bīrūnī and Al-Idrīsī.

All in all, Jack Goody's words seem as apt as anyone's in concluding this discussion:

> What we find in Italy was in essence a rebirth, recovery or re-creation of [institutions] that had existed in various forms in the Near East.... While the sequence of exchequer accounts, commercial accounts, market finance from the fairs of Champagne to more stable banking, of commercial documents and of commercial associations such as the *commenda* and joint stock company, was important to the [future] development of industrial capitalism, it was a sequence that had already taken place in other parts of the world.[41]

While early Islamic thinking had an impact that went beyond the European Renaissance, helping to inform Europe's Scientific Revolution, it also provided a crucial input into the European Navigation Revolution that underpinned Europe's transition to oceanic sailing after 1492 (as I explain in the next section), and which, in turn, enabled the diffusion of European commerce across the globe.

Returning to the narrative, I will now sketch the Muslim role in shaping Afro-Eurasian regionalization in the 1000–1492/1517 era. This whole Afro-Eurasian economy was nourished by three principal trade routes that were presided over for the most part by the Muslims. These have been dubbed the Northern, Middle and Southern routes by Janet Abu-Lughod (1989). However, here I shall focus on the two primary routes, the Middle and Southern, both of which were presided over by the Muslims. The Middle route began at the Mediterranean coast of Syria/Palestine, crossed a small desert and then the Mesopotamian plain to Baghdad, before finally splitting into a land or sea route. The land route continued across Persia to Transoxiana and then either south-east to northern India or due east to Samarkand and then across the desert to China. The sea route followed the Tigris River down to the Persian Gulf from Baghdad via Basra and then passed the trading kingdoms of Oman, Sīrāf, Hormuz or Qais (guardians of the link between the Gulf and the Indian Ocean beyond). While this route became particularly important after the sixth century, it was extremely influential when Baghdad was the prime Muslim centre of trade after 750. Yet, when Baghdad was plundered by the Mongols in 1258, the route underwent a temporary decline. However, when Iraq was subsequently ruled from Persia, the Gulf route revived. This Middle Route was also important because it enabled a deeply symbiotic trading relationship between the Crusader kingdoms and the Muslim merchants who brought goods from as far away as the Orient.

The chief Crusader port in the Middle East, Acre, was controlled up until 1291 by the Venetians, who excluded their Pisan and Genoese rivals. Nevertheless, although the Venetians dominated the European trading system, they always entered the global system on terms dictated by the Middle Eastern Muslims and especially the North African Muslims. When Constantinople fell to the Byzantines in 1261, the Genoese were favoured over the Venetians, thereby forcing the latter to focus on the Middle and Southern routes. But then, with the Fall of Acre in 1291, the Venetians had no choice but to rely on the Southern route, which was dominated by the Egyptians.

The Southern route linked the Alexandria-Cairo-Red Sea complex with the Arabian Sea, the Indian Ocean and beyond. After the thirteenth century, Egypt constituted the major gateway to the East. Importantly, '[w]hoever controlled the sea-route to Asia could set the terms of trade for a Europe now in retreat. From the thirteenth century and up to the sixteenth that power was Egypt'.[42] Indeed between 1291–1517 about 80 per cent of all trade that passed to the East by sea was controlled by the Egyptians. However, when Baghdad fell, Al-Qahirah – later Europeanized to Cairo – became the capital of the Islamic world and the pivotal centre of global trade (though this latter process had begun under the Fatimids in the tenth century).

Eurocentric scholars emphasize that European international trade with the East dried up after 1291 (with the Fall of Acre), because Egypt dominated the Red Sea trade to the East at the expense of the Christian Europeans. Supposedly, this prompted the Portuguese Vivaldi brothers to search for the more southerly route to the Indies via the Cape in 1291. But, despite the proclamation of various papal prohibitions on trade with the infidel, the Venetians managed to circumvent the ban and secured new treaties with the Sultan in 1355 and 1361. Right up until 1517, Venice survived because Egypt played such an important role in the global economy. Moreover, Venice and Genoa were not the pioneers of global trade but adaptors, inserting themselves into the interstices of the Afro-Asian-led global economy very much on terms laid down by the Middle Eastern Muslims and especially the Egyptians. In particular, European merchants were blocked from passing through Egypt. When they arrived in Alexandria they were met by customs officials, who stayed on board and supervised the unloading of goods. Christians required a special permit or visa and paid a higher tax than did their Muslim counterparts. The Europeans then retired to their own quarters, which were governed by their own laws and which they were not allowed to leave. They became wholly dependent upon the Egyptian merchants and government officials. Nevertheless, the Venetians and other Europeans accepted this regime because it was there that they gained access to the many goods produced throughout the East. Indeed the fortunes of Venice were only made possible through its access to Eastern trade via North Africa.

Of course, even if some of this was conceded, the conventional Eurocentric narrative insists that after 1500 the mainstream of international trade was decisively European, whether it was led by the Iberians, the Dutch, the English or the French. Yet, as the next section argues, even after 1517 the Islamic trading hegemony over Europe was maintained. For the baton of extensive Islamic power was passed from Egypt to the Ottoman Empire, which maintained its hold over the Portuguese in the Indian Ocean. Moreover, other centres of Islamic economic power – Mughal India and Southeast Asia – remained not only key players in the global trading system, but were strong enough to resist and dominate the European traders right up until about 1800.

The European Age of rediscovery and the Islamic origins of oriental globalization, c. 1517 to 1800

In standard Eurocentric world history the period following 1492 is described as the European Age of Discovery. With the trans-oceanic push initiated by Christopher Columbus and Vasco da Gama, it is assumed that the Iberians began to weave together the hitherto isolated regions of the East and far West. In effect, the Iberians allegedly began the process of proto-globalization, knocking down the high walls of the various isolated Asian regions and flooding them with the liberating effects of international commerce. But this scenario, in the context of Asia, needs to be inverted. For, as I have argued up to this point, India, and much of Asia for that matter, played a crucial role within the Afro-Asian-led global economy for many centuries before da Gama set off. The reality was that Columbus and da Gama were pre-empted by not much less than a millennium by the Afro-Asian Age of Discovery. Testimony on this point is revealed by

> When Da Gama sailed up the East African coast in 1498 he sailed into a familiar world, and one already linked to the Mediterranean and Europe. Arab traders had penetrated, converted, settled and intermarried as far south as Sofala [on the south-east African coast], and linked all littoral East Africa north of here with other parts of the Indian Ocean as well as the Red Sea and Europe.[43]

The irony was that when the Europeans arrived in Asia they soon found that they had little choice but to collaborate with, and sometimes kowtow to, the stronger Asian polities, merchants in general and Muslims in particular. For the fact is that despite the initial vainglorious proclamation of 'Death to the (Islamic) Infidel', when the Portuguese arrived in the Indies 'they also entered the domain of hegemonic Islam'.[44]

Moreover, the Indians were more advanced than their European 'discoverers'. Circumstantial testimony to this claim lies in the initial meeting between da Gama and the Indian Zamorin of Calicut. Indeed, far from being overawed or overwhelmed by the arrival of the Portuguese, the Indian Zamorin (ruler) was visibly underwhelmed. When Vasco da Gama was graciously granted an audience with the Zamorin, he presented some of the most advanced European products available. But the Indians could scarcely contain their amusement at the inferiority of the goods. As Needham put it

> The technological gap between the [East] and the West is well evidenced by Vasco da Gama's first visit in 1498 to Calicut. He presented various goods – cloths, hats, sugar, oil.... The king laughed at them and advised the Admiral rather to offer gold. At the same time, the Muslim merchants already on the spot affirmed to the

Indians that the Portuguese were essentially pirates, possessed of nothing that the Indians could ever want.[45]

In point of fact, it was the ruler's advisers who laughed. The ruler took great offence at the offerings, which he dismissed as unworthy of even the poorest merchant.

More generally, though, it was the Portuguese who were overwhelmed by what they experienced in India. Pedro de Covilhão reported back 'astonished at what he saw in the Indian ports: the lively commerce... and above all the lots of cinnamon and cassia bunches in the storehouses of the Arab merchants, the pepper climbing the trees, and the immense quantity of spices which grow in the fields just as wheat grows in Europe'.[46]

Cabral also returned home with similarly glowing reports and even brought back some of the Indian produce, especially the spices. Thus, if the Portuguese appeared to be motivated by an intense curiosity that the Asians were supposedly lacking it was only because on the one hand the Portuguese knew very little of the world (unlike the Asians), and on the other that the Asians had a great deal more to offer. In sum, neither the rounding of the Cape nor the Portuguese arrival in India deserved the label of a pioneering discovery. Though it was undoubtedly a revelation to the Europeans, it was merely yester-millennium's news to the Africans and Asians. All that was really happening was that the Europeans were directly joining the Oriental global economy. In this sense, the best that could be said was that da Gama opened up the European Age of Rediscovery.

It is possible to speculate at this point whether, without access to Islamic navigational and nautical knowledge, the Iberians would have ended up confined to the localized waters of the Mediterranean. For the, so-called, European Navigation Revolution owed a considerable debt to the Muslims (as well as the Chinese). First of all, European ships required a lateen sail to sail into headwinds, which were particularly onerous off the coast of Cape Bojador on the west coast of Africa, along which the Europeans plied their way to the Cape of Storms (later renamed the Cape of Good Hope). Although there is some circumstantial evidence to suggest that the Romans first invented the lateen sail,[47] there is no evidence to show that it was subsequently refined and developed by any European. This contrasts strikingly with the Islamic Middle Eastern tradition, where huge lateen mainsails were deployed on much larger boats. The contemporary, Ibn Shahriyā, even mentions one Arabic sail as tall as 76 feet in the mid-tenth century, which would have been roughly commensurate with the masts of the largest European ships of the early sixteenth century.[48] Moreover, Gerald Tibbetts tells us that the Arab ships of the fifteenth century – that is, *before* Vasco da Gama – were certainly as big as modern dhows (100 feet in length with a mast of 75 feet).[49] If nothing else, the development of large lateen sails demonstrates a clear 'adaptive capacity'. That is, to deploy a large lateen sail on a large vessel requires many refinements and a long period of experimentation (as White himself recognizes). In sum, it is not possible to conclude that the Persians or Arabs definitively invented the lateen sail, though equally it is not possible to dismiss that possibility. Nevertheless, it is highly probable that it was the Muslims who, having refined it over a long period of time, passed it on to the Europeans thereby enabling Vasco da Gama to set sail in 1498.

The lateen sail threw up a series of challenges that were solved by a string of Islamic innovations borrowed by the European Renaissance (the general outline of which I sketched earlier). First of all, because the lateen sail led to a zigzagging (or triangular) sailing path, this made it harder to calculate the linear distance travelled. This was solved by the use of geometry and trigonometry, which had been developed by, and was borrowed from, the Muslim mathematicians (as discussed earlier). A second challenge was posed by the strong tides south of Cape Bojador, which could beach or destroy a ship. To solve this required knowledge of the lunar cycles (since the moon governs the tides). At the end of the fourteenth century, this knowledge was developed by a Jewish cartographer resident in Portugal, Jacob ben Abraham Cresque, much of which was developed from Muslim knowledge.[50] A third challenge was the need for more accurate navigational charts than those already available (for example, the *Portolan*). This was solved by turning to Islamic astronomy to calculate the size of the earth and, thereby, calculate the distance travelled by using degrees.

The mariner's astrolabe was an important navigational instrument that enabled oceanic sailing by allowing the user to plot the ship's position against the stars or the sun. This directly enabled an extension of the European six-month voyaging season to the whole year, thereby doubling the number of voyages. The astrolabe first emerged in ancient Greece, though its details were never clear and the references to it are few and far between. It was, however, the Muslims who undertook all the major innovations, which can be traced back probably to Al-Fazārī in the mid-eighth century (and not Māshā'allāh as has been sometimes claimed). By the ninth century, the astrolabe was in regular production and had spread into Europe via Islamic Spain by the mid-tenth century.[51]

Interestingly, the apparently oldest Latin text on the astrolabe, *Sententie astrolabi* (from late-tenth century Northern Spain) is heavily reliant on various Islamic texts including Al-Khwārizmi's treatise on the astrolabe.[52] Yet, what was equally as impressive were the many refinements that were pioneered by various Islamic astronomers, which enabled the future regular use of the astrolabe by Europeans

Though the astrolabe was important it was complemented by a range of other navigational techniques. Here, the Iberians relied on suggestions made by the prominent Córdovan Muslim astronomer, Ibn as-Saffār (whose treatise had been translated into Latin). They also borrowed Islamic innovations in mathematics in order to work out latitude and longitude while relying on the Islamic tables developed by an eleventh-century Muslim astronomer. Moreover, calculating latitude also required knowledge of the solar year (since the sun's declination was pivotal to such calculations). Here, they turned to the sophisticated Islamic and Jewish solar calendars developed in the eleventh century. Pedro Nunes boasted in 1537 that: 'it is evident that the discoveries of coasts, islands, continents has not occurred by chance, but to the contrary, our sailors have departed very well informed, provided with instruments and rules of astronomy and geometry'.[53] Indeed, they were very well informed, but only because of the breakthroughs in Jewish, though mainly Islamic, science upon which the Portuguese Voyages of Rediscovery were based.

Finally, it is worth noting that various individual Muslims played an important role in guiding da Gama across to India in 1497–8. First, it is possible, though not certain, that Da Gama was shown a remarkably detailed map of India by a Gujarati Muslim, Malemo Cana, at Malindi before he set sail to cross the Arabian Sea. More certain though is that da Gama only made it across to the Indies with the help of an unnamed Islamic-Gujarati pilot (who was picked up at Malindi on the East African coast). Interestingly, it is often assumed that this navigator was the famous Ahmad Ibn Mājid, though Tibbetts has produced a number of convincing arguments that cast considerable doubt on this assertion.[54] That the influence of the Islamic-Gujarati pilot had been extremely important was revealed by the fact that his absence on the return journey meant that da Gama was extremely lucky to make it back at all.[55]

It is notable that one of the prime factors that sustained the Eurocentric belief that the Europeans dominated the Asian trading system lies in the exaggerated emphasis that has been accorded the Cape Route after 1500. Indeed, the consensus is that by 1500 the Islamic world economy had almost completely faded away as the declining Ottoman Empire was displaced by the 'all-conquering' Europeans. Typical of this is the conclusion that

> Central Asia was…isolated from the early sixteenth century…and therefore led an existence at the margin of world history.… The discovery of the sea route to East Asia [via the Cape] rendered the Silk Road increasingly superfluous.… From the threshold of modern times Central Asian history becomes provincial history. This justifies us in giving no more than a rapid sketch of the following centuries.[56]

In this Eurocentric portrayal, it is as if the European creation of a new route round the Cape had become mainstream, while Islamic trade was marginalized and left to fester in a kind of Islamic ox-bow lake. However, there are numerous problems with this Eurocentric formulation, not the least of which is that the Portuguese were merely joining the mainstream trade that was already presided over by the Ottoman Muslims as well as the Safavid Persians. More specifically, there are six main reasons why the Portuguese Cape route failed to displace Islamic trading power.

First, the new Cape route was not especially profitable, because it failed to lower transport costs. Second, considerably more trade flowed into Europe through the Levant and Venice via the Red Sea, the Persian Gulf and overland caravan routes. Indeed, even as late as 1585, over three times the amount of pepper and spices – the trade the Europeans were supposed to have a monopoly in – went via the Red Sea route and overland to Europe than circumnavigated the Cape.[57] Moreover, only ten per cent of the Moluccan clove trade that entered Europe went round the Cape.[58] Third, recent research reveals that before 1650 far more of Europe's bullion exports to the East went via the Ottoman and Persian Empires than via the Cape.[59] Moreover, the amount of silver passing through these empires increased in the 1650–1700 period, significantly outpacing that transported round the Cape.[60] Fourth, clear testimony to the insignificance of the Cape Route was that the Portuguese derived about 80 per cent of their trading profits within East Asia via intra-country trade. The myth of a Portuguese trading monopoly is nowhere more clearly revealed than by the fact that much of the Portuguese profit was derived from arbitrage rather than trade. Fifth, it is notable that even in the spice trade the Muslim merchants were dominant over the Portuguese. Key here were the Islamic Gujaratis, who plied the trade routes from South Asia across to West Asia and Africa. Interestingly, the Gujaratis enjoyed higher profit margins than the Dutch. This was naturally a source of considerable irritation for the VOC (the Vereenigde Oostindische Compagnie or Dutch East India Company), who enquired into the reasons for this. As Van Santen reports

> How was a humble Gujarati merchant able to compete with the mighty VOC? The answer given by the company servants themselves sounds quite convincing. The Indian trader simply operated at far lower costs.... Besides, as the Dutch servants admitted, he often had a much more thorough knowledge of how the market worked when he bought and sold his *baftas, tapechindes* or *chelas*.[61]

Sixth and finally, the concept of a Portuguese monopoly is falsified by the simple fact that in the sixteenth century only six per cent of total shipping tonnage employed in the Indian Ocean trading system was Portuguese.

This discussion, particularly of the Gujarati merchants, brings into play the role of Mughal India in the development of Oriental globalization in general and European commerce in particular. It is necessary to consider this, not merely as a topic in its own right, but also in the context of this book, for it would be reductive to conflate Islam only with the Middle East. To extend this anti-reductive logic further, I shall supplement this with the significant role played by Islamic Southeast Asia.

Mughal India and the promotion of global trade

Eurocentrism, in equating Mughal India with a regressive oriental despotic state, would assume that it could only be with the advent of the British Empire that progressive economic activity would emerge in India since the combination of a regressive Islam and an Oriental despotic state, which sucks all the resources out of society in order to maintain its despotic power, could only be fatal so far as Indian trade and development were concerned .[62] Yet, far from a backward and static economy that was isolated from the mainstream of international trade, this section advances various counter-propositions to reveal that before the advent of British imperialism the Indian economy and its trading capacity was developing of its own accord. Here, I want to pay special attention to the Islamic Gujarati merchants.

First, the assumption that the Mughal state crushed all capitalist activity is problematic because the state was, at worst, indifferent to capitalism, often tolerant of it and sometimes did much to promote it. One notable example of the positive help provided by the state concerns the case of the Gujarati merchants. Thus, while royal ships were important up to the early seventeenth century, a fundamental change occurred thereafter. The Gujarati merchants managed to persuade the rulers to withdraw the royal fleet and to grant them autonomy to ply their trade with their own ships, especially from Surat (a process that was complete by the mid-seventeenth century). It seems that the accompanying protection of Gujarati merchants offered by the state was an important factor in enabling the massive increase in Indian commercial shipping based in Surat by between 600 and 1000 per cent. Moreover, basing his claims on new primary research, Muzafar Alam shows how Mughal rulers frequently sought to protect Indian merchants. For example, letters were exchanged between the Mughal rulers, the Persian Shah and the Uzbeck Khans, in order to promote peace for the sake of maintaining the lucrative trade that linked these regions.[63] As Van Santen points out, the Mughal rulers engaged in a type of export promotion policy in order to attract precious metals into India.[64] Not surprisingly Indian traders often saw the rulers as their allies.

Indeed, it was this attitude that attracted the Gujaratis to migrate into Maharashtra in the seventeenth century. More generally, the long-distance Indian traders, the *Banjāras*, were largely Muslim and enjoyed high levels of prestige. Grover notes that

> On behalf of the state, the Zamindars of the regions were required to ensure their [the *Banjāras'*] free passage in their respective Zamindari jurisdictions. As the Banjara class kept up the supply pipeline from one place to another ... they were well respected in society. Whenever a caravan reached a village ... it was received with great warmth. The Chief Zamindars ... often offered robes of honour to Banjara chiefs on their safe arrival in their territories.[65]

A second problem is that the Eurocentric Oriental despotism thesis grossly exaggerates the centrality and power of the Mughal state. The central state actually devolved power and control to the localities and was happy to allow (and tolerate) the many provincial authorities that presided over trade. In general, the private 'shippers were free to run their vessels anywhere they wished; no shipping lines were the monopoly of any man or any group. Occasional attempts at monopoly in particular commodities were known but they were frowned upon and had no lasting effect'.[66] In any case, the system was simply too large and the Mughal state too weak for it to set up a command economy and monopolistic trading system in its own interests.

A third problem is that if the Oriental despotism thesis was correct, we would not expect to find significant sources of credit within the Indian economy. Yet financial institutions were both well developed and extensive, largely as a result of Islamic innovations.

Fourth, if the state had been an Oriental despot how can we explain the fact that many merchants became extremely rich? As Ashin Das Gupta concludes: 'The Hindu *bania,* [or equally the Islamic *Banjāras*] trembling in fear of the Mughal, unable to accumulate and retain property due to the [rapaciousness] of the government, is a figure largely conjured up by the ill-informed imagination of a few among India's western [Eurocentric] travellers. Large properties were freely accumulated in maritime trade.'[67]

Fifth, Eurocentrism asserts that one of the major signs of Mughal Oriental despotism lies in the claim that prior to the emergence of the British Empire, Indian commerce was insignificant and that it was but a mere appendix or footnote to the European commercial mainstream. There are two specific claims tied in here: first, that the minor extant trade was only in luxury goods and was, therefore, not extensive in nature; and, second, that Indian trade was allegedly conducted by small-scale pedlars who were but mere bit-players in the international arena. Let's take each briefly in turn.

One reason why Eurocentrism insists that Indian trade was only marginal comes about through the exotic imagery of Indian luxury textiles, which were sold to kings and the wealthy who comprised at most a mere ten per cent of the world's population. Yet, while luxury textiles were produced in places such as Bengal, Gujarat and Coromandel, the fact is that the majority of the textiles produced in India were aimed at mass markets. What Eurocentric scholars have missed is that a good deal of Indian textiles were of a coarse variety suitable only for the poorer consumers in mass markets. It is also interesting that these mass markets extended far and wide, to Indonesia in Southeast Asia all the way across to Hormuz and Aden in the west. Such markets were, therefore, hardly exceptional. Indeed, the poorer consumer groups in much of the Middle East provided the most demand for the coarse Indian cloth.[68] Mass-based consumer goods also took the form of everyday foods such as rice, pulses, wheat and oil, all of which were traded throughout the Indian Ocean and in considerable quantities.

The conventional Eurocentric image of Indian trade being conducted by pedlars is also fictitious, not least because there were many large-scale merchants plying their trade both inside and outside the Indian economy. As noted, key among these were the *Banjāras,* notably the Islamic-Gujarati merchants who were the largest of all the *Banjāras* and their role within the vast Indian Ocean network was extensive. No less significant is that the *Banjāras* were able to finance long-distance trade at much higher levels than did the British. Indeed, European ships were smaller and less capitalized. The English employed an average capital of 200,000 rupees at the beginning of the seventeenth century, while some Gujarati vessels trading to the Red Sea were worth five times this amount.[69] Thus, although there were many small-scale Indian merchants, the fact is that they (as well as the British) would have been unable to engage in trade without the help of the many large-scale Islamic merchants.

It is also important to note that the picture of Mughal India as isolated from international trade is clearly wide of the mark. While the Ottomans and Chinese, followed by the Safavid Persians, constituted the most important trading players in the global economy in the post-1500 period, Indian Muslim merchants increasingly came to play a complementary role, especially within the important Indian Ocean trading system. India was oriented more towards exports than imports and enjoyed a large trade surplus with Europe.[70] Not surprisingly, large amounts of silver flowed from Europe into India. That alone is surely a clinching argument that undermines the idea that Europe was the dominant trading region.

It is noteworthy that the Europeans ended up by cooperating with Asian merchants and rulers. Indeed, they were dependent on Asian goodwill if they wanted to continue to trade. One aspect of this saw the intermingling of Portuguese and Asian traders, to the advantage of both. Asian merchants often had more goods on a Portuguese ship than did the Portuguese traders. As M. N. Pearson notes:

> It seems that Portuguese sent goods on Gujarati ships, and vice versa, in a promiscuous and intermingled fashion quite typical of private Portuguese country trade in general. Here, rather than the grandiloquent state attempt at monopoly, was where the interest of most Portuguese was involved.[71]

However, Islam also extended into Southeast Asia; a region which also played an important role in spreading commerce from East to West, to a brief consideration of which I now turn.

A Southeast Asian appendix?

If Mughal India and the Islamic Indian merchants contributed significantly to global trade right down to the nineteenth century, this contribution was oiled by the role played by the Islamic Southeast Asian merchants. This, of course, flies in the face of Eurocentrism, which reduces Southeast Asia to the Straits of Malacca and then reduces Malacca to an appendix, or minor footnote, in the mainstream Western story. This is in part because the Straits are imagined as but a mere transit point or way station in the so-called mainstream trade between Europe and China, and in part because Malacca was allegedly dominated by the Portuguese after 1511 and the Dutch after 1641. Yet, not only does this obscure the region's role in trade that stems back to the early part of the Common Era, but it also obscures the vital role that the kingdom of Śrīvijaya in Sumatra played within Afro-Asian trade between the seventh and thirteenth centuries. Moreover, tracing Malacca's relevance only to the post-1511 period is problematic, not least because it was the voyages of the Chinese (Muslim) admiral, Cheng Hô, about a century earlier that enabled a major boost to Malacca and the Southeast Asian trade. For it was only then that Malacca replaced Java as the main centre of Indonesian trade, extending its trading links to Gujarat, Dhabol, Bengal and Coromandel in India, to China and the Ryūkyūs, and to the Persian and Ottoman Empires, as well as to the Mediterranean. Ultimately though, recounting the story of Malacca as a European outpost is problematic because, as was alluded to earlier, the Portuguese and Dutch were simply unable to monopolize Southeast Asian trade.

The Eurocentric dismissal of Southeast Asian trade, as with the denunciation of Indian trade, is made on two further grounds. Again, the first dismissal is based on the claim that trade was conducted only by small-scale pedlars; and second, trade was conducted only in luxury goods and was, therefore, marginal. The first Eurocentric claim is refuted by the existence of the *nakhodas*, who were large-scale and moderately wealthy junk owners. They were mostly Javanese and were the major carriers of foreign trade. Moreover, speaking of the Indonesian trade, M. A. P. Meilink-Roelofsz asserts: 'It is... clear that trade on such a [vast] scale... cannot be termed peddling trade. On the contrary, it forms a richly variegated pattern in which huge quantities of bulk goods, such as foodstuffs and textiles, alternate with smaller... quantities of valuable or even cheap commodities'.[72] This leads on to the rebuttal of the second claim. The familiar Eurocentric claim that Southeast Asian trade was dominated only by luxury goods appears to be based on the exaggerated emphasis that is accorded the spice trade, presumably because it was dominated by the Europeans. However, spices were in fact only a marginal trading item there.[73] Rather, bulk foods (including rice, salt, pickled and dried fish and palm wine), as well as cheap textiles and metal wares comprised the vast majority of the Southeast Asian boat cargoes.

So, to sum up the discussion thus far, it seems that the greatest legacy of the Portuguese (as well as the Dutch and English) seaborne empire was not how much, but how little things changed in terms of Islam's (and China's) leading position in the global economy between 1500–1750/1800. It is hard to avoid the conclusion that the European Age, or the Vasco da Gama Epoch of Asia, turns out to be but retrospective, Eurocentric wishful thinking. In light of all this it is instructive to compare the imperial boasts issued by the Portuguese king Manuel I and the Ottoman emperor Selim the Grim. Manuel boasted in a letter to the Pope of 28 August 1499 that he was: 'Lord of Guinea and of the Conquests, Navigations, and Commerce of Ethiopia, Arabia, Persia, and India'. While this might well have impressed the Pope, it proved to be an entirely fictitious claim. In this respect, Selim's proud boast was far nearer the truth:

> Now all of the territories of Egypt, Malaytia, Aleppo, Syria, the city of Cairo, Upper Egypt, Ethiopia, Yemen, the lands up to the borders of Tunisia, the Hijaz, the cities of Mekka, Medina and Jerusalem, may God increase the honoring and respecting of them completely and fully, have been added to the Ottoman Empire.

Also closer to the truth were the words of the Ottoman sultan, Suleyman (whom the Europeans called the Magnificent), pronounced in 1538: 'I am Suleyman, in whose name the Friday sermon is read in Mecca and Medina. In Baghdad I am the Shah, in the Byzantine realms the Caesar and in Egypt the Sultan, who sends his fleets to the seas of Europe, the Maghrib and India.'[74] In the light of this it seems necessary to correct the words of John Roberts, when he claims that

> It was only a comparatively small boast that the Portuguese king [Manuel] soon called himself 'Lord of Ethiopia, Arabia, Persia and India'.... The conquest of the high seas was the first and greatest of all the triumphs over natural forces which were to lead to the domination by Western civilization of the whole globe.[75]

And, as he goes on to say,

> Nowadays, people have come to use a specially minted word to summarise this state of mind – 'Eurocentrism'. It means 'putting Europe at the centre of things', and its usual implication is that to do so is wrong. But, of course, if we are merely talking about facts, about what happened, and not about the value that we place on them, then it is quite correct to put Europe at the centre of the story in modern times.[76]

However, in the light of this chapter's argument, it would be more accurate to say that 'if we are merely talking about the facts, about what happened [between 1500–1800]...then it is quite correct to put Islam and China at the centre of the story'.

Conclusion: redefining civilizational triumphalism

In this short conclusion I want to consider two interrelated issues, the first of which concerns the political implications of how we might think about Islamic/Western relations today, while the second offers up an alternative way of thinking beyond the Eurocentric discourse of civilizational triumphalism. Much of the current rhetoric concerning the clash of civilizations in general and the War on Terror in particular, presupposes a Eurocentric *weltanschauung*. Thus, when President George W. Bush justifies the War on Terror as necessary to protect the free world, which he conflates with Western civilization, the key implication is that the non-Western world, and especially the world of Islam, is a realm of un-freedom and un-civilization or barbarism. It also presumes that while the West has given much to the East, the latter has given very little to the former, bar terrorism and oil-based inflation. A little further behind this civilizational rhetoric are a series of unstated assumptions, which amount to the twin claims that the West single-handedly created the modern capitalist world, and that only the West has the power and goodwill to bequeath its own creation to the East. These twin claims underpinned America's most recent civilizing mission in the barbaric Middle East.

However, one of the key implications of this chapter is to reveal the point that this antithetical view of us and them is symptomatic of Eurocentric hubris, because what has not been recognized at the popular level is that directly and indirectly the East in general and Muslims in particular have bequeathed a great deal that enabled the West to make the final breakthrough to modern capitalism. Throughout the long period of European development – from roughly 650 through to the late eighteenth century – many of the major commercial ideas and institutions, as well as the sources of European trade more generally, that underpinned Europe's slow leap forward emanated from the East in general and Islam in particular. No less important was that Islam acted as the bridge of the world, serving to diffuse all manner of Eastern (as well as Islamic) resource portfolios into Europe, from which it benefited immeasurably. Another way of putting this is to say that beneath the overly dramatic headlines of the conflict between the Christian West and the world of Islam – often reduced to the Eurocentric notion of the clash of civilizations – lies a mundane, but far more important, story of the dialogue of civilizations. Indeed, it is particularly ironic that at the very time of the Crusades (1095–1291) the Europeans were avidly reading Islamic texts and enquiring into Islamic breakthroughs in mathematics, science, astronomy as well as many other areas of intellectual enquiry upon which the European Renaissance was later based.

It is for this reason that I began my chapter with the quote from Edward Said, whose message is that we need to explore and reveal the many symbiotic relations that have tied Europe and the world of Islam together for so many centuries. Overall, though, I would suggest that without these connections to the Muslim world it is debatable whether the Europeans would have ended up by tripping the modern light fantastic. In their absence they might never have arrived at the point where they could ignore the Islamic contributions that enabled their economic success in the first place when prosecuting the War on Terror with the barbaric Islamic infidel.

In the light of this, the question now becomes how to move forward politically and intellectually in order to overcome the neo-imperialist politics that emanate from Eurocentric hubris, which consistently celebrate only one small part of the world – the West of course – and to thereby think about creating a more just world beyond Western self-conceit. Nayef Al-Rodhan has performed a major task in setting out many of the issues that entail from such a normative project in his deeply learned book *Sustainable History and the Dignity of Man* (2009). Of course, in the limited space I have left here I cannot hope to do justice to his many arguments. Yet, what I can and do want to highlight is that his prescriptions emanate from a prior claim that we need to redefine the idea of civilizational triumph. For, rather than applying it only to the West's achievements in the last 500 years – which if nothing else is a tired, unimaginative and always a politically exclusivist, proclamation – we would be much better off thinking anew about world politics. The politics of Eurocentric neo-imperialism has proven little more effective than the old politics of empire and it is surely time to think creatively outside this box. For the cacophony of increasingly anxious Western voices who feel the need to constantly reiterate the inherent superiority of the West, surely only bears testimony to the deep well of Western insecurity and anxiety that has emerged since 1989 and especially since 9/11. Is this merely the latest phase of Western anxiety in the face of a rising East; one which returns us to the many anxious scientific racist Western voices that emerged after 1889 in the face of similar perceptions at that time?[77] Sadly, it would seem ever thus.

Al-Rodhan's notion of civilizational triumphalism moves us beyond the politics of Western Eurocentric anxiety by refusing to equate it with either the West or the East. As he puts it

> Rather than thinking in terms of multiple civilisations, we need to employ the ocean analogy. Human civilisation is more fruitfully conceived of as a great ocean, joined by many rivers that contribute to its overall growth. These rivers represent different geo-cultural domains that flourish at different points within the larger flow of human history due to mutual borrowing and encounters.[78]

From this, it is apparent that what matters is not which civilization is dominant at any one point in time, nor merely that different civilizations have contributed significantly at different times, but that, above all, it is global humanity that should be the focus of our attention. For the irony is that in all the Eurocentric discussions of inter-civilizational relations, it so often appears as though global humanity is a sideshow rather than the main event.[79]

Notes

1. G. Viswanathan (ed.) (2004), *Power, Politics and Culture: Interviews with Edward Said* (London: Bloomsbury Publishing).
2. For a full discussion of this, see J. M. Hobson (2004), *The Eastern Origins of Western Civilisation* (Cambridge: Cambridge University Press), chs 5–9.
3. G. F. Hourani (1963), *Arab Seafaring in the Indian Ocean in Ancient and Early Medieval Times* (Beirut: Khayats), pp. 36–8; A. Wink (1995), *Al-Hind: The Making of the Indo-Islamic World*, Vol. I (Leiden: E. J. Brill), pp. 48–55.
4. M. Rodinson (1974), *Islam and Capitalism* (London: Allen Lane), p. 14.
5. Ibid., pp. 16–17.
6. Cited in ibid., p. 29.

7. S. D. Goitein (1968), *Studies in Islamic History and Institutions* (Leiden: E. J. Brill), pp. 228–9.
8. M. G. S. Hodgson (1993), *Rethinking World History* (Cambridge: Cambridge University Press), pp. 111–16, 141.
9. Ibid., p. 133.
10. Rodinson, *Islam and Capitalism*, p. 56.
11. R. R. di Meglio (1970), 'Arab Trade Relations with Indonesia and the Malay Peninsula from the 8th to the 16th Century', in D. S. Richards (ed.) *Islam and the Trade of Asia* (Oxford: Bruno Cassirer), p. 126.
12. Hourani, *Arab Seafaring*, p. 62; J. L. Abu-Lughod (1989), *Before European Hegemony* (Oxford: Oxford University Press), p. 199; N. Chittick (1970), 'East African Trade with the Orient', in D. S. Richards (1970), *Islam and the Trade of Asia* (Oxford: Bruno Cassirer), p. 98.
13. Hourani, *Arab Seafaring*, p. 64.
14. Cited in J. Bloom and S. Blair (2001), *Islam: Empire of Faith* (London: BBC Worldwide), p. 164.
15. See E. R. Wolf (1982), *Europe and the People without History* (Berkeley: University of California Press), pp. 37–44.
16. E. W. Bovill (1933), *Caravans of the Old Sahara* (London: Oxford University Press), chs 5–6.
17. A. Bala, P. Duara and M. van Donzel (forthcoming), *The Bright Dark Ages: Rethinking Needham's Grand Question*.
18. F. Braudel (1992), *Civilization and Capitalism, 15th–18th Century* (Berkeley: University of California Press), p. 94.
19. A. Smith (1776/1937), *The Wealth of Nations* (New York: The Modern Library), p. 13.
20. Though this is not to ignore the considerable production of manufactured goods that occurred in the Islamic world.
21. Abu-Lughod, *Before European Hegemony*, p. 108.
22. Braudel, *Civilization and Capitalism*, p. 132.
23. For example, D. C. North and R. P. Thomas (1973), *The Rise of the Western World* (Cambridge: Cambridge University Press), p. 53.
24. M. J. Kister (1965), 'Mecca and Tamīm', *Journal of the Economic and Social History of the Orient*, Vol. 8, No. 2, p. 117ff.
25. A. L. Udovitch (1970), 'Commercial Techniques in Early Medieval Islamic Trade', in D. S. Richards (ed.) *Islam and the Trade of Asia* (Oxford: Bruno Cassirer), p. 48.
26. Ibid., p. 78; P. Kunitzsch (1989), *The Arabs and the Stars* (Northampton: Variorum),pp. 362–7.
27. Abu-Lughod, *Before European Hegemony*, p. 216.
28. S. D. Goitein (1967), *A Mediterranean Society*, Vol. I (Berkeley: University of California Press), pp. 197–9; A. L. Udovitch (1970), *Partnership and Profit in Medieval Islam* (Princeton: Princeton University Press), pp. 61–2.
29. Abu-Lughod, *Before European Hegemony*, p. 223.
30. Hobson, *The Eastern Origins of Western Civilisation*, pp. 173–83; J. Goody (2004), *Islam in Europe* (Cambridge: Polity), pp. 56–83; G. G. Joseph (1992), *The Crest of the Peacock* (London: Penguin), ch. 10; A. Bala (2006), *The Dialogue of Civilizations in the Birth of Modern Science* (Houndmills: Palgrave Macmillan); S. M. Ghazanfar (2006), *Islamic Civilization: History, Contributions, and*

Influence (Lanham: Scarecrow Press); C. K. Raju (2007), *Cultural Foundations of Mathematics*, Vol. X, Part 4, *History of Science, Philosophy and Culture in Indian Civilization* (New Delhi: Pearson Education).

31. Although they called themselves *can'ani* or Canaanites from Canaan and were situated on the east coast of the Mediterranean.
32. Joseph, *The Crest of the Peacock*, ch. 10; Bala, *The Dialogue of Civilizations*.
33. W. H. Abdi (1999), 'Glimpses of Mathematics in Medieval India', in A. Rahman (ed.) *History of Indian Science, Technology and Culture, AD 1000–1800* (New Delhi: Oxford University Press).
34. S. Nasr (1968), *Science and Civilization in Islam* (Cambridge, Mass.: Harvard University Press), ch. 5.
35. C. Singer (1956), 'Epilogue: East and West in Retrospect', in C. Singer, E. J. Holmyard, A. R. Hall and T. I. Williams (eds) *A History of Technology*, Vol. III (Oxford: Clarendon Press), p. 767.
36. E. S. Kennedy (1983), *Studies in the Islamic Exact Sciences* (Beirut: American University of Beirut), p. 41.
37. J. Needham and W. Ling (1959), *Science and Civilisation in China*, Vol. III (Cambridge: Cambridge University Press), p. 109.
38. G. Saliba (1994), *A History of Arabic Astronomy* (London: New York University Press), p. 64.
39. Kennedy, *Studies in the Islamic Exact Sciences*, pp. 50–83; Saliba, *A History of Arabic Astronomy*, pp. 245–305.
40. N. Swerdlow and O. Neugebauer (1984), *Mathematical Astronomy in Copernicus' De Revolutionibus* (Berlin: Springer), p. 295.
41. J. Goody (1996), *The East in the West* (Cambridge: Cambridge University Press), pp. 68, 72.
42. Abu-Lughod, *Before European Hegemony*, p. 149.
43. M. N. Pearson (1987), *The New Cambridge History of India* (Cambridge: Cambridge University Press), p. 11.
44. Wolf, *Europe and the People without History*, p. 234.
45. J. Needham (1990), *A Selection from the Writings of Joseph Needham*, edited by Mansel Davies (Lewes: The Book Guild), p. 176.
46. Cited in J. Desomogyi (1968), *A Short History of Oriental Trade* (Hildesheim: Georg Olms Verlagsbuchhandlung), p. 83.
47. L. Casson (1971), *Ships and Seamanship in the Ancient World* (Princeton: Princeton University Press); L. White (1978), *Medieval Religion and Technology*, Vol. I (Berkeley: University of California Press), pp. 255–60.
48. Cited in Hourani, *Arab Seafaring*, p. 100.
49. G. R. Tibbetts (1971), *Arab Navigation in the Indian Ocean before the Coming of the Portuguese* (London: The Royal Asiatic Society of Great Britain and Ireland), p. 49.
50. It is important to note that for centuries Jews, Christians and Muslims lived side by side for the most part perfectly amicably within the realms of Islam, including, of course, Al-Andalus and the Middle East. In particular, Jews entwined with Muslim traders and the *Rhadanite* Jewish merchants played a very important role within the trade and finance of the Islamic world – especially in Baghdad to about the tenth century and subsequently in Cairo after 969. Interestingly, the term appears to have been derived from the Persian term *rha dan* (meaning 'those who know the route').

51. E. Savage-Smith (1992), 'Celestial Mapping', in J. B. Harley and D. Woodward (eds) *History of Cartography*, Vol. II, Part 1 (Chicago: Chicago University Press), pp. 12–70; Kunitzsch, *The Arabs and the Stars*, chs 8 and 10.
52. Kunitzsch, *The Arabs and the Stars*, ch. 9.
53. Cited in P. Seed (1995), *Ceremonies of Possession in Europe's Conquest of the New World, 1492–1640* (Cambridge: Cambridge University Press), p. 126.
54. Tibbetts, *Arab Navigation*, pp. 9–11.
55. See the graphic description of the return journey reported in da Gama's diary. Cited in E. G. Ravenstein (1899) (ed.) *A Journal of the First Voyage of Vasco Da Gama, 1497–1499* (London: Bedford Press), p. 87.
56. P. M. Holt, A. Lambton and B. Lewis cited in A. Gunder Frank (1998), *ReOrient: Global Economy in the Asian Age* (Berkeley: University of California Press), p. 118.
57. N. Steensgaard (1974), *The Asian Trade Revolution of the Seventeenth Century* (Chicago: Chicago University Press), pp. 155–69.
58. Pearson, *The New Cambridge History of India*, p. 44.
59. N. Haider (1996), 'Precious Metals and Currency Circulation in the Mughal Empire', *Journal of the Economic and Social History of the Orient*, Vol. 39, No. 3, pp. 298–367.
60. S. Subrahmanyam (1994), 'Precious Metal Flows and Prices in Western and Southern Asia, 1500–1750: Some Comparative and Conjunctural Aspects', in S. Subrahmanyam (ed.) *Money and the Market in India 1100–1700* (Delhi: Oxford University Press), pp. 197–201.
61. H. W. van Santen (1991), 'Trade between Mughal India and the Middle East, and Mughal Monetary Policy, c. 1600–1660', in K. R. Haellquist (ed.) *Asian Trade Routes* (London: Curzon Press), p. 89.
62. See, for example, W. H. Moreland (1923) *From Akbar to Aurangzeb* (London: Macmillan); T. Raychaudhuri (1982), 'The Mughal Empire', in T. Raychaudhuri and I. Habib (eds) *The Cambridge Economic History of India, 1* (Cambridge: Cambridge University Press), pp. 172–3.
63. M. Alam (1994), 'Trade, State Policy and Regional Change: Aspects of Mughal-Uzbeck Commercial Relations, c. 1550–1750', *Journal of the Economic and Social History of the Orient*, Vol. 3, No. 3, pp. 225–6.
64. van Santen, 'Trade between Mughal India and the Middle East', pp. 94–5.
65. B. R. Grover (1994), 'An Integrated Pattern of Commercial Life in Rural Society of North India during the Seventeenth and Eighteenth Centuries', in S. Subrahmanyam (ed.) *Money and the Market in India 1100–1700* (Delhi: Oxford University Press), pp. 238–9.
66. A. Das Gupta (2001), *The World of the Indian Ocean Merchant, 1500–1800* (New Delhi: Oxford University Press), p. 124.
67. Ibid., p. 73.
68. Ibid., pp. 66, 92.
69. Goody, *The East in the West*, p. 128.
70. Gunder Frank, *ReOrient*, pp. 84–92.
71. M. N. Pearson (1987b), 'India and the Indian Ocean in the Sixteenth Century', in A. Das Gupta and M. N. Pearson (eds) *India and the Indian Ocean 1500–1800* (Calcutta: Oxford University Press), p. 78.
72. M. A. P. Meilink-Roelofsz (1970), 'Trade and Islam in the Malay-Indonesian Archipelago Prior to the Arrival of the Europeans', in D. S. Richards (ed.) *Islam and the Trade of Asia* (Oxford: Bruno Cassirer), p. 153.

73. K. N. Chaudhuri (1978), *Trade and Civilisation in the Indian Ocean* (Cambridge: Cambridge University Press), pp. 186–7.
74. Cited in Bloom and Blair, *Islam: Empire of Faith*, p. 158.
75. J. M. Roberts (1985), *The Triumph of the West* (London: BBC Books), p. 194.
76. Ibid., p. 201.
77. J. M. Hobson (2012), *The Eurocentric Conception of World Politics: Western International Theory, 1760–2010* (Cambridge: Cambridge University Press).
78. N. R. F. Al Rodhan (2009), *Sustainable History and the Dignity of Man* (Zürich: LIT Verlag), p. 218.
79. For the specific details concerning how the politics of global humanity might be advanced, see ibid.

6

Suppressed or Falsified History? The Untold Story of Arab-Islamic Rationalist Philosophy

Samar Attar

Bertrand Russell and Arab-Islamic philosophy

In his book *History of Western Philosophy*, Bertrand Russell, a distinguished British philosopher, displays a little understanding of what he calls 'Mohammedan Culture and Philosophy'. Ray Monk describes the book as 'the perfect introduction to its subject', while Sir Isaiah Berlin hails its arguments as 'not merely classically clear but scrupulously honest'.[1] *The Oxford Companion to Philosophy* depicts it as Russell's best-known philosophical work that 'exemplifies this breadth of interest and understanding, and shows that no two areas of philosophy can be guaranteed to be mutually irrelevant'.[2] Unfortunately, the reader is not given a chance to make up his mind since the gurus of philosophy have already attested to the greatness of the book. Exploring a foreign territory, such as Arabic-Islamic culture and philosophy, without having the appropriate tools or genuine knowledge, Russell refers briefly to two Muslim philosophers, the Persian Avicenna (Ibn Sina) (980–1037), and the Andalusian Averroes (Ibn Rushd) (1126–98) without clearly stating his sources. The information given is very shallow and he then concludes his chapter with the following statement:

> Arabic philosophy is not important as original thought. Men like Avicenna and Averroes are essentially commentators. Speaking generally, the views of the more scientific philosophers come from Aristotle and the Neoplatonists in logic and metaphysics, from Galen in medicine, from Greek and Indian sources in mathematics and astronomy, and among mystics religious philosophy

> has also an admixture of old Persian beliefs. Writers in Arabic showed some originality in mathematics and in chemistry – in the latter case, as an incidental result of alchemical researches. Mohammedan civilization in its great days was admirable in the arts and in many technical ways, but it showed no capacity for independent speculation in theoretical matters. Its importance, which must not be underrated, is as a transmitter. Between ancient and modern European civilization, the dark ages intervened. The Mohammedans and the Byzantines, while lacking the intellectual energy required for innovation, preserved the apparatus of civilization – education, books, and learned leisure. Both stimulated the West when it emerged from barbarism – the Mohammedans chiefly in the thirteenth century, the Byzantines chiefly in the fifteenth. In each case the stimulus produced new thought better than any produced by the transmitters – in the one case scholasticism, in the other the Renaissance (which however had other causes also).[3]

Russell, then, mentions Maimonides (Ibn Maymun) (1135–1204) as a separate category. He describes him as a Spanish Jew who went to Cairo at the age of 30 and remained there for the rest of his life. Then he dismisses the ideas of those who think that Maimonides influenced Spinoza. One wonders whether Russell's secondary sources about the subject matter mention other philosophers as well. Nothing is certain. There is not a single word on Al-Kindi (d. 873), Al-Farabi (d. 950), Ibn Gabriol (Avicebron, d. 1058), Ibn Bajja (Avempace, 1106–38/39), or Ibn Tufayl (Abubacer, 1100/10–1185). The British philosopher seems to be totally oblivious to Ibn Tufayl's book *Hayy Ibn Yaqzan* in this and the following chapters that deal with The Rise of Science, Francis Bacon, Hobbes's Leviathan, Descartes, Spinoza, Leibniz, Locke's Theory of Knowledge, Hume, Rousseau, or Kant. There is an unflattering remark about Al-Ghazali (Algazel, d. 1111) in reference to his debate with Averroes on philosophical speculation.[4]

For Russell, what 'distinguishes the modern world from earlier centuries is attributable to science, which achieved its most spectacular triumphs in the seventeenth century'.[5] Descartes is 'the founder of modern philosophy' and 'the first man of high philosophic capacity whose outlook is profoundly affected by the new physics and astronomy'.[6] The main reason for this, according to Russell, is that the French philosopher 'does not accept foundations laid by predecessors, but endeavours to construct a complete philosophic edifice *de novo*. This had not happened since

Aristotle, and is a sign of the new self-confidence that resulted from the progress of science.'[7]

Ignorance is mainly responsible for such a statement that confirms that Muslim civilization is only 'a transmitter' of the knowledge of others and not an innovator, that Avicenna and Averroes are mere 'commentators' on Greek philosophy, or that Al-Ghazali is only an orthodox theologian who sees 'no need of speculation independent of revelation'. It is not the fault of Bertrand Russell. He is simply repeating what other scholars had been saying in the West for decades. No one contested their views, or bothered to check the validity of their assumptions. But above all, no one thought of the dangerous implications of such statements which suggest that only Europeans are capable of innovation and independent speculation in theoretical matters. The rest of mankind is Other. Yet Russell observes that a transmitting civilization should not be underrated. So in this case, we even seem to have categories within the Other. There are those who receive knowledge and preserve it and those who prefer to destroy it. According to this view, then, the West is grateful to the Arabs and Muslims not for their innovation or high philosophy, but for protecting western heritage and preventing its loss to mankind. It is worth mentioning that since the recovery of the original Greek sources the need to use Avicenna's or Averroes's commentaries becomes unessential. This is, of course, reflected in the study of philosophy and other branches of science in western universities in the contemporary era. Arabic and Islamic philosophy is relegated now to Oriental Studies as a minor field quite irrelevant to Western philosophy. This is also reflected in the books and encyclopedias produced by western philosophers. Even those who allow a few entries on Avicenna or Averroes seem to encourage a peculiar discourse that does not show the continuation of human thought and the innovations of each philosopher, regardless of his religion or ethnic background. Indeed, most of these entries confirm our beliefs that East is East, and West is West, and the two can never meet.[8]

Plato and Aristotle did not spring out of nothing. They had mentors from other civilizations. They did not invent their philosophy. They borrowed from other nations and developed their ideas. The Arabs and Muslims continued this tradition. They were indebted to the ancient thinkers of the Near East, to the Greeks, the Romans, the Indians, the Persians and many others. Religion or ethnic background were never a barrier to the flow of ideas. Jewish, Christian, Muslim, Buddhist or atheist concepts all mingled together, and they were examined, developed, accepted or rejected on their merits. Thought (or Philosophy) had not stopped after Aristotle, as Bertrand Russell would like us to believe. Descartes (1596–1650), the founder of modern philosophy according to the West, did not start a revolution in world philosophy. He was simply standing on the shoulders of all these Arab and Muslim philosophers who, like their predecessors from other nations and religions, contributed hugely to this new philosophical trend in France and to the rise of Europe in general. Any schoolchild familiar with both Descartes and Ibn Tufayl, for instance, can pinpoint complete passages that may have been lifted out from the twelfth century Arabic book in order to establish a new philosophy in seventeenth-century France. Descartes' discussion of 'matter' and 'doubt' in his *Principles of Philosophy* and *Meditations* is a case in point. His sentences echo what Ibn Tufayl said centuries ago. 'A corner-stone of Descartes' approach', observes a modern philosopher, 'was that the matter throughout the universe was of essentially the same type, hence there was no difference in principle between "terrestrial" and "celestial" phenomena, and the earth was merely one part of a homogeneous universe obeying uniform physical laws'.[9] This is basically what Hayy Ibn Yaqzan began to discover after twenty-one years of his life on a desert island.[10]

Furthermore, Descartes has supposedly made 'doubt the cornerstone of a philosophical method', as another modern philosopher observes.[11] Yet, doubt was a philosophical method for decades prior to this outside Christian Europe. Although Al-Ghazali was at odds with Averroes, struggling most of his life with the tension between speculation and revelation in his thought, and had accused philosophers of incoherence, he nevertheless viewed skepticism as one of the most important criteria of the human mind. This was not lost on Ibn Tufayl, who adhered to a different philosophical trend. In his introduction to *Hayy Ibn Yaqzan*, he evaluates the contributions of other philosophers and acknowledges his debt to some of them, particularly Ibn Bajja. However, he also refers to Al-Ghazali and quotes an important passage on skepticism: 'If I [Al-Ghazali] did nothing but to make you doubt your inherited faith that would be beneficial enough. For he who does not doubt has not looked, and he who has not looked does not see, and he who does not see remains blind and confused.' Al-Ghazali then quotes an Arabic poem: 'Take only what you see and discard everything you have heard about from others.'[12] In short, opposing the old authorities does not mean wiping out all the foundations laid by them. The new philosopher is still able to find something original in his opponent's theories. In spite of his opposition to Al-Ghazali on philosophical grounds Ibn Tufayl hails his predecessor's concept on skepticism as the keystone for any inquiry.

All philosophers and scientists digest their predecessors' ideas. Some accept the foundations laid by those who come before them. Others contest these foundations and attempt to construct something new, but even then they will be always indebted to those who taught them how to doubt and how to find evidence. To my mind, there was never a rupture in philosophical thought after Aristotle, as Bertrand Russell and many other westerners claim. Modern philosophy did not start in France or England as 'a sign of the new self-confidence that resulted from the progress of science'. If there was no science in Europe before Descartes there was certainly science elsewhere in the globe.[13] It is only when we see that we share a common humanity and history that we begin to re-evaluate our biased political views concerning the barbarian Others and to understand ourselves as well. In this sense we are all transmitters as well as inventors of new knowledge regardless of our ethnic or religious background, or geographic location.

An Arab rationalist philosopher and modernity

In his essay *An Answer to the Question: What Is Enlightenment?* Immanuel Kant (1724–1804) defines the term as 'man's emergence from his self-imposed infancy. This infancy is the inability to use one's own understanding without the guidance of another'.[14] His words sum up a whole intellectual movement that supposedly began in England in the seventeenth century, spread to France and Germany in the eighteenth century, and eventually affected every facet of life in other European countries. Thus, the motto 'Have the courage to think for yourself and use your own reason' becomes an exclusively European one. Western theorists, who indulge in discussing the idea of progress or the triumph of the human mind over superstition or the scientific revolution, fail to trace the real origin and development of this drastically new concept of knowledge in the world as a whole. This is mainly due to an exclusive way of looking at Western societies as constituting separate and coherent entities very different from any other. The large divide created by historians, philosophers and literary critics between East and West seems to be responsible for many errors and misunderstandings in the transmission of knowledge in general.

My purpose here is to show how modernity, which Western scholars normally trace to European Enlightenment, travelled from Muslim Spain through a philosophical book written in the twelfth century in the guise of a novel that became well known in Europe after 1349. *Hayy Ibn Yaqzan* not only helped usher in the Scientific Revolution, but it also transformed Medieval Europe and nudged it toward modernity. Major European thinkers from Da Vinci to Locke, Descartes to Kant, Rousseau to Voltaire formulated and reformulated Ibn Tufayl's notions of freedom, equality and toleration. They gave Hayy different names and depicted him in different places. Yet, whether they admired him, ridiculed him or kept silent about him, they all imitated him in one way or another, subverted some of his traits and changed his basic humanistic message.[15]

Modernity in this context means the autonomous quest of man to master and fully understand the universe and live comfortably within it as a result of such understanding and mastery. It is reason that makes it possible for human beings to comprehend the mysteries of the universe, or to develop forms of government that will ensure human liberties. Jürgen Habermas (1929-), a second-generation member of the Frankfurt School, supports this definition of modernity. He tends to use modernity and enlightenment interchangeably. For him, the scientific and rational modern spirit is worth defending.[16] Alan Charles Kors also describes modernity in his Preface to the *Encyclopedia of Enlightenment* as 'an increasingly critical attitude toward inherited authority in a large variety of human spheres, a sense that, armed with new methods and new powers, the human mind could re-examine claims upon it in a growing set of the domains of human life, including religion.'[17] Furthermore, Kors highlights the ethical dimension of utility and the emergence of toleration as one of the most significant concerns of European culture from the 1670s to the early nineteenth century, including the American outposts of that culture.

Hayy Ibn Yaqzan, a philosophical novel, seems to exemplify what western scholars define as modernism. Written in 1160 or 1170 in Arabic by Ibn Tufayl, a mathematician, astronomer, philosopher and court physician of the Sultan Abu Ya'qub Yusuf of Morocco and Spain. The book was first translated into Hebrew by Moses of Narbonne in 1349 and into Latin by Pico della Mirandola in the second half of the fifteenth century. Another Latin edition appeared in 1671, based on a translation of the Arabic edition, by Edward Pococke, son of the well-known Orientalist professor at Oxford University. The translation was reprinted in 1700. There were numerous translations of the work into English during the second half of the seventeenth century. Dutch versions of *Hayy* also appeared in Amsterdam in 1672 and 1701 prior to the publication of *Robinson Crusoe* in 1719. It was reported that Spinoza, the Dutch philosopher whose family settled in Holland as refugees from the Inquisition in Spain and Portugal, had either translated the Arabic novel or recommended that it be translated into Dutch.[18] We know for sure that Alexander Pope (1688–1744), Gottfried Wilhelm Leibniz (1646–1716), Francois-Marie Arouet de Voltaire (1694–1778), Gotthold Ephraim Lessing (1729–81), Moses Mendelssohn (1729–86), Friedrich Wilhelm Joseph von Schelling (1775–1854) and Cotton Mather (1663–1728) among others had read it.

In his English translation of *Hayy Ibn Yaqzan* in 1708, Simon Ockley is very careful to disassociate himself from early translators, such as George Keith, a prominent Quaker, and George Ashwell, the Catholic vicar of Banbury well known for his naturalist theology. Ockley's reason is not only that these two translators were unable to read Arabic and would have carried out their translations from the Latin text, but mainly because 'there has been a bad Use made of this Book before',[19] and it was imperative for Ockley to make known his disagreement with certain views. In an appendix to his translation, entitled *The Improvement of Human Reason Exhibited in the Life of Hai Ebn Yokdhan*, Ockley referred to the dangerous influence of this book and assured his eighteenth century English readers that 'it contains several things co-incident with the Errors of some Enthusiasts of these present times'.[20] It is obvious that Ockley, a professor of Arabic at Cambridge University at the beginning of the eighteenth century, was very careful not to compromise his position in Anglican England and to associate himself with the views of dissenters, particularly the Quakers.[21]

But what is this dangerous book all about? *Hayy Ibn Yaqzan* (or *The Alive-One-Son of the Wakeful)* is one of the earliest philosophical novels that construct an autonomous individual who is born in nature, without parents, on a desert island.[22] He has no family, no religion, no history and no language. Neither his colour nor his looks are specified. He has no particular race. Yet, he belongs to all of humanity. In spite of his circumstances, or perhaps because of them, he learns how to be self-sufficient. Reason, which has been bestowed upon him and not upon the animals or plants around him, helps him to reflect on his own identity and the identity of other objects. No teachers, prophets or religious institutions play any role in Hayy's make up, or self awareness, or that of those around him, or of the heavenly bodies, or of the Mover of the Universe. His own search for the truth is based on objective criteria and the methods he uses at every stage of his development are appropriate to his age. Empirical investigations, deductive and inductive reasoning help him answer many difficult questions. Science and philosophy are not divorced from each other. Hayy has to become an astronomer, a biologist, a mathematician, a physicist, a psychologist, a sociologist and a physician before he attempts to solve his philosophical problems and is forced to apply analogous techniques to philosophy. It is only when he wishes to have a glimpse of the divine world that he recognizes the limitations of reason in this sphere. Intuition guided by the inner light, or reason, can eventually help the seekers of truth come face to face with the Eternal Being, who is not subject to the universal laws of creation and decay, and to grasp the meaning of the illuminating wisdom, the summit of human knowledge.

The principle of diversity and unity in the natural sciences that helps Hayy formulate his philosophical notion of the one and the many is crucial to our understanding of Hayy's identity *vis-à-vis* other identities, as well as his concern to maintain harmony between people and nature, people and people, people and the Divine Being. During the fourth stage of his development, for example, he examines 'all objects subject to creation and decay – the animals and plants in all their varieties, the metals and rocks and such things as soil, water, steam ... smoke and flames'.[23] He concludes:

> All of them had some qualities in common and some qualities were specific. When considered from the viewpoint of their common qualities they were all one. When considered from the viewpoint of their different qualities, they were a multiplicity. If he tried to set out the unique characteristics, those qualities that separated them from others, then the variety of difference was truly enormous and the whole of creation spread out into a multiplicity beyond classification. When he considered his own being and looked at the variety of his own organs, each with a unique function and a specific quality, then his being did indeed seem to be a multiplicity. On the other hand he could see that his organs, though many, were all interconnected and related and from this point of view his being was a unity. The different function of different organs depended on what reached them of the power of the spirit, the spirit itself being one. From this line of thought he concluded that spirit is a unity in its essence and is the reality beyond the self, all the organs being merely tools [machines]. His own self now appeared as a unity.[24]

This argument will prove helpful when the 50-year-old natural man moves temporarily from the wilderness to a human society ruled by a king. If there is no contradiction between the one and the many in the natural world, then there is no reason why there should be any contradiction between one personal identity and another in the human world. He extends his line of thought to other human beings when he meets Asal, a hermit who suddenly appears on the uninhabited island. According to Hayy, diversity and unity are two sides of the same coin. Such a belief will eventually lead him to the notion of toleration in human societies.[25]

After having learned Asal's language and familiarized himself with the stranger's religion and customs, he accompanies him to the inhabited island from which Asal has come. The king and a select group of his people have been shaped by their society and religion. They frown on religious speculations and accept the external interpretation of religion. The rest of the islanders seem to be diverted from thinking of God by their merchandise and trading. Hayy realizes that, although people are endowed with the same reason and the desire to do good, not all are willing at one point or another in their lives to apply these natural gifts to the right uses. For them, Hayy is a man who is only interested in pure truth. They withdraw from him, but still treat him kindly as a stranger. Finally, he opts for individual responsibility and comes to the conclusion that there is no reason to speak any more of pure truth. Fearing that he may cause more damage than good, Hayy goes back to the king, excuses himself and implores him to adhere to his own religion. Then he bids him farewell and returns to his desert island with Asal. His companion has reached similar conclusions about Man's happiness and ultimate goal in life by using different methods of inquiry to Hayy's, namely by attempting to understand the hidden meanings and spiritual contents of the scripture. The message of the novel is quite clear. People, we are told, are different although they belong to the same species. One must accept their multiplicity and unity at the same time. They happen to use various means in search of the ultimate truth. According to Hayy, there is a place for everyone on this Earth. Conformity is not recommended and arguments that may lead to violence and endanger the social and spiritual fabric of society are better avoided.[26]

In this context, Hayy is certainly someone who comes close to the sublime (as Kant defines the term), for he has no need for society without being unsociable. His departure from the civilized island is not seen as an act of misanthropy or anthropophobia (fear of people).[27] However, unlike many western thinkers of the Enlightenment, including Kant, Hayy does not lack a dialectical relation between knowledge and action.[28] He has acquired the widest possible range of autonomous and critical knowledge without the influence of any established authority. Yet, once he meets other humans who rely on authority in their judgement and neglect to use their critical reason he comprehends the significance of his findings and begins to possess a strong desire to bring about concrete changes in society. At the same time, he is convinced that his findings are not the only exclusive truth. Other people can reach where he has reached by other means. Therefore, he treads carefully. He is very concerned about the consequences of his actions. He concludes that if his crusade to alter society will definitely lead to discord and violence, he will then retreat and leave people to think for themselves, giving them a chance to reflect on the issues he has raised and to encourage them to reach judgements determined solely by their own critical reason.

Hayy Ibn Yaqzan is an optimistic treatise on human nature. Man is both body and soul. He is different from animals, for he can control his passions if he wishes. Humans are endowed with reason and free will.[29] If they use their rational capacity wisely they will be able to master nature. Everything can be learned by experience. Science is the key, which signifies certainty of observation. Mathematics, geometry and physics help solve everyday problems. Some bodies are in constant motion. The principle of mechanical cause and effect is of paramount importance. In short, material knowledge can be acquired through observation and experimentation. It is possible for man to control his universe and to progress to a higher form of rational knowledge. Yet, there is a dimension to Man's greatness, that is, his capacity to attain metaphysical truth. To acquire knowledge of what cannot be seen or tested by the senses, one needs intuition. However, this intuition is always tied to causes and sources. In short, the promotion of the autonomous rational individual, who is a moral agent by necessity, does not in any way undermine the stability of civil society. On the contrary, the more rational individuals we have in one place, the more we are likely to be able to create a polity based on justice and equality for all.[30]

Hayy Ibn Yaqzan advocates the primary importance of the individual and the virtues of self-reliance and personal independence. He is totally free of any external influence or control. He is independent of mind and judgement and may be considered the supreme ruler of himself. No one has supremacy or authority over him or his actions. His self-realization, the significance of his consciousness and self-development are necessary stages towards his ultimate freedom and happiness provided no harm is done to other beings, be they humans, animals or plants. As a moral agent an individual is normally content with very little. He eats no more than what would satisfy his hunger. Having more than one's shelter is not essential to survival. Although Man is motivated by self-interest, at first in order to survive in the wild, he quickly comes to the conclusion that it is also in his own interest to think of the general good. Human reason can create a balance between the Self and the Other. It is not difficult to check Darwin's state of continuous warfare. Harmony and peace can be established on Earth without need of policeman, judge or prince.

This thesis proves to be accurate in a natural state where a wild boy can change and be changed through different experiences and even surpass his original condition by making use of his inborn reason and intuition. Human nature at this juncture is supposed to be uniform. Yet, since Hayy has lived only in nature and is the sole individual on his island, he has no knowledge of human societies. His thesis must be tested in a political state, which is conceived as a body and moved by the natural desires of men. In his attempt to apply mathematical reasoning and psychology to social and political phenomena Hayy discovers that not all men are willing to use their rational power in order to control their passions, or to seek pure truth. However, there is no reason to believe that they cannot, or will not, change in the future, for men have great potential. Reason will eventually liberate them and show them the path to happiness. The antagonism between science and theology will cease to exist. Orthodox, or traditional, religion as we know it, will eventually diminish in status. In the meantime, the rational prince and his council ought to be pragmatic, keep peace at all costs for the general good of humanity and avoid violence and bloodshed. A contract between the ruler and the ruled is established. Human beings join together in the formation of a state, whereby individuals surrender some of their interests in exchange for security and the satisfaction of basic needs. The just sovereign, on the other hand, maintains peace and stability, and ensures the welfare of his people. In this context, the state is viewed as a rational construct meant to check men's greed and desires by rational means. It is worth mentioning that the problem of body and soul in this political state is quite pronounced. It is only when men fully utilize reason, derive their knowledge from science and overcome their excessive desires that this problem can be solved. In short, conflict between the individual and the group need not exist if individuals utilize their rational power and strive to balance their responsibilities towards others and themselves. It is important to understand that while individuals are ends in themselves, at the same time they are extensions of all others in the universe. Equality is a key concept in Hayy's theories.[31] Every individual is unique and can be autonomous if he strives to be. The emphasis is on the notion that there is no contradiction between the one and the many, that identities are similar and different, and that it is possible for individuals to coexist peacefully in spite of their differences, or to live separately as they choose.

Hayy's ethical and evolutionary theories were not totally accepted by western thinkers. Daniel Defoe, the father of the English novel, who seems to have plagiarized a significant portion from this Arabic book in *Robinson Crusoe* could not envision a totally ethical individual such as Hayy. For Defoe, a nation cannot consist purely of saints. If commerce is not allowed to go on, the nation could be easily transformed into beggars.[32] Thus, he heralded the age of slavery and exploitation. In contrast, Locke, who borrowed liberally from Hayy, advocated private property, which eventually led to the rise of capitalism. He had no difficulty justifying the appropriation of foreign land without consent and excluding Catholics and Muslims from the body politic.[33] Kant, who exalted the autonomous rational individual as a moral agent, did not hesitate to differentiate between races and described the white race to which he belonged as humanity's greatest perfection in contrast to the inferior 'yellow Indians' and the 'negroes'.[34] Similarly, Darwin's concept of survival of the fittest has acquired a racist and sinister overtone. According to the father of evolutionary biology and promoter of natural selection, competition is the essence of everything in life. Self-interest guides all species on Earth.[35]

Nevertheless, Hayy's notion of the greatness of man, with emphasis on his significant rational power and empirical ability, became one of the prominent themes in the Renaissance and seventeenth- and eighteenth-century Europe. The image of the self-made man was glorified by Leonardo Da Vinci (1452–1519) and later by Francis Bacon (1561–1626), Spinoza (1632–77), Locke (1632–1704), Leibniz (1646–1716) and many others. This exalted view of man also appeared in the works of Descartes who differentiated sharply between men and animals and spoke of the freedom of the mind. Many ideas were discussed, accepted or discarded. Is man nothing but a machine? How can one solve the dichotomy of mind and body? Is there a relationship between freedom and determinism? How can one explain the imperfection and limitation of human nature? Some, like Hobbes (1588–1679) adopted mathematics and geometry as their scientific method and attempted to apply it to politics. Others, like Leibniz, made mathematics the basis of their political projects in the hope that they would discover universal characteristics in man and be able to eradicate conflicts.

The metaphor of Leviathan, or commonwealth, suggested by Hobbes, evokes Hayy's description of man's organs and its interconnected relation not only within a single body, but also within other bodies in nature.[36] Motion and mechanical cause and effect govern everything in the universe. The state and nature are juxtaposed in the work of both Ibn Tufayl and Hobbes. Yet, while Hobbes clearly depicts the Leviathan as a giant whose body consists of smaller bodies of men, who has a soul and possesses reason and will, Ibn Tufayl leaves it to the intelligence of his readers to apply what is in nature to the political state and make the link between the two. In his attempt to make a connection between physics, politics and psychology, Hobbes likens the body politic to an engine continuously moving by means of springs and wheels. The suggestion is that the state is a rational being made by men. Ibn Tufayl, on the other hand, does not elaborate on this issue although he has previously likened Man's organs to machines. However, he makes it abundantly clear that the state visited by his protagonist, Hayy Ibn Yaqzan, is a rational construct meant to check men's greed and desires by rational means.[37]

In his book, *Classical Individualism: The Supreme Importance of Each Human Being,* Tibor Machan argues that many people across the political spectrum deem individualism to be problematic. 'The central charge is that the individualism that classical liberalism embodies is simply incapable of making room for morality...Classical liberalism,' he observes, 'has been accused of fostering licentiousness, libertinism, hedonism, and moral subjectivism, as well as promoting atomism, alienation, and the loss of community and human fellowships.'[38] These accusations may be levelled at the political economists who followed Hobbes and encouraged individuals to amass great material wealth, or to build empires based on inequality and racism. In contrast, Ibn Tufayl exalted the autonomous enlightened individual, who strives for self-perfection and the preservation of all species on Earth. His allegorical novel suggests a social contract in the political state to be endorsed not by an absolute monarch as in the case of Hobbes, but by a group of just and rational human beings presided over by a prince.[39] It is understood that when other men begin to emerge from their 'self-imposed infancy', to use Kant's term, and show their courage in using their own understanding, then there will be no need for a state or a contract of any kind.[40] The enlightened individual thinks and wills for himself without violating the freedom of others. Returning to nature is not dangerous or undesirable. Society's regulations and constraints are only meant for those who would rather have others check their desires and passions. Yet, the essence of all humans is the same whether in the state of nature or in society. Our capacity for consciousness and agency elevates us all beyond the materialistic physical realm. Artificial civilization might corrupt us, but it is our task to cultivate our capacities and to act as moral agents. There are many different humans on the face of the Earth, yet they are all one. We should celebrate their differences and similarities.[41]

In a short essay on individualism, Bryan S. Turner argues that individualism has 'its modern roots in seventeenth-century religious dissent, especially the Protestant sects and it is interpreted as a fundamental ideology of capitalism. In economic theory', he says, 'the fictional character Robinson Crusoe is often taken to be the quintessential representative of individualistic capitalism.'[42]

It is true that the notion of individualism 'had its modern roots in seventeenth-century religious dissent'. However, Turner seems to be unaware of the impact of a dangerous book such as *Hayy Ibn Yaqzan* on the dissenters.[43] Robert Barclay (1648–90), a Scot and a prominent Quaker theologian referred to *Hayy* in his book *Apology,* which was printed in 1678. Yet, the reference was omitted in most of the subsequent editions.

Whatever the nature of the controversy, there is no doubt that the Quakers have been influenced by certain ideas that feature in Hayy's story, particularly those that exalt personal experience above dogmatic, external teaching, emphasize the significance of the inner light given as a gift by God to each one of us, and stress the principle of toleration and the futility of hatred and violence. For the Quakers, Hayy was the prototype of the individual who thought for himself without the help of priests or scriptures. He was also an independent scientist who advocated the importance of experiment and evidence. Without intuition, believed to be always tied to causes and sources, he would not have been able to prove the existence of God, or what he preferred to call the Mover of the World. Doubt became the point of departure for his rationalist world view. This skepticism, which challenged people's ability to obtain reliable knowledge and reach the truth, was put to the test.

According to Alan Macfarlane, individualism is a modern word. He traces its usage to the English translation of Tocqueville's *Democracy in America* and quotes Tocqueville as saying in a later work 'our ancestors had not got the word "Individualism" – a word which we have coined for our own use, because in fact in their time there was no individual who did not belong to a group, no one who could look on himself as absolutely alone'. In modern societies, such as the USA, 'Men being no longer attached to one another by any tie of caste, of class, or corporation, of family, are only too much inclined to be preoccupied only with their private interests... to retire into a narrow individualism'.[44]

Obviously Tocqueville is not familiar with the story of Hayy Ibn Yaqzan that postulates the existence of an autonomous individual in both nature and society who is not totally preoccupied with himself and his own interests. On the contrary, he symbolizes the self-sufficient and ethical person, who thinks for himself without the help of social, political or religious institutions, and makes his own judgement within a moral framework. His love for Self and Other is a cornerstone in his philosophy. The word individualism might not have been coined in the West until the nineteenth century, and the autonomous individual might not have been discussed in Europe till the seventeenth and eighteenth centuries, but both linguistic term and person were certainly known elsewhere in the world and had varieties of definitions and implications.[45]

In sum, philosophical and scientific activities are 'not simply creative but cumulative'. Each philosopher, or scientist stands upon the shoulders of previous predecessors, 'and because of that he can see further'.[46] There is no superior or inferior culture. Eurocentrism has created Europe and the Other. It is a fallacy to believe that everything originated in Europe. This imperialist attitude has kept Arab and Muslim philosophers and scientists out of any philosophical, scientific or literary debate, and ensured their permanent segregation. With the appearance of radical Islam on the political stage, this binary opposition between East and West has intensified, creating two distinct categories of human beings, namely one Muslim or Arab and the other a Westerner. As a result of this vicious political climate, a whole culture is denigrated; its people are depicted as primitive and inferior. Ignorance of the contribution of Ibn Tufayl and other philosophers and scientists to modern Europe has turned Islam, Muslims and Arabs in general, to use Henri Pirenne's term, 'into the very epitome of an outsider against which the whole of European civilization from the Middle Ages on was founded'.[47]

Shared history is a bridge to peaceful co-operation, not permanent conflict

In his book, *The Clash of Civilization*, Samuel Huntington, a prominent political scientist and a Professor of Government at Harvard University, argues that,

> [t]he West differs from other civilizations not in the way it has developed but in the distinctive character of its values and institutions.

> These include most notably its Christianity, pluralism, individualism and the rule of law, which made it possible for the West to invent modernity, expand throughout the world, and become the envy of other societies. In their ensemble these characteristics are peculiar to the West. Europe, as Arthur M. Schlesinger, Jr., has said, is 'the source – the unique source' of the 'ideas of individual liberty, political democracy, the rule of law, human rights, and cultural freedom.... These are *European* ideas, not Asian, nor African, nor Middle Eastern ideas, except by adoption.[48]

The West did not invent modernity, or the sovereign individual. Christianity, pluralism, individualism and the rule of law may be the characteristics of the West today. But they were certainly not always specific western traits. They originated at some point in the Near East. Only a person who has no knowledge of world history can utter a statement such as this.

In sum, critical reason has no colour, no race, no ethnicity and no gender. Every human being is endowed with reason. This is what distinguishes us from animals. But some of us at one point or another prefer to rely on the judgement of others rather than use our own. It is the responsibility of the rational among us to remind the rest of this natural gift given to all mankind. This idea must be the cornerstone for our understanding of the world.

All cultures are dependent on each other. One day we contribute something new, another day we borrow from someone else. History is never static. The idea of individual liberty, political democracy, the rule of law, human rights and cultural freedom are all universal human aspirations. Europe did not invent them. They flourished in different societies at different times. If Europe enjoys a relative cultural freedom today it is its responsibility to remind others by peaceful means of our shared history and the joy that such ideals can bring to humanity.

Nayef Al-Rodhan's ocean model of human civilization is a shining metaphor of what a generation of Arab and Muslim philosophers always advocated in the past, though the words might sound different. Al-Rodhan suggests that human civilization 'is like an ocean into which rivers representing geo-cultural domains run. The histories and cultures of geo-cultural domains are inseparable, and we would do humanity a great service by recognizing this and acknowledging our mutual debts'. In short, '[t]he development of human civilisation is built on foundations to which everyone has contributed.... The future... of geo-cultural domains will depend on a *collective civilisational triumph*, facilitated by the creation of conditions under which human needs are met, including broadly defined needs, the need for a positive identity and the need to have a sense of purpose and knowledge. This implies conditions under which human dignity and justice are ensured.'[49] Thus, Huntington's thesis of the clash of civilizations is rejected in its entirety, and a new positive proposition based on dialogue and peaceful interaction is suggested.

Perhaps the Arab philosopher Ya'qub Ibn Ishaq Al-Kindi, who died in 873 in Baghdad, illustrates Al-Rodhan's thesis in very simple terms. For Al-Kindi the truth must be taken wherever it is to be found, whether in the past or among foreign peoples. Most of his works were lost, but some survived in Latin translations.[50] Unlike today, Baghdad, the city in which he worked, was once a vibrant metropolis and a microcosm of Al-Rodhan's ocean model, where various ethnic and religious groups contributed to the development of civilization. Hunayn Ibn Ishaq (Joanitius, 809–73), for example, a Nestorian Christian from Al-Hirah who translated the works of Aristotle, Galen, Hippocrates, Dioscorides and Plato from the Greek into Syriac, was his contemporary.[51] His son Ishaq translated his father's manuscripts from Syriac into Arabic. Thabit Ibn Qurrah, who was born around 836, was a heathen Sabian of Harran. He translated the bulk of the Greek mathematical and astronomical works. Yahya Ibn 'Adi who was born in Takrit at the end of the ninth century and died in Baghdad in 974 was a Jacobite or Monophysite, and a church bishop, who introduced neo-platonic speculations and mysticism into the region.[52] No one threatened these scholars, or denounced them for being Christians or star-worshippers or bishops of certain churches. On the contrary, the state, along with its majority Muslim population, venerated them and appreciated their scholarly activities, which helped promote the knowledge of various geo-cultural domains and facilitated borrowings from foreign cultures. Al-Kindi's Baghdad was once a pluralistic society, just like that of Ibn Tufayl in Muslim Spain, where people of different backgrounds lived side by side, or separately as they chose. No one was excluded. Every one of them contributed in one way or another to the development of human civilization. The future of Iraq and the rest of the Arab-Islamic region will largely depend on 'a collective civilizational triumph' whereby equality, dignity and justice are ensured for all. But this triumph will not be complete unless the West too understands its history and recognizes its debts to other nations. Such an understanding will facilitate the formation of genuine multicultural societies and allow every individual to flourish and grow. Eventually, the dominated and the dominant worlds will dissolve into one, yet remain different.

Modern philosophers and politicians alike assume that tolerance and inclusion are Western ideas. John Lachs, for instance, in his book *A Community of Individuals* argues that '[i]nclusion in a single species guarantees rights to all; differentiating us into a variety of natures safeguards against a natural consequence of such inclusion, namely the oppressive demand that all of us pursue the same ideals. Our shared nature forms the foundation of decency, our divergent natures provide the ground of toleration'.[53] Lachs does not seem to be aware of the fact that this thesis has been floating for decades, not in the West that is associated with colonialism and exclusion, but in the Arab-Muslim world.

Reflecting on our shared history enables us to build bridges instead of destroying the ties that bind us together. As a result, the I and the Other will become One. The Constitutive Other, who is deemed in western contemporary philosophy as the Opposite of the Same and identified as Different, will eventually come to denote the Self, or even constitute its likeness. The modern Othering of Arabs, and Muslims in general, not only by western philosophers and literary scholars but also by politicians, both on the right and the left, leads to the demonization and dehumanization of specific ethnic and religious groups and justifies the constant calls to civilize them by all means. We are different people, yet we are similar, as Ibn Tufayl assures us. Differences and similarities, diversity and unity, the one and the many are two sides of the same coin.

This line of thinking has a political significance, not only for the dominant but also for the dominated cultures. The analysis of Western national and global security that depends heavily on biased scholarship, the media and popular culture tends to see the Other as a threat or, at best, as someone very different, but in both cases as inferior. This view leads by necessity to war and violence. It also helps the proliferation of terrorism around the world. The constant denigration of other people's religion and messenger, the disparaging remarks against those Others who are deemed to be different, can only lead to the destruction of everyone involved, the accused and the accuser. Unless the dominant culture acknowledges the fact that we have different, but similar, histories, we will always face tremendous challenges to our existing orders. Our achievements and failures are interwoven. We all move in different directions, but in the end we meet at the same spot. There is no superior or inferior culture. Global security may be achieved if we all believe in one collective human civilization that comprises of the Self and the Other, the Same and the Different, and denounces the concept of domination and imperialist thinking. On the other hand, dominated cultures must examine themselves thoroughly and freely, past, present and future, and allow their philosophers, particularly those who have discussed at length the conflict between religion and philosophy, and highlighted toleration as a vital principle in any society, to be studied in depth at schools and universities, clarifying the misunderstanding about East and West, ethnic majority and minority, and the various religions and sects, not only in the world at large, but mainly in one's own domain. Suppressing or falsifying history always leads to a rigid dichotomy and a nonsensical formula, such as Us versus Them. Thus, the untold story of Arab and Muslim rationalist philosophy, if it is allowed to be told freely in both East and West, might re-shape our deteriorating human relations in the present era, and facilitate a new constructive dialogue between perceived old enemies.[54]

Notes

1. See the back cover of B. Russell (1961 rpt. 1996) *History of Western Philosophy* (London: Routledge).
2. 'Russell, Bertrand (1872–1970)', in Ted Honderich (ed.) (1995), *The Oxford Companion to Philosophy* (Oxford: Oxford University Press), p. 782.
3. Russell, *History of Western Philosophy*, p. 420.
4. Ibid., p. 419.
5. Ibid., p. 512.
6. Ibid., p. 542.
7. Ibid.
8. Averroes (1126–98) is given only 18 lines in *The Oxford Companion to Philosophy*. Although his books were studied in the West to the mid-seventeenth century and caused lots of controversies, his influence, not only as a great Aristotelian commentator, but also as an innovator who enabled the rationalist philosophers in Europe to rise, is not discussed. Of course, in such a short space one can hardly discuss anything in depth. Avicenna (980–1037), who is also belittled by Bertrand Russell as someone 'more famous in medicine... though added little to Galen', is given 42 lines, Al-Farabi 19 lines, Al-Kindi 18 lines, Ibn Maymun (Maimonides, 1135–1204), who is presented as a Jewish philosopher, 50 lines, and Ibn Gabriol (1022–58) 20 lines. There is no mention of Ibn Tufayl or his book *Hayy Ibn Yaqzan*. In general, all these entries have no comparative tendencies or any inclination to hint at the possible continuation of some ideas at a later date in a different continent. See Honderich, *The Oxford Companion to Philosophy*, pp. 70–1, 269, 386, 517–18.

   In contrast, P. Adamson and R. C. Taylor (eds) (2005), *The Cambridge Companion to Arabic Philosophy* (Cambridge: Cambridge University Press), designate a separate volume for a philosophy that seems to have nothing to do with European philosophy and would be of interest only to Arabists and Islamists.

There is nothing strange about this state of affairs among western philosophers. See, for example, W. Durant (1926 rpt. 1961), *The Story of Philosophy* (New York: Washington Square Press). The book, which is described as 'one of the best-loved works of our time', has a 'Table of Philosophic Affiliation', on pages 102–3 that begins with the Greco-Roman philosophers, then proceeds to westerners, such as Thomas Aquinas (1225–74), Francis Bacon (1561–1626), René Descartes (1596–1650) and others, and concludes with John Dewey (1859–1952) and Bertrand Russell (1872–1970). The philosophic association is based on European, rather than human kinship. In this sense, Europeans are somehow a species apart. Unlike the Oxford and Cambridge Companion to Philosophy, which are designed for scholars, Durant's book is meant to bring philosophy to the common man. Unfortunately, the message in all cases is the same; specialists and non-specialists alike are told that Europeans have nothing to do with other races. Their philosophy is strictly theirs.

9. See the entry on 'Descartes' in Honderich, *The Oxford Companion to Philosophy*, p. 189. Compare this with what Ibn Tufayl says in *Hayy Ibn Yaqzan* when discussing the matter in general. Faruq Sa'd (ed.) (1980), *Hayy* (Beirut: Dar Al-Afaq Al-Jadida), pp. 152, 166–70. See Descartes (1985), 'Principles of Philosophy', 'Meditations on First Philosophy' and 'The World, or Treatise on Light', translated by J. Cottingham, R. Stoothoff and D. Murdoch, *The Philosophical Writings of Descartes* (Cambridge: Cambridge University Press). In his 'Discourse on Method' (1637), Descartes argues, just like Ibn Tufayl's protagonist, Hayy Ibn Yaqzan, that 'good sense or reason, is by nature equal in all men', that he exercises his reason in all matters and does not accept anything as true, which he does not clearly know to be such. Having armed himself with logic, mathematics, algebra and geometrical analysis, his attention becomes solely focused on the search for truth and the endeavour to acquire some knowledge of nature. In 'Meditations on the First Philosophy' (1641) Descartes observes that he has accepted, even from his youth, many false opinions as truth. However, later on, he becomes 'convinced of the necessity of undertaking once in [his] life to rid [himself] of all the opinions [he has] adopted, and of commencing anew the work of building from the foundation, if [he desires] to establish a firm and abiding superstructure in the sciences'. Furthermore, he postulates that all that he has accepted up to this moment is received either from or through the senses. But then he discovers that the senses sometimes have misled him and 'it is the part of prudence not to place absolute confidence in that by which we have even once been deceived'. See the translation of 'A Discourse on Method' and 'Meditations on the First Philosophy' in J. Veitch (1960), *The Rationalists* (New York: Dolphin Books, Doubleday & Company Inc.), pp. 39, 51, 53, 96, and 112–13. These are only a few examples that may have been taken from Ibn Tufayl's book. Since Hayy is born in nature without parents, he is forced from the beginning of his life to depend on his senses, observations, experiments and, ultimately, his reason in establishing a firm superstructure in the sciences. His life is divided into seven-year periods. Each period represents a natural foundation in man's progress and spiritual development.

10. See a new translation by Riad Kocache (1982), *The Journey of the Soul: The Story of Hai bin Yaqzan As Told by Abu Bakr Muhammad bin Tufaiy* (London: The Octagon Press), p. 28.
11. See the entry on 'doubt' in Honderich, *The Oxford Companion to Philosophy*, p. 205. See *Descartes, Meditations on First Philosophy*, translated by J. Cottingham (Cambridge, Cambridge University Press, 1986), pp. 9, 12.
12. Quoted by Ibn Tufayl in his introduction to *Hayy Ibn Yaqzan*, p. 114. The translation from Arabic into English is mine.
13. Western historians usually jump from the Greeks to the Renaissance as if the years 750 to 1100 never existed. Yet, there were many prominent Arab and Muslim scientists during these years. See M. Ilyas (1996), *Islamic Astronomy and Science Development: Glorious Past, Challenging Future* (Selangor Darul Ehsan, Malaysia: Pelanduk Publications), pp. 1–17. Also consult H. F. Cohen (1994), *The Scientific Revolution: A Historical Inquiry* (Chicago: Chicago University Press), p. 418. Note that Ibn Tufayl had written at least two books on medicine. He had advanced useful theories in astronomy, unlike those of Ptolemy, or Al-Bitruji, his own student (d. 1185–6). However, all his books and treatises were lost. Yet, there are still many old Arabic manuscripts in different libraries around the world awaiting serious scholars to edit them. One cannot be sure if Ibn Tufayl or other Muslim scientists had, in fact, advanced some new ideas, which might have helped Copernicus, Kepler and Galileo, for the complete story of Arabic science has not been told yet.
14. Immanuel Kant, quoted in L. Goldman (1973), *The Philosophy of the Enlightenment: The Christian Burgess and the Enlightenment*, translated by H. Maas (London: Routledge & Kegan Paul), p. 3. See W. Beck's translation of Kant: 'Enlightenment is man's release from his self-incurred tutelage', in L.W. Beck (ed.) (1963), *On History* (Indianapolis: Bobbs-Merrill), p. 3.
15. For the influence of *Hayy Ibn Yaqzan* on these western philosophers, see S. Attar (2007), *The Vital Roots of European Enlightenment: Ibn Tufayl's Influence on Modern Western Thought* (Lanham: Lexington Books). Chapters 5 and 6, for example, are on the influence of Hayy on Da Vinci, Hobbes, Voltaire and Rousseau. Also consult S. Attar (2009), 'Europeans' Betrayal or Ignorance of the Other's Achievements? The Influence of Ibn Tufayl on Modern Western Thought.' Published online by Deutsche Morgenlandische Gesellschaft. Ausgewahlte Vortrage Herausgegeben im Auftrag der DMG von Rainer Brrunner, Jens Peter Laut and Maurus Reinkowski, http://orient.ruf.uni-freiburg.de/dotpub/attar.pdf.

    Note that Arabic influence on Europe is not restricted to philosophy, but to all fields of knowledge, including literature. See S. Attar (2010), 'An Islamic *Paradiso* in a Medieval Christian Poem? Dante's *Divine Comedy* Revisited', in S. Guenther and T. Lawson (eds) *Roads to Paradise: Eschatology and Concepts of the Hereafter in Islam* (Leiden: E. J. Brill).
16. See J. Habermas (1987 rpt 1991), *The Philosophical Discourse of Modernity Twelve Lectures*, translated by Frederick Lawrence (Cambridge, Mass.: MIT) and J. Habermas (1983), 'Modernity – An Incomplete Project', in H. Foster (ed.) *The Anti-Aesthetic: Essays on Postmodern Culture* (Port Townsend, Washington: Bay Press), pp. 3–15.
17. A. C. Kors (ed.) (2003), *The Encyclopedia of the Enlightenment*, Vol.1 (New York: Oxford University Press), p. xvii. For further definitions of modernity

in various fields, see J. Rée and J. O. Urmson (2005), *The Concise Encyclopedia of Western Philosophy*, 3rd edn (London; New York: Routledge).

18. The most recent German translation is P. O. Schaerer (2006), *Der Philosoph als Autodidakt Hayy Ibn Yaqzan Ein philosophischer Inselroman* (Hamburg: Felix Meiner Verlag). In his introduction, Schaerer quotes Voltaire as being unimpressed by *Hayy*. It is clear the translator/critic is not aware of Ibn Tufayl's influence on the French writer, particularly in *Zadig* and *Candide* and the French novel during the seventeenth and eighteenth centuries. For further discussion, see Attar, *The Vital Roots of European Enlightenment*, chs 5 and 6. On a different note, however, Schaerer refers to the Marxist philosopher Ernst Bloch (1885–1977), who rediscovered *Hayy* in 1952, and considered the book as the embodiment of the basic belief of the European Enlightenment – for example, in that 'man does not need any faith beyond his reason'. See Schaerer, 'introduction', pp. lxxxi, lxxxv.
19. See the Appendix to S. Ockley (1708 rpt 1983), *The Improvement of Human Reason Exhibited in the Life of Hai Ebn Yokdhan* (London; rpt Hildesheim: George Olms Verlag), p. 168.
20. Ibid., p. 167.
21. For further discussion, see Attar, *The Vital Roots of European Enlightenment*, p. 37.
22. For the text of *Hayy Ibn Yaqzan*, I have consulted the Arabic versions of A. N. Nadir, published by Dar Al-Mashriq in Beirut in 1968 and that of F. Sa'd, published by Dar Al-Afaq in Beirut in 1980; and that of J. Saliba and K. 'Ayyad, published by Damascus University in Damascus in 1962, and the English translations of L. E. Goodman (1972), *Ibn Tufayl's Hayy Ibn Yaqzan* (New York: Twayne Publishers) and the Kocache translation, *The Journey of the Soul*.
23. Kocache, *The Journey of the Soul*, p. 17.
24. Ibid., pp. 17–18.
25. See Attar, *The Vital Roots of European Enlightenment*, p. 73.
26. Ibid., p. 74.
27. See I. Kant (2000), 'Analytic of the Sublime', in Paul Guyer (ed.), *Critique of the Power of Judgment*, translated by P. Guyer and E. Matthews (Cambridge: Cambridge University Press), pp. 5, 276.
28. Lucien Goldmann argues, 'The thinkers of the Enlightenment in general lack all sense of the dialectical relation between knowledge and action, between self-awareness and practice.' See Goldmann, *The Philosophy of the Enlightenment: The Christian Burgess and the Enlightenment*, p. 2.
29. Although women are absent in Ibn Tufayl's allegorical novel, there is no reason to believe that they, as human beings, are not endowed with reason and free will. There is no explicit or implicit statement about women in the text. Also, we never think of Hayy or Asal as men, rather as human beings with no specific gender. However, at the beginning, when Hayy is an infant and a boy, the image of the female deer as a mother is overpowering. She represents all that is good in nature. One should never forget that she is the boy's first mentor. Furthermore, the position of women in Muslim Spain during Ibn Tufayl's life was quite good. Women were highly educated and played an important role in society. Men sought knowledge from learned women. See J. C. Bürgel (1992), 'Ibn Tufayl and His Hayy Ibn Yaqzan', in S.

Khadra-Jayyusi (ed.) *The Legacy of Muslim Spain* (Leiden: E. J. Brill), p. 832. Bürgel observes that the presence of the female as represented by the gazelle is essential for Hayy's survival.

One may contrast what Kant specifically says about women and their rational ability in his essay 'An Answer to the Question: What is Enlightenment?' [1784] in (1996) *Practical Philosophy*, translated and edited by M. J. Gregor (Cambridge: Cambridge University Press), pp. 8:35, 8:36.

30. For further discussion, see Attar, *The Vital Roots of European Enlightenment*, p. 81.
31. Unfortunately, Ibn Tufayl is never discussed alongside those that Western scholars call classical theorists, such as Locke, Kant and Rousseau. No one seems to be aware of his existence or influence on these thinkers. Scholars continue to produce books either praising the men who wrote about the state of nature and the social contract or condemning them for their racism and capitalism. See, for example, S. Muthu (2003), *Enlightenment against Empire* (Princeton; Oxford: Princeton University Press) and C. W. Mills (1997), *The Racial Contract* (Ithaca; London: Cornell University Press).
32. See S. Attar (1996), 'Serving God or Mammon? Echoes from Hayy Ibn Yaqzan and Sinbad the Sailor in Robinson Crusoe', in L. Spaas and B. Stimpson (eds) *Robinson Crusoe: Myths and Metamorphoses* (London: Palgrave Macmillan; New York: St. Martin's Press), pp. 78–89. See M. Weber [1904–5] (1958), *The Protestant Ethic and the Spirit of Capitalism*, translated by T. Parsons (New York: Charles Scribner's Sons), pp. 155–83. Weber discusses the issue of wealth and its acquisition in a number of Christian theological books including Robert Barclay's *Apology for the True Christian Divinity* as a representative of the Quakers' views in this regard. He concludes that all theologians under study, except Calvin, have frowned on the acquisition of earthly goods. Yet, the reason for this is their fear of Man's laziness and relaxation that may result from such an acquisition. Labour, he assures his reader, is 'an approved ascetic technique, as it always has been in the Western Church, in sharp contrast not only to the Orient but to almost all monastic rules the world over', p. 157. In the final analysis, Christian theologians, according to Weber, support the rational and utilitarian uses of wealth for the needs of the individual and the community. It is obvious that Weber is not aware of *Hayy Ibn Yaqzan* and the book's tremendous influence on Barclay and the Quakers, who borrowed from it, misinterpreted some of its ideas and discarded the rest. It is ironic, of course, that Weber thinks that only the Western church emphasizes work and its significance 'in sharp contrast to the Orient'. If there is any book that highlights the importance of work it is *Hayy*. Yet, as for the rational and utilitarian uses of wealth for the needs of the individual and the community on the inhabited island, it is the task of the just king to prevent exploitation and greed. Hayy himself has no need for wealth on his desert island. He works to support himself and the environment around him.
33. J. Locke (2003), *Two Treatises of Government and a Letter Concerning Toleration*, edited and with an introduction by I. Shapiro (New Haven; London: Yale University Press). See also J. Tully (2000), 'Aboriginal Property and Western Theory: Recovering a Middle Ground', in A. Pagden (ed.) *Facing Each Other: An Expanding World*, Vol. 31, Part 1 (Aldershot, Burlington: Ashgate Variorum),

pp. 53–80; H. M. Bracken (1973), 'Essence, Accident and Race', *Hermathena*, No. 116, p. 84; A. Pagden (1998), 'The Struggle for Legitimacy and the Image of Empire in the Atlantic to C. 1700', in N. Canny (ed.) *The Oxford History of the British Empire. The Origins of Empire: British Overseas Enterprise to the Close of the Seventeenth Century*, Vol. 1 (Oxford; New York: Oxford University Press), pp. 34–54.

34. Examine, for example, Kant's notorious comments on the mental capacity of blacks in I. Kant (1960), *Observations on the Feeling of the Beautiful and Sublime*, translated by J. T. Goldthwait (Berkeley: University of California Press), pp. 111–13. See also I. Kant [1777] (2000), 'Of the Different Human Races', in R. Bernasconi and T. L. Lott (eds) *The Idea of Race*, translated by J. M. Mikkelsen (Indianapolis, Cambridge: Hackett Publishing Company Inc.), pp. 8–22. See Kant's 'On the Different Races of Man' [1775] in E. W. Count (ed.) (1950), *This is Race* (New York: Henry Schuman), pp. 16–24. Note that Kant had appropriated David Hume's racist dogma. In a footnote to his essay 'Of National Characters' [1748], Hume argued that blacks in general were inferior to whites. See E. F. Miller (ed.) (1987), *Essays: Moral, Political and Literary* (Indianapolis: Library Fund). See E. C. Eze (1995), 'The Color of Reason: The Idea of Race in Kant's Anthropology', in K. M. Faull (ed.) *Anthropology and the German Enlightenment: Perspectives on Humanity* (London; Toronto; Lewisburg: Bucknell University Press), pp. 200–41.
35. Consult C. Darwin (2003), *On the Origin of the Species by Means of Natural Selection*, edited by J. Carroll (Peterborough, Ontario; Orchard Park, NY: Broadview Press). Darwin's views on racial issues can also be found in 'On the Races of Man', the seventh chapter of *The Descent of Man*, published in 1871 and reprinted in Bernasconi and Lott, *The Idea of Race*, pp. 54–78.
36. See T. Hobbes [1651] (1996), *Leviathan*, edited by R. Tuck (Cambridge: Cambridge University Press).
37. For further discussion, see Attar, *The Vital Roots of European Enlightenment*, pp. 83–4.
38. T. R. Machan (1998), *Classical Individualism* (London: Routledge), p. 1. See P. Hopper (2003), *Rebuilding Communities in an Age of Individualism* (Hampshire; Burlington: Ashgate), pp. 29–30.
39. Contrast Ibn Tufayl's social contract with that of Rousseau. See *Discourse on Inequality* [1755] (1984), translated with an introduction and notes by M. Cranston (New York; Harmondsworth: Penguin Books). According to C. Mills, 'Rousseau argues that technological development in the state of nature brings into existence a nascent society of growing divisions in wealth between rich and poor, which are then consolidated and made permanent by a deceitful "social contract". Whereas the ideal contract explains how a just society would be formed, ruled by a moral government, and regulated by a defensible moral code, this non-ideal/naturalized contract explains how an unjust, *exploitative* society, ruled by an *oppressive* government and regulated by an *immoral* code, comes into existence.' Mills, *The Racial Contract*, p. 5.
40. Unlike Ibn Tufayl, many Western theorists saw danger in an unregulated state of nature and envisioned only chaos and savagery. It is interesting to see how Kant, in his *Anthropology from a Pragmatic Point of View*, read and understood Rousseau. In a revealing passage on 'The Character of the

Species' Kant argues: 'One certainly need not accept the hypochondriac (ill-tempered) picture which Rousseau paints of the human species. It is not his real opinion when he speaks of the human species as daring to leave its natural condition, and when he propagates a reversal and a return into the woods. Rousseau only wanted to express our species' difficulty in walking the path of continuous progress toward our destiny.... Rousseau wrote three works on the damage done to our species by (1) our departure from Nature into culture, which weakened our strength; (2) civilization, which resulted in inequality and mutual oppression; and (3) presumed moralization, which caused unnatural education and distorted thinking. I say, these three works, which present the state of Nature as a state of innocence...should serve only as preludes to his *Social Contract*, his *Emile*, and his *Savoyard Vicar* so that we can find our way out of the labyrinth of evil into which our species has wandered through its own fault. Rousseau did not really want that man go back to the state of nature, but that he should rather look back at it from the stage which he had then reached. He assumed that man is good by nature...but he is good in a negative way. He is good by his own decision and by intentionally not wanting to be evil. He is only in danger of being infected and ruined by evil or inept leaders and examples. Since, however, good men, who must themselves have been trained for it, are required for moral education, and since there is probably not one among them who has no (innate or acquired) depravity himself, the problem of moral education for our species remains unsolved.' See I. Kant (1978), *Anthropology*, translated by V. L. Dowdell, revised and edited by F. P. Van De Pitte (Carbondale; Edwardsville; London; Amsterdam: Southern Illinois University Press), pp. 243–4. Author's emphasis.

41. See Kocache, *The Journey of the Soul*, pp. 60–2.
42. B. S. Turner (2005), 'Individualism', in George Ritzer (ed.) *Encyclopedia of Social Theory*, Vol. 1 (Thousand Oaks; London; New Delhi: Sage Publications), p. 399. Also examine B. Turner, N. Abercrombie and S. Hill (1986), *Sovereign Individuals of Capitalism* (London: Allen & Unwin). Note that Alan Macfarlane refers to the importance of seventeenth-century religious dissent in England as one of the possible factors that led to the emergence of individualism. However, like Turner, he is not aware of the influence of *Hayy Ibn Yaqzan* on the Quakers in this regard. See A. Macfarlane (2002), *The Making of the Modern World: Visions from the West and East* (New York: Palgrave).
43. See S. Attar (1997), 'The Man of Reason: Hayy Ibn Yaqzan and His Impact on Modern European Thought', *Qurtuba* 2 (Cordoba), pp. 19–47.
44. A. Macfarlane (2004), 'Individualism', in A. Kuper and J. Kuper (eds) *The Social Science Encyclopedia*, Vol. 1, 3rd edn (London; New York: Routledge), p. 486.

    Ibn Tufayl's thesis is that the individual is prior to society and history. Many classical western theoreticians of the social contract must have been familiar with the translation of *Hayy* into Latin or other European languages, in addition to their familiarity with Daniel Defoe's *Robinson Crusoe*. Their basic assumption is that the autonomous individual in the state of nature depicts the true characteristics of humankind. Contrast the views of Norbert Elias who might not be aware of Hayy's existence. Elias argues against the case of the individual being prior to society. For him,

Robinson Crusoe 'bears the imprint of a particular society, a particular nation and class. Isolated from all relations to them as he is on his island, he behaves, wishes and plans by their standard, and thus exhibits different behaviour, wishes and plans to Friday, no matter how much the two adapt to each other by virtue of their situation.' See M. Schroter (ed.) (1991), *The Society of Individuals*, translated by E. Jephcott (Oxford; Cambridge, Mass.: Basil Blackwell), p. 27.

Note that the influential New England Puritan minister, Cotton Mather, who condemned the 'Mohammedans' as 'infidels', saw in Hayy the noble savage, and through him, he attempted to understand Native Americans, determined to convert them to Puritan Christianity. In the Arabic book, however, no one converts anyone to his religion. Indeed, the noble savage is wiser than the civilized people who adhere to a specific scripture.

45. See K-P. Kopping, M. Welker and R. Wiehl (eds) (2002), *Die Autonome Person – Eine Europaische Erfindung? (The Autonomous Person- A European Invention?)* (München: Wilhelm Fink Verlag). The question mark in the title may indicate the editors' uncertainty about the origin of this European concept. My thesis is that Europeans have appropriated this notion from Ibn Tufayl's allegorical novel, but later on deformed it. Then, Americans borrowed the concept from Europeans and reinvented it. Most recently, some scholars are coming much closer to Ibn Tufayl's original position. See, for instance, K. J. Gergen (2002), 'Beyond Autonomy and Community. Relational Being', in Kopping, Welker and Wiehl (eds) *Die Autonome Person*, pp. 177–92. Speaking about the many problems surrounding individualism, Gergen argues, 'My particular hope in this regard is placed in concepts and practices that give realization to forms of what might be called *relational being*, that is, intelligibilities and actions that transcend the binaries of self/other and individual community and create a sense of fundamental inseparability. How may we understand ourselves in ways that render us palpable within processes that unite, solidify, or otherwise celebrate relationships over identity and division?' (p. 184).
46. Examine George Sarton's letter to Henry James dated 17 May 1935. Sarton papers, Houghton Library, Harvard University. Quoted by R. K. Merton in his 1988 book *The History of Science and the New Humanism: With Recollections and Reflections* (New Brunswick, NJ; Oxford: Transaction Inc.), p. xi.
47. Henri Pirenne quoted by E. Said (1979), *Orientalism* (New York: Vintage Books), p. 70.
48. S. P. Huntington (1996), *The Clash of Civilizations and the Remaking of World Order* (New York: Simon & Schuster), p. 311.
49. See N. R. F. Al-Rodhan (2009), *Sustainable History and the Dignity of Man: A Philosophy of History and Civilisational Triumph* (Berlin: LIT Verlag), p. 438. See also pages 29, 36–7, 39 and 214.
50. For more information on Al-Kindi's scientific activities consult M. Th. Houtsma (ed.) (1993), *E. J. Brill's First Encyclopaedia of Islam 1913–1936*, Vol. III (Leiden; New York; Koln: E. J. Brill), pp. 1019–20 and C. E. Bosworth, B. Lewis and Ch. Pellat (eds) (1986), *The Encyclopaedia of Islam: New Edition* Vol. V (Leiden: E. J. Brill), pp. 122–3. See also P. Hitti (1970), *History of the Arabs*, 10th edn (New York: Macmillan, St. Martin's Press), pp. 370–1; A. Hourani (1991), *A History of the Arab Peoples* (Cambridge: The Belknap Press of Harvard University Press), pp. 76–7 and M. Fakhry (1970), *A History*

of Islamic Philosophy (New York; London: Columbia University Press), pp. 82–112.

51. For the full story of Hunayn Ibn Ishaq, see Ibn Abi Usaybi'a (1882), *'Uyun al-Anba' fi Tabaqat al-Atibba'* edited by A. Muller (Cairo), pp. 184–200. See B. Lewis, V. L. Ménage, C. H. Pellat and J. Schacht (eds) (1986), *Encyclopaedia of Islam: New Edition* Vol. III. (Leiden; London: E. J. Brill and Luzac & Co.), pp. 578–81. See also Hitti, *History of the Arabs,* pp. 312–16.
52. For more information on Thabit Ibn Qurrah and Yahya Ibn 'Adi consult Hitti, *History of the Arabs,* pp. 314–15.
53. J. Lachs (2003), *A Community of Individuals* (New York, London: Routledge), p. 55.
54. To my mind, the Danish cartoonist who drew the image of the prophet Muhammad with a bomb on his head in the newspaper *Jyllands-Posten* in September 2005 had abused the meaning of the freedom of speech in Denmark and deliberately engaged in that crusading spirit that had demonized Islam and its prophet since the Middle Ages. Many European newspapers have reprinted the 12 representations of the prophet Muhammad in solidarity with the cartoonist, asserting their right to freedom of expression without giving the slightest thought about the accuracy of the information delivered to the public, or to the effect of the cartoons on Muslim immigrants in Europe. Similarly, the extremists who threatened the cartoonist's life abused the spirit of Islam and engaged in criminal acts. Both parties denied the use of reason as a path to solving endemic problems between East and West. Islamophobia in Europe was highlighted as the end result of the cartoons and violent demonstrations against Denmark took place in the Muslim world.

    Europeans must draw a sharp line between freedom of speech and hate speech that provokes the weak-minded and incites some of them to commit crimes. The US protects most forms of speech, including hate speech by fringe groups like the Ku Klux Klan. Denmark is one of the most liberal countries in Europe in its enforcement of free speech. In my view, censorship is perhaps not the answer. Rather, education and a serious debate about knowledge and the responsibility of the individual in the modern world may alleviate this continuous trend of attack and counterattack on the Other. Dialogue is the only means to bridge the differences between cultures.

    On a different note, the Dutch filmmaker, Theo Van Gogh, along with the Somali-Dutch MP, Ayaan Hirsi Ali, who wrote the script, are just as responsible for the death of the director as the Moroccan Dutch migrant who killed him. All of them acted hysterically, without thinking of the consequences of their actions. The film *Submission,* which I saw at Harvard in 2006, is not a rational critique of Islam, or the *Quran,* rather a series of derogatory remarks made by hysterical characters. Its aim is not to engage our reason in discussing women's position in Islam. I witnessed how the highly educated audience jumped up and down in horror, quite excited by what they were watching on the screen. I thought at the time, if this is the effect of the film on this type of people, what would be the effect then on downtrodden migrants in Holland who are reminded on a daily basis of their Otherness? The Dutch Somali MP, who was treated as a celebrity, came to visit the campus in May in order to give some lectures at the university. I truly felt sorry for her. She had to escape death and become a fugitive in the US. Yet, I was also very bitter about her provocative role in the making of the film that tragically resulted in the murder of Theo Van Gogh in 2004. When I questioned the wisdom of her actions during the discussion session that was very well-guarded, the chair of the session, a prominent physician and an Afro-American professor, stopped me from explaining my views. He did not want me to utter any criticism of his famous guest. However, I was grateful to the university newspaper that reported my critical remarks. I am totally against censorship as well as violence in both East and West. But I distinguish between a work that engages our reason and a work that excites the hidden and deep prejudices within us. Similarly the interviews given by the ultra-rightist Dutch politician, Geert Wilders, that are often shown on international television screens are sheer hate speeches. I have not seen his film *Fitna*, but I have read about it. This is the stuff that provokes terrorism in the world.

On the other hand, criminals who recently attacked churches in Iraq and Egypt, and killed and maimed dozens of worshippers must understand that Christianity is not a Western trait, and that Christians are part and parcel of the Arab and Muslim world. For many years now, the killing of innocent people who belong to different ethnic or religious groups, particularly in Iraq, Pakistan and Afghanistan, is on the rise. This criminal trend is abhorrent to the majority in the Arab and Islamic world. It has nothing to do with Islam, or its prophet. Religion, in this case, is perverted and used as an expression of anger and dissatisfaction with Western policies in the region. It is an anarchistic cry against injustice that kills friend and foe alike. Local governments that opposed or collaborated with the West for decades, regardless of their ideology, have utterly failed to be heard. Now the extremists who pervert Islam and wear an Islamic mantle are trying to tell the world that the problems of the region will be solved only through terror. It is not only their weird philosophy that is responsible for the current state of affairs. Israel, created by the West on Palestinian soil in 1948, must also be manipulating some elements among them, as well as Geert Wilders et al in the West. It is to its advantage that Arabs and Moslems are killing each other and westerners, so that the attention of the world will not be focused on the dispossession of the Palestinians and their horrible treatment by the Israeli state and its European settlers.

Curbing terror is the responsibility of both East and West. Demagogues and criminals must be punished for their actions. Enlightened education is the only key to peaceful coexistence and harmony between nations. Our triumph will occur only when we, in the dominant and dominated world, acknowledge our kinship and our debts to each other, both within and outside our geographical domain. Provocation under the guise of the freedom of speech is not helpful. Instead, we urgently need to talk to each other, examine our intentions and fully understand our mutual history. Equality, freedom and toleration ought to be the cornerstone in our life. We cannot defend human rights in one part of the world and turn a blind eye to another. Basic human needs must be met in both the dominant and the dominated world in the hope that domination itself will gradually be phased out.

7

A Forgotten Debt: Humanism and Education, from the Orient to the West

Mohammad-Mahmoud Ould Mohamedou

The passage of the West from Classical Antiquity to the Renaissance was facilitated by the Islamic civilization, whose contribution was central to the emergence of the modern enlightened West as we have come to know it. Yet, this essential fact of world history has been almost systematically overlooked in leading humanism studies, thus perpetuating a crucial chasm in the sequence of world history and the genealogy of ideas. In his poem *To Helen*, the great Edgar Allan Poe could just as easily have bridged that gap by adding to the famous lines 'the glory that was Greece, the grandeur that was Rome',[1] a proper reference to 'the magnificence that was Baghdad'. Artistic licence aside, such oversight is indicative of a long-standing amnesia developed in the Western world over recent centuries and which has functioned as a mode of invisibilization of the magnitude of the impact of Arab and Islamic cultural thought and practice on the rise of the modern Western world.

The phenomenon was lengthy and widespread, manifesting itself systemically in education, science, arts and politics, and it was primarily the result of a history of revisionist self-perception. For in experiencing its entry into the modern era, and in rising to dominate that new world, the West relied just as much on its own revolutionary innovations and socioeconomic and cultural re-examinations as it did on the achievements of past civilizations passing on a well-lit torch of culture. Yet amongst these, only 'glorious' Greece and 'grand' Rome have been the mainstay of the Renaissance narrative. A shortcut excising the contribution of the Arab and Islamic world from that account appeared early on in the eighteenth century, it was rapidly cemented in the context of the imperial age of Great Britain and France during the nineteenth century and then endowed with normality throughout the twentieth century. When, in the first decade of the twenty-first century, the West and the Orient were pitted anew against each other perceptually in an apparent clash of civilizations and the post-September 11 world, the narrative and its lacunae re-emerged, at times antagonistically, when, in fact, by that critical point it should have been revealed as merely lacking factuality.

At its height in the twelfth century, the Arab and Islamic Empire – the first truly globalized world dominion stretching from Spain to Zanzibar to China – was the theatre of dynamic thinking and multifaceted creativity that, by the time of the *Reconquista,* had made a substantial impact in creating, indeed signposting, the path upon which a reborn Europe would soon embark. Yet, as the dominant narratives goes, the sum total of knowledge accumulated during the previous eight centuries could simply not come to influence, immediately and directly, the direction which Western Europe, and in time North America, would take in the subsequent centuries. Yet, the Arab and Islamic achievements were admittedly important. However, (i) those achievements were essentially confined to translations of Greek classical works, and as such were not necessarily original in and of themselves, (ii) they functioned primarily as a transmission belt of works originating elsewhere and passed on to others and, consequently, (iii) the Arab-Islamic impact on the overall picture of the rise of the West is secondary, if not negligible.

Against this background, the experience and discourse about the particular traits of Western identity have led it often to regard itself as the sole legitimate locus and promoter of ethical norms. The resulting narrative is concerned with the West's historical ability to situate itself at the heart of what is good and desirable for humanity, and to proceed to subjugate, force, rally, or merely convince others of the normalcy of that self-designed and self-serving reality, whereas such confiscation of universality rests, fundamentally, on a historical subterfuge as regards the roots of Western enlightenment.

Contesting the historical accuracy of this interpretative perspective, and examining primarily humanist and educational aspects, this essay argues that the Arab and Islamic civilization has made a direct, central and consequential contribution to the rise of the Western world. In contradistinction to the above narrative, which understates such a bestowal, it is argued that not only did the methods of thinking and learning developed in the Arab and Islamic world impact those conceived of and adopted later in the West, but that the very essence of contemporary questioning and critical thinking prevalent in the West traces its ancestry to the Arab and Muslim culture and its supremacy over eight centuries, from the 700s to the 1500s. This oft-overlooked historical reality stands, it is put forward, in stark contrast to the recent dominant analyses negating such contribution or diminishing its importance. The chapter concludes that it is precisely on such unearthing of a common past that the future of mutually-respecting and constructively-engaging Western and Muslim worlds rests, and not on alleged civilizational clashes and war on terror hysteria.

The genesis of Western exceptionalism

The progression of ideas is at once an unswerving and a non-linear phenomenon with individuals building on and expanding earlier contributions. History thus moves forward through both repetition and accumulation, societies replaying age-old patterns and developing new ones. These two dimensions, which can be posited as axioms of knowledge production and action definition, stand at the heart of this discussion. They point to an ultimately singular process whereby the intellectual lineage of a given civilization, the Western one (one, too, invariably insisting on its universality), has been paradoxically pictured in most accounts as almost *sui generis* when it is the visible inheritor of a grand legacy.

Beyond the conscious disappearance of the Arab-Islamic contribution to the writing of that episteme, the incomplete account of the emergence of the West is inextricably linked to political developments in Europe from the Middle Ages onwards. For all the intentionality of the oblivion towards the Arab-Islamic contribution – a phenomenon as widespread, lasting, and with mutually-reinforcing instances cannot be random – the fact of the matter is that this story has as much to do with the reinvention of the West as it does with the recasting of the Arab-Islamic world in a supporting role. Yet, it begs credulity that a Dark Ages Medieval Europe could rush into modernity solely on the strength of its own innovations without so much as incorporating the revolutionary transformations that were playing out around it and, indeed, in its very midst in Arab Andalusia and Muslim Sicily. As Prince Faysal Bin Hussayn Bin Ali Al-Hashemi is depicted as saying to T. E. Lawrence with respect to that historical asymmetry: 'But you know lieutenant, in the Arab city of Cordoba, there were two miles of public lighting in the street when London was a village.'[2]

Hence, it is roughly with the reclaiming of Spain by Isabella of Castile and Ferdinand II of Aragon that came, in the post-1492 world, the beginning of the writing of a new religious-political narrative about the historical anchoring of a self-produced Western cultural identity and its educational underpinnings harkening back overwhelmingly, if not exclusively, to the Greco-Roman period. The dual discourse of invisibilization and of demonization working in tandem appears early on with the *Crónica Sarracina* [Saracen Chronicle] of Pedro Del Corral, also known as *Crónica del Rey Don Rodrigo* [Chronicle of King Don Rodrigo], which is put forth as a historiographic work when, in fact, it partakes in a political discourse informed centrally by resentment towards the Muslim colonizer. As Patricia Grieve notes, the *Crónica* 'changed the way Spain viewed its national origins.... In fifteenth-century histories and poetry written by the nobility and upwardly mobile, what we find especially is *the importance of identifying with those who resisted the Muslims*' (emphasis added).[3] It is hence a story of fall and redemption that sets the stage for the birth of a discourse of exceptionalism, which per force functions according to a mode of negation. In this sense, the fulfilment of the new-old Western project is associated with foundational myths of identity.

Indeed, the specificity of Western culture has seldom been the subject of in-depth inquiry. The West has devoted attention and resources to the study of other civilizations, but other cultures have rarely sought to examine what is inherently constitutive of Western identity. Southern intellectuals have documented Western domination of the world and its impact on their societies. Similarly, the mechanisms of colonialism and imperialism have been unpacked and their political and cultural logics revealed.[4] However, these approaches have been concerned with Western attitudes towards others, not necessarily with what was intrinsic to Western society.

In so doing, historians and social scientists from the South have been mostly reactive in their intellectual posture. Denouncements of Western policies – from historical colonial actions to neo-colonial adventures – have been the order of the day, rather than a clinical inspection of Western attributes. Whereas Western intellectuals have painstakingly assembled a body of knowledge about other civilizations, approaching these cultures with dispositions ranging from contempt to infatuation, the non-Western thinker has remained, for the most part, confined to a posture of protest, justification, or defence – unable or unwilling (or, indeed, blind to such a possibility) to match the West's ambition to map the world, and beam back a dispassionate, nuanced, and scientific statement on Western ethos.

By declaring a coincidence between the desired state of modernity, which other cultures seek to achieve, and the West's stance and corpus, it is implied that the others have to graduate to that position; doing so, as it were, essentially by emulating 'the free world'. From civilizing mission to humanitarian intervention, by way of the 'white man's burden', the provincializing of the West's ideas was always associated with a deep-rooted self-perception of exceptionalism and, therefore, claimed concomitant rights and responsibilities. The Western argument proceeds thus: the universal norm of modernity has been attained by the West, which, after the Renaissance, completed its intellectual migration to that stage, and other cultures have merely to emulate the West to achieve what is presented as universal modernity. Such political expansion has succeeded to the point that its investigation (let alone its questioning) by non-Westerners has always been confined mostly to a victimhood perspective. Consequently, the West's success in universalizing its specific history rests in its ability – from one global political order to another (colonialism, neo-colonialism, the Cold War, the post-Cold War era, the post-9/11 period) – to maintain this supremacy, ever mutating as long as it can remain the central locus of the modernity's origin. Consequently, even when highly effective, intellectual resistance was just that. Beyond stigmatization, no equivalent examination of the Western metropolis was, for a long time, conceivable.

In the post-September 11, 2001 world, the late Edward Said argued that 'more than ever before, it is true to say that the new generation of humanist scholars is more attuned than any before it to the non-European, genderized, decolonized, and de-centered energies and currents of our time.'[5] To be certain, we have, in recent years, witnessed works unpacking the historical implications of Western self-perceptions.[6] Still, the perception of supremacy remains dominant both in the North and the South. As Richard Rorty notes, 'for most white people, until very recently, most Black people did not so count'.[7] Indeed, Francis Fukuyama wrote in a seminal piece in 1989 that 'for our purposes, it matters very little what strange thoughts occur to people in Albania or Burkina Faso'.[8] For most leading Western thinkers, an alternative paternity of modernity – which can be associated with a strong past, as in the case of Islam – is not really conceivable. Forcing or convincing the other to adhere to the existing status quo is a condition that is always at the ready.

In the final analysis, the infinite ability to state that values designed in the West (must) apply internationally, because they are allegedly global, assumes that a reverse, reciprocal process, whereby values originating elsewhere – significant beliefs and norms, not cosmetic incorporations of, say, particular traits of some cultures that can be reconciled with the basic Western curriculum – are adopted in the West, is inconceivable. This contradiction is at the heart of the existing equation between the West and the rest. More importantly, it is the result of a conscious set of historical actions that have cast aside an intellectual debt towards the Arab and Islamic world. As the Moroccan philosopher Mohammed Abed Al-Jabri remarks, 'the Orientalist reading... merely seeks to understand how much Arabs have "understood" the cultural legacy of their predecessors'. Such a process of alienation negates the historical weight of Arab thought itself.[9]

History is assuredly written by the victors and, as such, it can be stubborn. 'The scientific study of other cultures is almost exclusively a Western phenomenon, and in its origin was obviously connected with the search for new and better ways, or at least for validation of the hope that our own culture really is the better way, a validation for which there is no felt need in other cultures,'[10] erroneously argues Allan Bloom, for intellectual curiosity about others is precisely where what we can term the Arab 'Naissance' began. In that respect, we must explicitly come to terms with the fact that the West does not solely originate in eighteenth century Germany or sixteenth century French or Italian humanism (*mos gallicus* and *mos italicus*). To the extent that historiography is a process concerned with the changing ways of viewing the past and its relationship to the present,[11] unearthing the proper sequence of that past could help enable a sober contemporary civilizational balance. Let us examine it.

Arab-Islamic cultural 'naissance'

Higher learning is deeply rooted in the history and societies of the Arab Middle East.[12] The Arab-Islamic contribution has, indeed, taken the form of the preservation of ancient works, but it has also generated new contributions which were wholly original. As Philip Hitti reminds us:

> [A]fter the establishment of Baghdad as the seat of the Caliphate, the Arab-speaking peoples were in possession of the major works of Aristotle, the leading Neo-Platonic commentaries, the mathematical and astronomical compositions of Euclid and Ptolemy and the medical writings of Galen and Paul of Aegina. These translations into Arabic, transmuted in no small degree by the Arab mind during the course of several centuries, were transmitted together with many new contributions to Latin Europe mainly through Moslem Spain and Norman Sicily and crusading Syria. They laid the basis of that

> canon of knowledge which lay at the bottom of the modern European renaissance.... In their Latin translations, the...works of the Arab authors were used in such early universities as Naples, Bologna, and Paris.[13]

The missing link in relation to the Arab-Islamic contribution is specifically here concerned with a whole period that is skipped in the contemporary study of humanism in the Western canon. Working backwards, such study usually depicts a modern period founded during the Renaissance, whose power and originality are stressed almost as if it emerged *ex nihilo* and then, much earlier, from Greco-Roman literature. The intervening centuries, and in particular the medieval period of the twelfth and thirteenth centuries are almost always just not studied, much less presented as key to the (re)configuration of the *Re*naissance.

A missing module, which we can term the Andalus Enlightenment, predated the Classical Renaissance of Europe. Yet, if erudition became respected in those ages of an early modern world, the struggle against feudalism, gnosticism and fatalism began immediately with the emergence of the Islamic Empire in the seventh century. 'Creatively assimilated',[14] the Greek works were translated during the Abbasid period under Al-Ma'mun, the seventh Abbasid caliph (813–33), founder of *Beit al Hikma* or the house of wisdom, where texts were compiled and thoroughly studied in an organized, specialized and permanent setting. The bulk of translations was carried out in Baghdad and the *Banu al Munajjim* (eminent intellectual figures of ninth century Baghdad) played a key role with lead translators such as Hunayn Ibn Ishaq (known in Latin as Joannitius), Thabit Ibn Qurra, Qusta Ibn Uqa, and Hubaysh. Muslims also worked alongside Christians such as Yuhanna Ibn Bukhtishu and translations were submitted to corrections and revisions. The translators aimed hence at a correct (*sahih*) text, but with an equal emphasis on intelligibility (*fasaha*) and eloquence (*balagha*). As Roger Arnaldez notes: 'The culture that was born at this period in the Muslim world was not solely about the books. It did not confine itself to a pale imitation of Antiquity. It drew inspiration from original research and realized a genuine progress for civilization and the history of humanity.'[15]

Al Mam'un also called to his court the Persian mathematician, Mohammad Ibn Musa Al-Khawarizmi who devised the first articulated theory of algebra, *Al Maqala fi Hisab al Jabr wa al Muqabala*, subsequently translated into Latin in the twelfth century under the title *Liber Algebrae et Almucabola*. Others produced their works within their professional activity. As in the case of Abu Bakr Mohammad Ibn Zakariya Al-Razi who authored a major medical reference guide, *Al Hawi* (also referred to as *Al Jami*), which became *Liber Continens* in 1279 and was widely available throughout Europe. Examples abound of such a process in the fields of astronomy, linguistics, theology and logic. Similarly, the Caliph Al-Mu'tadid provided shelter to several scientists in his palace. Thus, such institutionalization of the production of knowledge went beyond the immediate dimensions of translation and dissemination. Consequently, a sense of respect for tradition (*al turath*), not merely a sense of the past, but of a spiritual heritage as a whole, which also allows for forward projection, combined with a practice of codification that took place immediately after the early Muslim conquests. Known as *'asr al tadwin* ('the era of codification'), and enacted throughout the eight century, this period saw Muslim scholars organize the body of knowledge produced at the time of the Prophet to introduce a pre-Cartesian three-tiered dialectical reasoning built around *al bayan* ('the statement or indication'), *al 'irfan* ('the understanding or illumination' and *al burhan* ('the demonstration or validation'). In so doing, the Muslims introduced a cognitive structure and an ontological process whose systematic and replicable nature was a departure from earlier discursive thinking whose epistemological nature was much less pronounced.

Such reasoning was endowed with persistence as it was displayed and nurtured in *madariss* (schools), where students undergoing apprenticeship would be encouraged to engage in *tafsir* ('exegesis'), *fiqh* ('jurisprudence') and, indeed, *ikhtilaf* ('divergence'). The creative process during that phase of world history was, therefore, not merely one of renewal or regeneration, but of actual innovation. The value of dialectic (*jadal*) and logical reasoning advanced in large part thanks to the work of Abu Hamid Mohammad Al-Ghazali. Author of some 457 titles, Al-Ghazali produced critical inquiries into Greek philosophy (in particular Plato and Aristotle), as well as Arab philosophy (in particular Ibn Sina or Avicenne and Al-Farabi), the most famous of which were *Maqasid Al Falasifa* [The Objectives of Philosophers] and *Tahafut Al Falasifa* [The Incoherence of Philosophers]. Similarly, Al-Ghazali's work strongly emphasized the importance of the principles of education. He argued that schools – and teachers, whose centrality he highlighted – played a fundamental role in 'filling up' the pupils with knowledge about their social environment as well as about their selves. He was amongst the first to introduce the experience of education as a 'total' experience drawing attention to both the acquisition (concepts, methods, categories, and aims) and practical (plenitude and fulfillment) use of knowledge.[16] As Philip Hitti notes, 'Al-Ghazali's influence...was effective and lasting. Through it, theology became more rational, more relevant, and at the same time more spiritual. Jurisprudence became more sensitive to changing conditions, expanded beyond the narrow bounds of religion, and was lifted to a higher intellectual level.'[17]

The conspicuous role that Al-Ghazali played would be furthered by Ibn Hazm and Ibn Tumart, who would take critical thinking beyond Aristotle or Plato. Yet again we find that the contribution of these Muslim thinkers has been reduced to commentary, when it was constitutive of original thought. Thus, Ibn Hazm is usually known for *Tawq al Hamama* [The Ring of the Dove], an eloquent treatise on love, when he produced more in terms of legal studies and a system of thought characterized by the prevalence of three key concepts, namely the principles of discontinuity, contingency and analogy. For his part, Ibn Rushd introduced the distinction between philosophy and religion, planting the seed for the Enlightenment and the rebellion against the Church. Similarly, in opposing religious orthodoxies, Ibn Tumart stressed (and actively practiced) the importance of judgement and the legitimacy of questioning established order. Overall, the contribution concerned the bridging of known and unknown variables, and how to systematize their interrelationships within an increasingly organized and structured scholarly environment.

What was particularly novel was the process of turning reflections into axioms to be used (or questioned) systematically. The endeavour was aimed at individual enlightenment, and was an invitation to exercise personal judgement in the face of received information. Ibn Rushd devoted a section of his law treatise to this very aspect, *Bidayat al Mujtahid wa Nihayat al Muqtasid* ('The beginning of the one concerned with interpretation and the end of the one concerned with the received information'). The second significant humanist innovation concerned the relationship between science and thought. The world was no longer merely observed (as in the Hellenic tradition, albeit insightfully), but questioned in relation to an independent tool, namely the mind, which is itself now the subject of systematic rules. For instance, a fellow colleague of Ibn Rushd – both students of Abu Bakr Mohammad Ibn Abdelmalik Ibn Tufayl – Abu Ishaq Al-Batruji, precedes Galileo Galilei and Nicolaus Copernicus in working towards a symbiotic relationship between science and reasoning.

The scholasticism that was being born was also characterized by its emancipation from both religion and politics. Part of the initial focus on older hard sciences (mathematics, astrology and logic) was to avoid politicization of knowledge. Yet, their insights were often meant as a commentary on current affairs, much like Voltaire's later. This was the case, for instance, with Ibn Tufayl's 1170s allegorical novel *Hayy Ibn Yaqzan* [Alive, Son of Awakening], which was translated into Latin as *Vivens Filius Vigilantis*. Ibn Tufayl, known for his keen insights on his contemporaries, introduced Ibn Sina to the Almohad caliph Abu Ya'qub Yusuf in Andalusia, thus making an important connection that allowed Ibn Sina to benefit from the Caliph's patronage.

The historical importance of such critical consciousness and its centrality in relation to the subsequent rise of Western reason and enlightenment cannot be overestimated. What is more, the emerging humanism features dynamic fertile (*ikhtilaf*) debates between, for instance, Ibn Sina, Ibn Rushd and Al-Ghazali. In that respect, in a famous reply to Al-Ghazali's *Tahafut al Falasifa* [The Incoherence of Philosophers], Ibn Rushd published *Tahafut al Tahafut* [The Incoherence of The Incoherence]. Omnipresent culture, as a way of life, is something that was eminently characteristic of the Arab-Islamic world during this period. Much later, for instance, Raymond Williams, in his study of the transformation of British society in the period 1780–1950, would discuss at length how the Western mutation of 'civilization' and 'the general progress of society' took place in the context of democratization and industrialization without necessarily seeing how such diffusion of 'culture' had been imported during the previous centuries as a powerful matrix for aesthetics, which had similarly transformed the Arab and Islamic world. Indeed, the novelists whose works Williams examines – Edmund Burke, Charles Dickens, D. H. Lawrence and T. S. Eliot – had all been influenced by William Shakespeare's works, where the structure of such Arab-influenced omnipresent concern with culture was eminently visible.[18]

In that respect, the Italian humanists of the sixteenth century had developed a multidisciplinary and comprehensive *studia humanitatis* (poetry, ethics, history, language and politics), which in many ways was precisely the perpetuation of the tradition previously developed in the Arab and Islamic world as *adab* (a *sui generis* terms approximated by civilization, customs or manners). For example, Al-Ghazali's *Ihiya Ulum al Din* [Revival of the Religious Sciences] preceded the *Summa Theologiae* of Thomas Aquinas, and his *Al Munqidh min al Dalal* [Deliverer from Error] St. Augustine's *Confessions*, as did Abdallah Ibn Al-Qutayba's *Kitab al Adab* [Book of Customs]. Yet, whereas the Muslim humanists had generally been independent thinkers opposed to religious thinkers and the dogma of their time, the Italian and French humanists were often men of the Church or under its patronage and tutelage.[19] Thomas Aquinas, in particular, had been influenced by Muslim authors while a student at the University of Naples, where the Norman King Frederick II sought and translated Arabic works into Latin. Aquinas studied Al-Ghazali in depth, from whom he borrowed the notion of 'perfect knowledge' (his 'grace') to be found in contemplation as did Blaise Pascal with the concept of 'bliss' in his *Les Pensées* (1669). Christian beatification came, as it were, from Islam. At the other end of this spectrum, Muhyiddin Ibn 'Arabi influenced the seven heavens notion of Dante Alighieri in his *Divina Commedia*. In addition to Dante's own quoting of Ibn Sina and Ibn Rushd (magnanimous, he places them in Limbo instead of Inferno), Miguel Asin Palacios convincingly demonstrated how the *Divine Comedy* had substantially borrowed from Ibn 'Arabi.[20] As Rachida El Diwani remarks: 'Muslim philosophy influenced Western thought in several ways. It mainly initiated in the West the humanistic movement and helped the Western scholastics in harmonizing philosophy with faith. Muslims gave a humanist bent to the Western mind. They revealed to the West that outside the prevailing Catholic church it was not all darkness and barbarism but immense wealth of knowledge.... By harmonizing faith with reason, Muslim thinkers made possible for themselves and for Europe an unhampered development.'[21]

Yet again – although it had been uncontested contemporaneously, 'the Francs learned early on what Islam was and to admit in the Muslims a people more civilized than themselves'[22] – the influence of the Oriental was both ignored and transformed into a negative picture as the Latin humanists claimed to be in pursuit of 'the sources' (*ad fontes*), namely Classical Greek works. As Nabil Matar remarks on this issue: 'In their discourse about Muslims, Britons produced a representation that did not belong to the actual encounter with the Muslims. Rather, it was a representation of a representation.'[23] Initially, however, there is a perceptible ambivalence as competition, fear, admiration and hostility are alternately present in relation to Muslims at the time of an Elizabethan England engaged in substantial commerce and diplomacy with North Africa and the larger Muslim world (the Barbary Company was established by Queen Elisabeth I in 1585 to engage in exclusive trade with the Kingdom of Morocco). As José Pimienta-Bey aptly notes: 'Western scholarship has characteristically dragged its feet on the issue of the historical significance of the Moor.... The Moor's largely obscure fate, however, is not due to his insignificance in the history and development of Western civilization, but, rather, to the judgment passed upon him out of jealousy at his great influence. The religious and ethnic/racial prejudices of several European historians seem to have prevented most contemporary histories from presenting a more thorough and balanced view of the Moor and Islam, especially as they relate to Christian Europe.'[24]

Humanism has also developed in the West on the heels of great poetry. Here too, we note in this founding Arab period a strong influence that was subsequently forgotten and which had primarily taken the form of the definition of the then predominant mode of poetry, chivalry. Poetry flourished notably in the Abbasid Empire from the mid-eighth to the thirteenth century. As Wacyf Boutros-Ghali sums it up: 'There was in the twelfth century between the Orient and the West an exchange of ideas and of sentiments: the West provided the shield and the organization which sustained the noble traditions of the Arabs; the Orient gave in exchange a refined civilization and his loving understanding of the virtue that enriched the make-up of European chivalry.'[25] Most paradoxically, Arab poetry contributed to forming the moral ideals of French knights who would engage in crusading. 'Those who have studied the history of the Crusades do not have to be taught that in these struggles, the virtues of civilization: magnanimity, tolerance, genuine chivalry and loving culture were all on the side of the Saracens.'[26] As Gustave Le Bon aptly remarks, this was also the basis of the gender respect that came later on in the West, but which was prevalent in Arab and Islamic circles early on: 'It is to Arabs that the inhabitants of Europe borrowed the rules of chivalry and the gallant respect of women that such laws imposed. It was not then Christianity, as is generally believed, but indeed Islam that gave woman her standing.'[27]

All in all, the scholastic method introduced by the Muslims aimed at a synthetic form of knowledge within a culture of tolerance, of valuing compelling expression, of sophisticated chivalrous poetry and, indeed, intellectual competition. To wit, the approach was that the search for the truth puts the thinker or debater in a position where he has even to find arguments for his opponent; a form of argument which would become *disputatio* in the Latin tradition. Above and beyond this particular disposition that looked upon knowledge as a core component of social affairs, the Arab-Islamic world developed, as noted, a tradition of centres for scholarship which were the direct ancestors of Western universities. The *madariss* ('schools') furthered this conception of higher learning by introducing standards (gradual specialization), structure (different programs) and academic freedom (protection of the sanctity of debate). In time, the prevalence of higher learning came to be illustrated throughout the Arab and Islamic world from

Al Qarawiyin in Fes, Morocco founded in 859, the world's oldest academic degree-awarding university, to Al Azhar in Cairo established in 970, the world's second oldest degree-granting university. Other organized centres of learning with regular curricula, specialized faculties and organized libraries spread throughout the Arab world, notably in Baghdad (Iraq), Damascus (Syria), Mecca (Arabia), Kairouan (Tunisia) and Chinguetti (Mauritania).

The modern nature of Arab and Islamic humanism and the modernizing bent of its emphasis on education is best illustrated by the work of Abdulrahman Mohammad Ibn Khaldun. With his 1377 *Muqaddima* [Introduction] and his 1375 *Kitab al Ibar* [Book of Advice], Ibn Khaldun puts forth both a comparative universal history of the world and a policy analysis of historical development. In tackling the universal mechanics of civilization (*umran*), notably in relation to economic growth, social mobility, political competition, dynastic evolution and generational transformation, Ibn Khaldun came to represent a new, unprecedented form of independent critical and comparative historiography, which established him as the founder of modern sociology. In addition to sociology, Ibn Khaldun's work was particularly important for humanism and education as regards its focus on the role of the state and specifically the correlation between statehood and historical significance. As Aziz Al-Azmeh notes: 'The object of the prolegomenon [*The Muqaddima*] is eminently historical, in that it corresponds to, and consciously takes as its model, the conception which historical writing in Arab-Islamic culture has of the object of historical study, a conception that, immanently, devolves upon the category of the historically significant unit: the state. It is the state in its historiographic physiognomy that is carried over from this field and elaborated in the *Muqaddima*'.[28] Indeed, Ibn Khaldun presents a problematization of history beyond narrative and his introduction of the concept of *asabiya* ('kinship' or *esprit de corps*) would influence lastingly sociopolitical analysis, incorporated as early as Niccolò Machiavelli's use of the notion in his *virtù*, setting the stage for Classical Republicanism and, later, Hans Baron's civic humanism.

In ushering an age of thorough reflection about the world around them opposed to superstition, fanaticism, fatalism and irrationality – at a time when these were dominant in Medieval Europe – the Arab and Muslim thinkers of that period enacted a widening progression from hearsay (*sama'a*) to reading (*qara'a*) to belonging to a school of thought (*qaraa 'alaa*), which built the foundations of higher learning leading to our modern *cursus studiorum* and core curriculum.

A proximate and lasting bequest

As early as the 680s, the Umayyad, notably Khalid Ibn Yazid Ibn Muawiya, commissioned translations of Greek works and grammarians, from such as Abi Ishaq Al-Hadrami, which appeared less than a century after the Quran was fully revealed. As noted, the movement gathered momentum with Al-Ma'mun who dispatched envoys to the Emperor of Byzantium requesting philosophy books. With the advance of Muslims in Europe and the simultaneous internal expansion of the breadth of those cultural works, the direct points of transmission to Europe were southern Italy and southern Spain. If the excellence of the work is perceived as vestigial today, it bears reminding that the Arab-Islamic Empire was culturally rich, precisely because it was open and welcomed innovation. For all the indelible imagery of the savage 'Sarasin', holy book and sword in hand forcing 'infidels' to convert (regardless of the Quran's explicit command 'Let there be no compulsion in religion (10:99)'), the imperial Muslim was a man (and a woman[29]), whose initial and general disposition was above all else tolerant and, more often than not, translated into a *zeitgeist* of exchange.

The transmission of this disposition to the West takes place from post-Late Antique Italy to the fifteenth century. The leading figures of Western thought in the period preceding the Renaissance, Thomas Aquinas, Roger Bacon and Adelard of Bath (who journeyed to Sicily and spent several years in the Arab East in the 1110s studying what he termed 'the wisdom of the Arabs' and translating many of their works), had all been exposed to Arab-Islamic works and methods, which they adopted and, in turn, transmitted to the Western canon. Whether it is the work of Abu Yusuf Yaqub Ibn Ishaq Al-Kindi (known as the father of Arab philosophy, whose many works, insisting on the rules of reasoning, were translated into Latin and circulated in Medieval Europe generating positivist thinking), or Al-Farabi (working on the harmony of agents, his *Ara Ahl al Madina al Fadila* [Book of Opinions of the People of the Ideal City] stands as a precursor to Jean-Jacques Rousseau's *Social Contract),* they pervaded the coming of age of a Western cosmology directly indebted to these revolutionary ideas of the organized relationship between man, humanism, education and society.

By and large, we witness a reaction against irrationality looked upon as the mainstay of ignorance. Ibn Sina's greatest work, *Kitab Al Shifa* [The Book of Healing], for all its universalist appeal, nonetheless makes specific reference to another work in which he discusses the Oriental philosophy or wisdom characterized by, as he notes, 'exhaustive research and extended reflection'.[30] The rejection of obscurantist thinking that is being produced is, therefore, fully conscious of its own Arab and Islamic identity, in particular that which it is rejecting (*al jahiliya*[31]), and what it may be transmitting.

The conveyance to the West ultimately produces, firstly, a methodical approach and exegesis that go beyond the apparent meaning (*al dhahir*), in order to unearth the meaning of a text or contribution and the meaning attributed to it by the author. Secondly, it establishes the imperative link between the veracity of facts (*al waqi'*) and their objective conformity to the world to produce science. Within a dynamic context of reinvention, re-examination and production of new canons and methods – and indeed, the devising of overarching laws for history, for example, Ibn Khaldun's *Muqaddima* – what emerges is a mindset treasuring competence (*kifaya*) and thoroughness.

In the tenth century, an Ismaili group in Iraq known as Ikhwan al Safa (the Brethren of Purity) produced the world's first encyclopedia with educational and training purposes. Titled *Rasail Ikhwan al Safa wa Khulan al Wafa* [Epistles of the Brethren of Purity and the Sincere Friends] and deepening the work of Plato and Pythagoras, the work was a multidisciplinary collection of articles on mathematics, physics, psychology and law. All the encyclopedias produced in Europe in the thirteenth century and later would find direct inspiration from it through a translation into Spanish that was prepared in Al-Andalus by Maslama Al-Majriti. This was the case for Alexander Neckham's *Speculum Speculationum* (1215), Bartholomeus Anglicus' *De Proprietatibus Rerum* (1240), Vincent of Beauvais' *Speculum Maius* (1264), and in time Denis Diderot and Jean le Rond D'Alembert's *Encyclopédie ou Dictionnaire raisonné des sciences, des arts et des métiers* (1751–72).

Such initiatives were forerunners of any in the West, since they did not limit themselves to (an already laudable work of) translations in the context of religion,[32] and because of the officially sanctioned nature of intellectual activity. As noted, the Umayyad and the Abbasid urged their courts 'to seek knowledge' ('until China' the Prophet Mohammad is reported to have advised). If, arguably, we can trace such characteristic eloquence to an Arabia that predated Islam – the most complex and rich poems are the seven *Mua'laqaat* [The Suspended Odes], which were composed during the *jahiliya* – it is fundamentally the post-Islam period that is revolutionary in its positive embrace of the value of knowledge (*'ilm*), the importance of education (*adab*), the social and political empowerment of savants (*'alem*) and the resulting openness to the world. For example, the Abbasids were contemporaneously surrounded by different traditions (Persians and Byzantine) and were themselves the result of expansion, following the Umayyads, as they would have a foot in Baghdad and one in Spain. Such globalization of its day functioned according to a mode of furthering of physical centres of learning.

The implications of this legacy were profound, notably due to the concomitance of (i) the intellectually 'empty' nature of Europe during that period and (ii) the acceleration of quality production in an Andalusia where thinkers, benefiting from the solidity of higher learning structures devised earlier in Baghdad and elsewhere in the East, were engaged in a sophisticated contest of scholarly one-upmanship. Going beyond the immediacy of discourse (*Al Kalaam*) and Greek sophism, they subjected language itself to rigorous practice, subjugating the previously dominant custom of imposing discursive tendencies to a requirement to articulate a construct guided first and foremost by objective rules. Hence, Ahmad Bin Abdulrahman Ibn Mohammad Ibn Mada authored a *Kitab Al Rad 'ala Al Nuhat* [Book of Response to the Grammarians] in which he, among others, attempted to systematize the respect of grammatical rules refuting the *ta'lil* ('motivation') through which nouns and verbs were excessively adapted to specific context; hence leading to a multiplication of special cases and undisciplined improvisation. Indeed, the dominant themes of the day were *ijtihad* ('interpretation'), *ijma'* ('consensus'), *ilham* ('inspiration'), *dalil* ('proof'), *istiqra'* ('examination'), *sabab* ('cause') and *qiyas* ('reasoning'), allowing for a qualitative progression from indication or statement to the inevitable demonstration.

In spite of the linearity of this bequest, as the Arab world lost ground in the fifteenth century, first to the *Reconquista* and then to the Ottomans, a twofold mutually-reinforcing phenomenon of reappropriation of the Muslim contribution and the rendering invisible of this tradition materialized. In time, and before the German Orientalist T. J. De Boer and his *Geschichte der Philosophie im Islam* (1901), Ernest Renan – famously of the view that 'the conquest of a country of inferior race by a superior race is nothing shocking'[33] – could argue in a racialized study of Ibn Rushd, *Averroes et l'Averroïsme* (1823), that philosophical thinking amongst the Arabs could only be an imitation of the Greeks. Later, Carra de Vaux is equally explicit in perpetuating the new myth: 'We must not expect to find among the Arabs the same powerful genius, the same gift of scientific imagination, the same "enthusiasm", the same originality of thought that we have among the Greeks. The Arabs are before all else the pupils of the Greeks; their science is a continuation of Greek science which it preserves.'[34]

The new narrative that emerges after the Renaissance and throughout the imperial age of the nineteenth century is the one that would remain the canon of contemporary 'admitted truth' on this issue.[35] With new focal points and establishing a revisionist historical symmetry between The Antiquity and The Renaissance, it would proceed to surgically remove all Arab and Islamic contributions from the educational and humanist march of the world. This endeavour was essentially facilitated by the fact that it took place in the context of the colonial expansion of the West. For how could the now-rendered-in-terms-of-savagery Muslim be an inspiration for the Enlightenment? How could his defeated religion be a basis for a victorious Church and a nascent imperial republic? As Sigmund Freud famously demonstrated, 'It is always possible to bind together a considerable number of people in love, so long as there are other people left over to receive the manifestations of their aggressiveness.'[36]

Initially, Christianity is positioned as the preliminary to republicanism and the religious legacy to be shed is paradoxically the very religion that will become anathema to the West. In other words, the tenets of the Muslim faith helped build Western secularism.

> Christendom (*Christianitas*) was the form of Western unity that emerged in the High Middle Ages. Medieval writers spoke of Christendom when they talked about themselves and their civilization, investing the idea of Christendom with their hopes for temporal as well as spiritual unity in this world.... One finds the full articulation of the notion of *Christianitas* in crusading chronicles.... The launching of the Crusade can be seen as marking the symbolic point when Christendom became a 'living reality', when it was transformed into what could be called a society.... An essential moment in the articulation of the self-awareness of the Christian commonwealth was the construction of the Muslim enemy. The antagonistic difference between themselves and the Muslims was a constitutive element of the Latin Christians' collective identity... [The Muslims] were regarded as precisely the fundamental enemy of Christendom.... The Muslim world became no less than 'the antithetical system'.... This determined the nature of Christian war against the Muslims, which was harsher and more ferocious than wars against any other adversary.[37]

The amnesia therefore has political underpinnings. Ironically, as the West increasingly associated itself with science and rationality in its practice and discourse – 'Everyone here is fully convinced that this is the most just war, because it is against barbarians; who would believe in this age such atrocities could be committed in a Christian civilized country'[38] – the facts on the ground were evidence of a rewriting of history primarily by means of violence. Sven Lindqvist captures the subterfuge:

> When Europeans went east as Crusaders in the twelfth and thirteenth centuries, they came across people who were superior to them in culture, diplomatic cunning, technical knowledge, and not least in experience of epidemics. Thousands of crusaders died because of their inferior resistance to bacteria. When Europeans went west in the fifteenth century, they themselves were the bearers of those superior bacteria. People died everywhere the Europeans went.... Preindustrial Europe had little that was in demand in the rest of the world. [Its] most important export was force.... Thus the backward and poorly resourced Europe of the sixteenth century acquired a monopoly on ocean-going ships with guns capable of spreading death and destruction across huge distances.[39]

Regardless, the colonial movement is schizophrenic as it cannot fully erase the influence of the world that it is subjugating. So, from the end of the eighteenth century onwards, Western artists travelled throughout the Islamic world and brought back powerful ideas and visuals. Once a source, and even as a target, the Orient became an inspiration further fuelling the Western cultural project and its accelerated rise in the nineteenth and twentieth centuries. The 'voyage to the Orient' becomes all the rage and many – François René de Chateaubriand in Palestine (1806), Eugène Delacroix in Morocco (1832), Alphonse de Lamartine in Syria (1833), Gérard De Nerval in Egypt (1843) and Guy de Maupassant in Algeria (1881) – succumbed to it. In 1856, Owen Jones published a *Grammar of Ornament* in London in which he organized Islamic designs as universal models. Simply put, modern creation was regenerated thanks to the earlier advances of Cordoba, Baghdad or Cairo.

During the early twentieth century, religious and biological[40] explanations were replaced by cultural ones and we witnessed the transformation of an adventure into an enterprise and then into an administration.[41] However, the amnesia remained throughout the twentieth century.[42] Therefore, if the West and Islam are often presented as antagonistic,[43] it is largely because of the impact of political discourse prevalent between the eighteenth and twentieth centuries, which successfully sought to erase the historically consequential trace of Arab and Islamic influence on the West. In recent decades, this storytelling has gained momentum. As Mahmood Mamdani writes: 'Islam and the Middle East have displaced Africa as the hard premodern core in a rapidly globalizing world.... Whereas Africa is seen as incapable of modernity, hard-core Islam is seen as not only incapable of but also resistant to modernity.'[44] Yet, the very notion (objectivity) that is being levelled as missing in the Muslim translations is the one absent in the case of the latter-day Western world. Citing Charles Malik, Nabih Amin Faris summarizes the issue of a necessary reciprocity, away from a relationship of domination: 'When will it become possible for a Muslim scholar to write a treatise on Christianity to which Christians could refer, for the next thousand years, as a standard and a reliable work on the subject?'[45]

Conclusion

This chapter has argued that the progression of the West is historically indebted to the Arab and Islamic world, although this debt has been subject to amnesia, notably as regards humanism and education. The duty of recognition that is so reflexively expressed in relation to the Classical Greek and Roman periods is almost systematically denied to the Muslim golden age. Yet, the latter's is a central contribution to a Western story generated from and built upon knowledge produced over eight centuries in Baghdad, Cairo, Cordoba, Seville and elsewhere under the Islamic Empire. Much as it has been said to be 'pre-scientific',[46] the world before the Arab contribution was arguably pre-humanistic.

The Greeks influenced the Arabs who in turn influenced Westerners. No sleight of hand could erase that linearity. The notion of an intransigent and independent reason able to transcend and join rigorously two opposed viewpoints was actively articulated during the golden age of the Arab and Islamic Empire. Demonstrative methodology beyond inquisitive mind, and rigorous dialectic beyond discourse and sophistry were tangible contributions which the Muslims developed in higher learning centres for a lengthy period and over a vast stretch of territory. By the early Renaissance, the sum total of this knowledge had been known to the Italian and French, and later British and German, scholars. Three centuries later, it would have been re-appropriated and its lineage erased for political reasons.

Amnesia or theft of meta-historical units?[47] As academe is increasingly tackling the profoundly problematic nature of the Eurocentric or Occidentalist account of the genesis of the contemporary era, we must come to terms with the revisionist nature of the account of a 'backward

East' and an 'inventive West' as a normative referential. Stripped of all legendary accretions and the anaemic language of translated works, the enormous legacies remain of, among others, Al-Ghazali, Al-Shafi'i, Al-Kindi, Ibn Sina, Ibn Rushd, and Ibn Khaldun to whom the likes of Thomas Aquinas and those that followed are indebted as they invariably walked in their footsteps.

In the post-September 11 world, it is even more necessary than ever to re-establish the facts in this sequence, with a view to re-founding a new, more positive relationship between the Orient and the Occident and unearthing their shared history. Above and beyond that relationship, ultimately humanism and education cannot be reduced to a history of subjective representation. Their very appeal requires the nurturing of the sanctity of their universality and never-ending expansion from one culture to the other.

Notes

1. Before Edgar Allan Poe revised the poem in 1845, the original lines composed in 1831 had been: 'the beauty of fair Greece and the grandeur of old Rome'.
2. Dramatized dialogue in the screenplay by Robert Bolt from the 1962 motion picture *Lawrence of Arabia* directed by David Lean. Also see T. E. Lawrence's own major work *Seven Pillars of Wisdom*, published in different versions since 1922.
3. P. E. Grieve (2009), *The Eve of Spain – Myths of Origins in the History of Christian, Muslim, and Jewish Conflict* (Baltimore, MD: John Hopkins University Press), p. 69. The, at times, schizophrenic disposition of actively repressing and passively appropriating Muslim achievements is tackled, in the case of Spain, by Barbara Fuchs (2008) in *Exotic Nation – Maurophilia and the Construction of Early Modern Spain* (Philadelphia: University of Pennsylvania Press).
4. Notably by Edward Said (1978), *Orientalism – Western Conceptions and the Orient* (New York: Routledge); and (1994) *Culture and Imperialism* (New York: Vintage Books). See, also, U. Singh Mehta (1999) *Liberalism and Empire – A Study in Nineteenth-Century British Liberal Thought* (Chicago: University of Chicago Press).
5. E. W. Said (2004), *Humanism and Democratic Criticism* (New York: Columbia University Press), p. 47.
6. See, in particular, S. Bessis (2002), *Western Supremacy: The Triumph of an Idea* (London: Zed Books); C. Hall (2002), *Civilizing Subjects – Colony and Metropole in the English Imagination, 1830–1867* (Chicago: University of Chicago Press); and V. Forrester (2004), *Le Crime Occidental* (Paris: Fayard).
7. R. Rorty (1997), 'Human Rights, Rationality, and Sentimentality', reprinted in M. R. Ishay (ed.) *The Human Rights Reader* (New York: Routledge), p. 263.
8. F. Fukuyama (1989), 'The End of History?' *The National Interest* 16, p. 9. The sentence was excised from the book of the same title published in 1992 by the Free Press.

9. Mohammed Abed Al-Jabri (1995), *Introduction à la critique de la raison Arabe* (Paris: La Découverte), p. 37; translated compilation of Al-Jabri's two major works: *Nahnu wal Turath: Qiraat Mu'asira fi Turathina Al Falsafi* [Tradition and Us: Contemporary Readings in Our Philosophical Heritage] (Casablanca: Dar Al Nashr Al Maghribiya, 1980) and *Al Turath wal Hadatha* [Tradition and Modernity] (Beirut: Al Markaz Al Thaqafi, 1991).
10. A. Bloom (1987), *The Closing of the American Mind* (New York: Simon & Schuster), p. 36.
11. Z. Sayre Schiffman (1985), 'Renaissance Historicism Reconsidered', *History and Theory*, Vol. 24, No. 2, p. 170.
12. V. Romani (2009), 'The Politics of Higher Education in the Middle East: Problems and Prospects', *Middle East Brief*, No. 36 (Crown Center for Middle East Studies, Waltham, Massachusetts), p. 2.
13. P. K. Hitti (1944), 'America and the Arab Heritage', in N. A. Faris (ed.) *The Arab Heritage* (Princeton: Princeton University Press), pp. 2–3.
14. To use George Makdisi's phrase. See his 1974 'The Scholastic Method in Education: An Inquiry into Its Origins in Law and Theology', *Speculum*, Vol. 49, No. 4, p. 661.
15. R. Arnaldez (1985), 'Les traductions du grec: naissance des sciences profanes et de la philosophie dans les pays musulmans', in *Les grands siècles de Bagdad*, Vol. I (Algiers: Entreprise Nationale du Livre), p. 257.
16. See N. Nofal (1993), 'Al-Ghazali', *Prospects* (UNESCO), Vol. 22, Nos 3–4, pp. 519–42.
17. P. K. Hitti (1968), *Makers of Arab History* (New York: St. Martin's Press), p. 160. Hitti also notes Al-Ghazali's influence on Jewish scholars. He writes: 'Less than a century after al Ghazali's death, a Jewish convert to Christianity in Toledo had his philosophical works translated into Latin. In the mid-thirteenth century, *Mizan al 'Amal* [The Balance of Deeds], a compendium of ethics, was done into Latin by a Jew in Barcelona. Maimonides of Cordova, the most celebrated Jewish philosopher of the Middle Ages, used his *Maqasid*. The compendium on mysticism, *Mishkat al Anwar* [The Niche of Lights], was translated and aroused much speculation among Jewish scholars' (p. 163).
18. Besides Othello and the Prince of Morocco, other Arab-Islamic figures, such as Caliban and Aaron, feature in Shakespeare's plays *Othello, The Merchant of Venice, The Tempest* and *Titus Andronicus*. For a critique of Shakespeare's Eurocentric perspective, see G. de Sousa (2002), *Shakespeare's Cross-Cultural Encounters* (Houndmills: Palgrave Macmillan).
19. See F. D. Logan (2002), *A History of the Church in the Middle Ages* (London: Routledge).
20. M. A. Palacios (1919), *La Escatologia Musulmana en la 'Divina Comedia'* (Madrid: Real Academia Española). Also see his 1931 *El Islam Cristianizado* (Madrid: Editorial Plutarco).
21. R. El Diwani (2005), 'Islamic Contributions to the West', paper presented at Lake Superior State University.
22. E. Lavisse and A. Rambaud (1894), *Histoire Générale du IVème Siècle à Nos Jours – Vol. II: L'Europe Féodale, Les Croisades (1095–1270)* (Paris: Armand Colin), p. 346.

23. N. Matar (1999), *Turks, Moors, and Englishmen in the Age of Discovery* (New York: Columbia University Press), p. 15.
24. J. V. Pimienta-Bey (1992), 'Moorish Spain: Academic Source and Foundation for the Rise and Success of Western European Universities in the Middle Ages', in I. van Sertima (ed.) *The Golden Age of the Moor* (Rutgers: Transaction Publishers), p. 182.
25. W. Boutros-Ghali (1996), *La tradition chevalresque des Arabes* (Casablanca: Eddif), p. 33; originally published in Paris by Plon in 1919. The etymology of 'chivalry' is from the Arabic 'chelval' or 'cherval' used to mount a horse.
26. S. Lane Poole (1898), *Saladin and the Fall of the Kingdom of Jerusalem* (New York: G. P. Putnam's Sons), p. 306.
27. G. le Bon (1884), *La Civilisation des Arabes* (Paris: Firmin-Didot), p. 428. Barthelemy Saint-Hilaire writes similarly: 'To the commerce of Arabs and their imitation, the rough masters of our Middle Ages softened their boorish habits and the knights without losing their bravery came to know more delicate sentiments, more noble, and more humane. It is doubtful that only Christianity, however beneficent, would have inspired them thus.' See J. B. Saint-Hilaire (1865), *Mahomet et le Coran* (Paris: Didier et Cie), p. 223.
28. A. Al-Azmeh (1982), *Ibn Khaldun* (London: Routledge), p. 11.
29. See F. Mernissi (1997), *The Forgotten Queens of Islam* (Minneapolis: University of Minnesota Press).
30. Cited in Al-Jabri, *Nahnu wal Turath*, chapter on 'Ibn Sina wa Falsafatuhu al Mashriqiya' ('Ibn Sina and His Oriental Philosophy').
31. On *Al Jahilia*, see D. O'Leary (1927), *Arabia before Muhammad* (London: K. Paul, Trench & Trubner).
32. On this issue, see L. D. Reynolds and N. G. Wilson (1991), *Scribes and Scholars – A Guide to the Transmission of Greek and Latin Literature* (Oxford: Clarendon Press).
33. E. Renan (1871), *La réforme intellectuelle et morale de la France* (Paris: Hachette). Renan adds: 'One sees that in all things the Semitic race appears to us to be an incomplete race, by virtue of its simplicity... [T]he Semitic nations... have never been able to achieve true maturity.'
34. C. de Vaux (1931), 'Astronomy and Mathematics', in T. W. Arnold and A. Guillaume (eds) *Legacy of Islam* (Oxford: Clarendon Press).
35. See, for example, D. R. Kelley (1970), *Foundations of Modern Historical Scholarship – Language, Law, and History in the French Renaissance* (New York: Columbia University Press); or P. Burke (1970), *The Renaissance Sense of the Past* (New York: St. Martin's Press).
36. S. Freud [1930] (1961), *Civilization and its Discontents*, translated and edited by J. Strachey (New York: W. W. Norton), p. 59.
37. T. Mastnak (2002), *Crusading Peace – Christendom, the Muslim World, and Western Political Order* (Berkeley: University of Los Angeles Press), pp. 91–2, 117.
38. C. Darwin (1839), *The Voyage of the Beagle* (London: Henry Colburn), ch. 5.
39. S. Lindqvist (1996), *Exterminate All the Brutes* (New York: The New Press), pp. 46–7; 111.
40. The State Institute for Racial Biology in Uppsala was still in existence in the 1950s.

41. S. Venayre (2002), *La gloire de l'aventure – genèse d'une mystique moderne, 1850–1940* (Paris: Aubier), p. 89.
42. In France, for example, those features were shared by radically different regimes before and during World War II. See P. Ory (1994), *La Belle Illusion – Culture et Politique Sous le Signe du Front Populaire, 1935–1938* (Paris: Plon); and C. Faure (1989), *Le Projet Culturel de Vichy* (Lyon: CNRS).
43. Among many such titles, see for instance A. Pagden (2008), *Worlds at War – The 2,500-Year Struggle Between East and West* (New York: Random House).
44. M. Mamdani (2004), *Good Muslim, Bad Muslim – America, the Cold War, and the Roots of Terror* (New York: Random House), p. 19.
45. N. A. Faris (1957), 'The Muslim Thinker and His Christian Relations', *The Muslim World*, Vol. 47, No. 1, p. 62.
46. Robert Briffault writes: 'The debt of our science to that of the Arabs does not consist in startling discoveries of revolutionary theories; science owes a great deal more to Arab culture, it owes its existence'. See R. Briffault (1928), *The Making of Humanity* (London: G. Allen and Unwin), pp. 200–1.
47. On this issue, see the work of Jack Goody, notably his 2006, *The Theft of History* (New York: Cambridge University Press); in particular chapter 2, 'The Invention of Antiquity', pp. 26–67 and chapter 9, 'The Appropriation of Values: Humanism, Democracy, and Individualism', pp. 240–66.

8

The Arabic-Latin Intercultural Transmission of Scientific Knowledge in Pre-Modern Europe: Historical Context and Case Studies

Mohammed Abattouy

During the rise of Islamic civilization, Europe was still at an early stage in science, medicine and technology. The Arabic-Latin translation movement in the Middle Ages led to the transformation of almost all scientific, medical and philosophical disciplines in the Medieval Latin world. The impact of Arabic knowledge on Western learning was particularly strong in mathematics, astronomy, chemistry, medicine and philosophy. However, the influence of Arabic works in fertilizing Western culture and in providing the foundation for scientific progress in pre-modern Europe is hardly recognized in the mainstream of literature outside academic circles of professional historians.

This chapter summarizes the debt that the West owes to Arabic-Islamic civilization in the field of science and technology. Recent Western interest in Arabic-Islamic achievements in science, technology, medicine and arts was awakened by current social and political events of the last decades. It is time to recognize such a debt and use it to found a universal history of science as a field of intercultural influences and mutual fertilization between successive cultural traditions.[1]

In the universal history of science, the scientific tradition of Muslim civilization, understood as synonymous with Arabic and Islamic science, refers to the scientific activity developed in the Muslim world between the seventh and seventeenth centuries (all dates refer to the Common Era), in the large region where Islam was the dominant religion and culture, a vast territory stretching from the borders of China to Southern Europe.

Whilst most scientists belonging to this tradition were Muslims, they were from different ethnic and religious origins: Arabs, Persians, Central Asians, Indians, Andalusians, Berbers, Turkish; they believed in different faiths, the principal ones being Islam, Christianity and Judaism, besides minorities such as the Sabians and Zoroastrians. The language in which they wrote their treatises, worked out their investigations and interacted with their intellectual milieu was essentially Arabic, which was the dominant vehicle for science and knowledge throughout the Muslim world.

The tradition of science in Muslim civilization, as reconstructed by successive generations of historians since the nineteenth century, has revealed itself to be a cornucopia of scientific theories, results, discoveries and inventions, in all the fields of science practised in ancient and medieval times, from mathematics, astronomy and physics, to geography, chemistry, life sciences, medicine, pharmacy and social sciences. With these features, science in Muslim civilization stands among the most dynamic world traditions. After it emerged in the late eighth century, it lasted for more than seven centuries, longer than that of modern science (seventeenth to twenty-first centuries).

A major impetus for the blossoming of science in the early Islamic world under the Abbasid Caliphate came from the patronage of the new elite that came to power in Baghdad. These patrons, including several Caliphs, court officials and notables, supported a large scientific community for generations, first to translate Indian, Greek, Syriac and Persian works into Arabic, and then to produce original scientific results. The patronage of science was to be a constant feature of the institutional setting of science throughout the Muslim world for centuries. The foundation of social institutions for the practice of science and the dissemination of its results served as cradles of intellectual activity. Royal institutions such as *Bayt Al Hikma* ('House of Wisdom') in Baghdad and *Dar Al-'ilm* ('House of Knowledge') in Cairo played a decisive role. Yet, many other institutions also played a key role: numerous private libraries, which grew rapidly from the ninth century onwards; hospitals, which also hosted teaching, training, and clinical research facilities; mosques, temples of prayer and institutions of learning throughout Islamic history; observatories, from small ones in Baghdad and Damascus under the Abbasids to large-scale institutions in Maragha and Samarkand; and, finally, the school system, initiated with the *madrasas* as autonomous endowed colleges established from the eleventh century.

Scholarly interest in the symbolic, intellectual and scientific legacy of Islamic civilization has experienced great progress in the last few decades and takes the form of a paradigm shift. Thousands of original texts were edited, translated and analysed, and whole traditions of Islamic science, technology and medicine were reconstructed through the long term, sustained research of successive generations of scholars since the nineteenth century. As a result, the contribution of the Islamic world to human knowledge is widely recognized, and its decisive influence on the rise of Western Europe in pre-modern times became a necessary key for the understanding of the early phases of the modern world's intellectual history.

Indeed, we know much more today than we knew a few decades ago. Whole fields, from mathematics, astronomy, optics, medicine and pharmacy, mechanics, technology and engineering, to agriculture, architecture, history, economy, sociology and anthropology, were completely rewritten. This reconstruction was conducted with various fortunes and in-depth analyses. To take just a few examples, the contributions of Al-Khwarizmi, Al-Biruni, Ibn Sina, Ibn Al-Haytham, Al-Zahrawi, Al-Jazari and Nasir Al Din Al-Tusi up to Al-Kashi, Ibn Khaldun, and Taqi Al-Din Ibn Ma'ruf in the late sixteenth century, were well documented and their status in the history of science made clear, to the point that it should be obvious to any impartial eye in science studies today that those scholars deserve the highest distinctions. With our present standards, we can confidently say that several among them deserve, were they still living among us, to be awarded a Nobel prize.[2]

Historical context of the transmission of Arabic knowledge to Medieval Europe

With this scholarly background in mind, we may claim that we are now well informed about the impact Muslim science exerted on the emergence of science in Europe. The translation into Latin of Arabic scientific texts enabled the first appearance of serious scientific knowledge in Europe in the twelfth century. This interest in scientific knowledge coming from the East lasted until the late seventeenth century in European scientific circles. However, long before that, at the turn of the millennium, around 1000, European scholars became aware of the vast storehouse of knowledge held in the Islamic world. In the ensuing centuries, much of this Arabic knowledge, including earlier Greek works of science, medicine and philosophy, was translated into Latin and transmitted to European centres of learning.

Centres of transmission

The transfer of Islamic science and technology to pre-modern Europe occurred in various urban and cultural centres and through historical events such as military confrontations, commercial relations, migration of artisans, movement of scholars, converts, diplomats and commercial agents. I give below an outline of these factors.

In the eleventh through to the thirteenth centuries, there were three main geographical areas in which contact between the Islamic and Latin worlds allowed for the transmission of knowledge from one culture to the other: Spain, southern Italy and Sicily, and the Middle East.

Al-Andalus and Spain

Spain was the most important centre of direct transmission of Arabic knowledge to Medieval Europe. While some copies of Arabic works were brought to Europe by the crusaders, Italian traders and ambassadors, the most important role played in awakening European scholars to the intellectual riches of the Islamic civilization happened in the Iberian peninsula, where, over several centuries, the coexistence of different communities permitted friendly relations between Muslims, Christians and Jews.

Most of this geographic area of Southern Europe had been under Islamic rule since the eighth century. For several centuries Muslims, Christians and Jews coexisted peacefully under Islamic rule, and Arabic scholarship flourished in the eleventh and twelfth centuries under the Umayyad dynasty and continued later on in the various principalities. Bilingual and multilingual Spanish scholars facilitated the translation of Arabic works into Hebrew and Latin. However, it was not only native Spaniards who produced translations, but foreign scholars as well, who came to Spain, learnt Arabic and took their translations back to their homelands. As early as 967, the scholar Gerbert of Aurillac, who became Pope Sylvester II, crossed the Pyrenees from France into Spain to study Arabic mathematics. What began as a trickle turned into a flood as the Christian re-conquest of Spain during the eleventh and twelfth centuries placed Arabic centres of culture and libraries of Arabic books into Christian hands. Toledo, the cultural centre of Spain, fell in 1085 and its intellectual riches attracted scholars from all over Europe.

The greatest of all the translators was Gerard of Cremona (d. 1187). Around 1140, he travelled from northern Italy to Spain in search of

Ptolemy's *Almagest,* which he had learnt about but had been unable to locate elsewhere. He found a copy in Toledo and learnt Arabic in order to translate it into Latin. While there, he became aware of numerous Arabic texts on many other subjects and he devoted several decades of his life to translating this corpus into Latin. He produced an astonishing number of books, between 70 and 80, including works on astronomy, mathematics, optics, natural philosophy, and medicine. Among these translations were many great and important texts, such as Euclid's *Elements,* Al-Khwarizmi's *Algebra* (early ninth century), Aristotle's *Physics* and *On the Heavens,* and Ibn Sina's (980–1037) *Canon of Medicine.* Perhaps most impressive, though, was the skill with which Gerard rendered these works into Latin. Often translators resorted to literal word-for-word replacement from Arabic into Latin, which resulted in nonsensical sentences and mangled meanings. Gerard, however, had such a good command of the languages and a clear understanding of the subject matter that he was able to produce translations that were true to the original meaning and nuances of the Arabic works.

The Spanish historian Américo Castro (d. 1972) argued[3] that Christian Spain has always been an importer of technologies, and after the fall of Toledo in 1085 the exporters of technology were the Muslim Mudéjars,[4] who formed enclaves of technological expertise. The Mozarabs[5] also played an important role in transferring Arabic culture and technology to Christian Spain. The Christian kingdoms could only continue to expand by successfully colonizing the territories that they occupied. The policy practiced by Alfonso III to attain this aim was to repopulate them by attracting Mozarab immigrants from Al-Andalus. The Mozarabs built important buildings, monasteries and fortresses that constituted typical examples of Mozarabic architecture. They brought with them their knowledge of the language that enabled them to compile Arabic glosses on Latin manuscripts, and to translate Arabic works, thus providing the base of the intellectual movement of the School of Translators of Toledo.[6]

Sicily

While Italy was much less important than Spain in the activity of translating from Arabic into Latin, its role in the accumulation of knowledge was not insignificant. Southern Italy and Sicily were important both for the translations of Constantine the African in Salerno in the eleventh century and especially for the translations directly into Latin of Greek works during the twelfth and thirteenth centuries. There had always been Greek-speaking communities in Italy and strong ties with the Byzantine Empire. Libraries of Greek works were rediscovered and translators such as James of Venice (c. 1140) and William of Moerbeke (c. 1270) attempted to provide European scholars with new or revised Latin translations of Aristotle, Plato, Archimedes and Euclid from the Greek.

Due to its proximity to mainland Italy, Sicily played an important role in the transmission of Arabic science and technology to Europe. During the Arab (827–1091) and Norman (1091–1194) eras, the island was a bridge between Arabic-Islamic civilization and Europe. The Arab tradition of tolerance toward other religions was perpetuated under the Norman kings in Sicily. Under the rule of Roger II, Sicily became a clearing house where eastern and western scholars met and exchanged ideas, debates and texts. The Arab presence in Sicily was the stimulus for artistic activity which characterized Norman Sicily. Virtually all monuments, cathedrals, palaces and castles built under the Normans were of an Arab style. Monuments and vestiges still show the Arabic influence on architecture in several Italian cities.[7]

Byzantium

Another point of cultural contact with the Christian medieval world and the lands of Islam was through the East via Byzantium. The proximity of Byzantium to Islamic territories and their common borders resulted in active commercial and cultural contacts. As a result, Arabic scientific works were translated into Greek through this channel. As we shall see below, the discovery of the Tusi Couple in a Greek manuscript that could have been accessible to Copernicus accounts fairly well for the possible transmission of that theorem through the Byzantine route.[8]

Military confrontations

Although the influence of the Crusades on the transmission of science to Europe was small, the Crusaders, while in the Near East, experienced the attractive and useful sides of Islamic life, and attempted to imitate these on their return home. These aspects of material civilization mean that the Crusaders transferred to Europe several technological ideas from the Near East.[9]

The military confrontations between Muslims and Christians in Spain resulted in various kinds of technology transfer. One of these was the use of gunpowder and cannon. It is reported that this technology was also transferred to England in 1340–2. The English earls of Derby and Salisbury participated in the siege of Al-Jazira in Muslim Spain and it is related that they carried back with them to England the knowledge to make gunpowder and cannon. A few years later, the English used cannon for the first time in Western Europe against the French in the battle of Crecy in 1346.[10]

Waves of migration

The cultural transfer of science, techniques and various forms of knowledge and practices occurred also as a result of human movement, travel and migration around the southern and northern borders of the Mediterranean in medieval times. These waves of migration contained artisans and various social categories, from scholars and diplomats to commercial agents.

An effective method of transfer was the migration of craftsmen and artisans. This concerned mainly techniques and procedures in technology, architecture, industry and trade. Hence, in the eleventh century, Egyptian craftsmen founded two glass factories at Corinth in Greece, then they emigrated westwards after the destruction of Corinth by the Normans. In the thirteenth century, large numbers of Syrian glassworkers were driven to glassmaking centres in the West. In 1277, Syrian craftsmen were sent from Syria to Venice as a result of a treaty between Antioch and Venice.[11]

In Spain, the migration of Muslim craftsmen to Christian territories took place in parallel and as a result of the wars of re-conquest. Al-Andalus was an emporium from which Christians were importing the products they did not produce themselves. The techniques, however, were transferred upon the conquest of Muslim towns. The technologies were practised by resident Muslim craftsmen, who diffused manufacturing technologies throughout the Christian kingdoms.

In the thirteenth and fourteenth centuries, the economy of Provence in the south of France was affected by contact with both Muslim west and east. Imported crockery from Spain became popular in Provence. Archaeology attests to the importation of techniques from the Muslim west for the manufacture of ceramics in imitation of the Muslim ones. During this period, a large proportion of artisans and workers in Marseilles and Provence were foreigners including Muslims and Jews from Spain.[12]

The fall of Muslim Sicily to the Normans resulted in the emigration of many Sicilian Muslims to North Africa, although others remained. Around 1223, Frederick II deported the remaining Muslims to Lucera in Apulia, Italy, and some settled in other parts of southern Italy. The Muslims of Lucera practiced several occupations including the manufacture of arms, especially crossbows and other industrial products, such as ceramics. When the colony was destroyed in 1230, the manufacturers of arms were allowed to stay in Naples to practise their craft.[13]

In addition to the translators who flocked to Spain during the twelfth and thirteenth centuries, there was a continuous movement of persons to and from the West, the Near East, Southern Europe and the Maghreb countries. This movement of persons contributed to the transmission of science and technology from Islamic lands to the West.

Gerbert of Aurillac was a French educator and mathematician, who spent three years (967–70) in the monastery of Ripolli in northern Spain during which time he studied Arabic science. He is considered the first ambassador to carry the new Arabic science across the Pyrenees. Constantinus Africanus was the first to introduce Arabic medicine into Europe. He was born in Tunis (c.1010–15) and died at Monte Cassino in 1087. He travelled as a merchant to Italy and having noticed the poverty of medical literature there, he decided to study medicine for three years in Tunis. After collecting several Arabic medical works he departed to Italy and settled first in Salerno then in Monte Cassino. Constantinus translated into Latin the most important Arabic medical works of the time and attributed them to himself. However, these works were later traced back to their real Arabic origin. Nevertheless, he was responsible for introducing Arabic medicine into Europe and in heralding the start of a proper medical education in medieval Italy.[14]

One of the earliest Western scholars to travel to Arab lands was Adelard of Bath (fl. 1116–42). He travelled to Sicily and Syria where he spent seven years, during which time he learnt Arabic and became acquainted with Arabic learning. Beside his important scientific translations, Adelard was instrumental in the transfer of Islamic technology. He issued a revised edition of *Mappae Clavicula*, a very important treatise on Western medieval technology in the form of a collection of recipes on the production of colours and other chemical products.[15]

Another important figure from the same era was Leonardo Fibonacci, who was born around 1180. He was a great mathematician who received his education in mathematics and Arabic in Bougie in Algeria. He also visited Syria and Egypt and had access to Arabic manuscripts in mathematics. His writings include the important book *Liber abaci* (1202, revised 1228) and *Practica geometriae* in which he explained the use of geometry in surveying (*'Ilm Al Misaha*) as it was practised by Muslim engineers.

The famous Leo Africanus, who was born in Granada between 1489 and 1495 and was raised in Fez, Morocco, was, in fact, Hasan Al Wazzan, who was captured by Sicilian corsairs who presented him to Pope Leo X. During his stay in Italy of around 30 years, he learnt Italian, taught Arabic at Bologna and wrote his famous book *Description of Africa*, which was completed in 1526. He collaborated with Jacob ben Simon in compiling a Arabic-Hebrew-Latin vocabulary.

In the Renaissance period, Guillaume Postel (d. 1581), a French scholar, who was well versed in Arabic and other languages, procured a large number of Arabic manuscripts during two trips to Istanbul and the Near East. The first trip in 1536 was undertaken to collect manuscripts on behalf of the king of France. During the second trip, Postel is believed to have spent the years 1548 to 1551 travelling to Palestine and Syria to collect manuscripts. After this trip, he earned an appointment as Professor of Mathematics and Oriental Languages at the College Royal in Paris. Two Arabic astronomical manuscripts from his collection are now in the Bibliothèque Nationale in Paris and in the Vatican, and they contain the Tusi theorems and carry heavy annotations and notes made by Postel himself. It is possible that among the manuscripts that he collected were some written by Taqi Al-Din Ibn Ma'ruf, who was the foremost scientist in Istanbul at that time, and who wrote treatises on astronomy, machines and mathematical subjects.[16]

Another important scholar from this period is Jacob Golius (1590–1667). He was appointed Professor of Oriental Languages at the University of Leiden. He spent several years (1625–9) in the Near East and brought back a harvest of 300 Arabic, Turkish and Persian manuscripts. He was an Arabist as well as a scientist, and it is reported that he translated some works of Jabir into Latin and had them published.

Another important figure from the Renaissance period was Patriarch Ni'meh who emigrated from Diyar Bakr in northern Mesopotamia to Italy in 1577. He carried with him his own library of Arabic manuscripts. Ni'meh was well received by the Pope Gregory XIII and by the Medici Family in Florence and was appointed to the editorial board of the Medici Oriental Press, which published Arabic books. His own library is still preserved at the Laurenziana Library in Florence. During his service with the press several Arabic scientific works were published.[17]

Towards a theoretical framework

The primary motivation behind the effort of translation from Arabic into Latin was utility.[18] Astronomical and medical works were sought out and translated first. Medical treatises had an obvious value, and Ibn Sina's *Canon of Medicine* was the most complete, scholarly compilation of medical knowledge to be found anywhere during the Middle Ages.

Astronomy (and astrology) was also very useful in the medieval world. Astronomy was essential for calendar keeping and the prediction of celestial events. To fully understand and utilize complex astronomical works, such as the *Almagest,* scholars also needed to translate and learn mathematical treatises of Greek and Arabic origin. Moreover, medicine and astronomy both rested on certain philosophical underpinnings found in Aristotle and other Greek philosophers. Thus, translators who sought medical and astronomical works also found themselves delving into the natural philosophy and metaphysics of Greek and Arabic philosophers.

By the middle of the thirteenth century, the flood of translation had slowed again to a trickle, as most of the Greek and Arabic philosophical and scientific works were by then available in Latin at the various European centres of learning. Throughout the next century and a half gaps in the translations were filled and the new learning spread to the farthest reaches of pre-modern Europe, where it was incorporated into, or inspired, new educational institutions. It was at these universities and schools that the final phase of assimilation occurred, as the influx of Greco-Arabic knowledge became absorbed and institutionalized in Latin theology, culture and science.

The earliest translations from Arabic into Latin were made in tenth-century Aragon, in Northern Spain. A major translation activity began in the eleventh century in Spain, in particular in Tarrazona and Tudela. In the twelfth century, Toledo became the main centre of the translation movement. Early translations were primarily from Arabic into Latin, some into Hebrew, and then subsequently into the vernacular languages of Europe.

Centres of transmission where texts were systematically translated emerged along the boundaries between the Christian world and the Islamic and Byzantine Empires. The emphasis on specific types of knowledge transmitted depended on local circumstances and interests. Toledo, re-conquered from the Arabs in 1085, thus became preeminent for the translation of philosophical as well as scientific texts in the Aristotelian tradition; from the eleventh century in Salerno, not far from Byzantine settlements in Puglia, Greek texts on medicine were translated into Latin; in the twelfth century, Palermo, on the outskirts of Europe, became a meeting point for Latin and Arabic scholars, generating translations as well as new joint contributions. Between these centres at the boundary, a network of scholarly migrations began to develop in the twelfth and thirteenth centuries, now also covering the urban centres sustaining scholarship in the heart of Europe, such as

Oxford and Paris. The varying ways in which the different cultures met depended on the local manifestations of a conflict with geopolitical dimensions, ranging from the courtly encounters between Catholics, Byzantine Christians and Muslims in Palermo, to the appropriation of the scholarly and technological achievements of a besieged enemy after the *reconquista* of Toledo. In any case, the Arabic-Latin translation movement, just like the Greek-Arabic translation movement in the ninth and tenth centuries, was not only a matter of the transmission of texts. It was the result of a clash between two worlds, both embodying universal claims to political and ideological dominance, which resulted in the opportunity for Latin scholars to encounter an active scientific culture previously almost inaccessible to them.

The sequence of works selected for translation by Latin scholars testifies to the fascination exerted by an alien and hostile culture supposedly in possession of a superior knowledge that was believed to potentially constitute a powerful asset also for the Latin culture. In fact, texts on astrology and divination were the preferred subject of the early translations. The earliest scholarly compilation in Latin based on Arabic sources and written in the tenth century, is the *Liber Alchandrei* or *Mathematica Alchandrei*, a 'sum of astrology'. Almost two dozen astronomical tables and works concerning the astrolabe were translated in the decade 1140–50. These scholarly endeavours are inconceivable without astrology in the background as part of a popular culture drawing on techniques of science. The great translators Adelard of Bath and Michael Scot, for instance, are said to have been fascinated by practices of astrology and divination displayed in the streets of Al-Andalus and other Muslim towns, such as Tunis, by gypsies and fortune tellers, employing astonishing mathematical skills. Mathematical works in general entered the horizon of the Latin scholars as a spin-off from an interest in astrology. For example, in the twelfth century, Adelard of Bath not only composed introductions to astrology, a set of astrological aphorisms and a work on making talismans, but also translated Euclid's *Elements* and Al-Khwarizmi's astronomical tables.

Another kind of practical interest drove the translation movement in Salerno where Galen's medical works, popular in the Arabic world, were rendered from Greek into Latin from the beginning of the eleventh century onwards. By the middle of the twelfth century, the range of topics covered by the translators was substantially enlarged to include philosophy and the physical sciences. In Sicily, for instance, works by Plato, Anaxagoras, Aristotle, Plutarch, Themistius, Ptolemy, Euclid, Hero and others were translated from Arabic and Greek into Latin. In

Toledo, Gerard of Cremona set up an exhaustive translation program, which was guided by Al-Farabi's classification of the sciences and aimed at systematically filling the gaps in the corpus of ancient writings available in the West. In particular, numerous works of Aristotle were accessible due to his efforts. Medical, mathematical, astronomical and philosophical works formed the core of the translation activities that spread in the thirteenth century to other cities of northern Spain, such as Tarragona, Leon, Segovia and Pamplona.

The translators were a group of self-appointed men, mostly from among the lower clergy, who travelled to the emerging transmission centres from all over Europe in an effort to gather new knowledge from their translation activities. The conscious character of their efforts is evident from the fact that several of them devised more or less systematic programmes for their work, such as Gerard of Cremona of whom no less than 67 translations are preserved. While a few translators happened to be born, so to speak, in the right place, such as John of Seville in Al-Andalus or Hugo of Santalla in northern Spain, most of them came from remote parts of Europe: Gerard of Cremona and Plato of Tivoli from Italy, Adelard, Robert of Ketton and Daniel of Morley from England, Rudolph of Bruges from the Low Countries, and Hermann of Carinthia from the Alps. Only a few of them actually knew Arabic. A key role was, therefore, played by mediators and, in particular, by Jewish scholars, who either cooperated with the Christian scholars or produced translations into Hebrew. Scholars such as Petrus Alfonsi, Avendauth, Abraham Ibn Ezra, Judah Halevi, or Abraham bar Hiyya, were familiar with both the Arabic and the Latin world and mastered Arabic as well as a language accessible to the Latin scholars, whether Hebrew, Latin, or a vernacular tongue.

Several translators also cooperated with Arabic assistants. For instance, Robert of Ketton and Hermann of Carinthia worked with a certain Muhammad, while Gerard of Cremona was supported by a certain Gallipus (Ghalib?) in his translation of the *Almagest*. The Arabic-Latin translation movement was hence, just like the Greek-Arabic translation movement, characterized by intercultural cooperation, in this case involving Christian, Jewish, and Muslim scholars.

Patronage, on the other hand, played a lesser role in the Arabic-Latin translation movement than in the Greek-Arabic transmission, as is evident from the biographies of prominent figures such as Adelard of Bath or Gerard of Cremona. Adelard travelled from England to the border between Latin Europe and the Islamic Empire without any official protection or support, just in order to seek what he saw as the superior knowledge of another civilization. Gerard went from Italy to Spain, entirely at his own expense, just in order to find a copy of Ptolemy's *Almagest*.

Nevertheless, on a smaller scale than in Baghdad during the high times of translation from Greek into Arabic, patrons, mostly of the clergy, did play a role. These patrons shared the same interest in acquiring new knowledge as the translators they supported and had, in general, no ulterior motives, such as the legitimation of their power. Bishop Michael of Tarrazona, for instance, was eager to learn about astrology and astronomy and encouraged Hugo of Santalla to translate Al-Khwarizmi's astronomical tables. He entertained friendly relations to the nearby Muslim court of the Banu Hud, who had retreated after the fall of Saragossa to the town Rueda de Jalón. Thanks to such good neighbourhood relations Bishop Michael had access to the manuscript collection of the Banu Hud. Another patron, stimulated by the close neighbourhood of a different culture to pursue its treasures of knowledge, was Raimond of Toledo who supported John of Seville in translating works of astronomy and astrology. Later, Dominicus Gundissalinus, Archdeacon of Toledo, set up a systematic program of translations in the context of which he supported translators such as Gerard of Cremona, who, in turn, developed his own translation program. Patrons in the heart of Europe became involved only after they had been activated by translators who convinced them of the relevance of their enterprise. Great monasteries of the twelfth century, in particular, were engaged in reforms that also included revisiting ancient knowledge in the context of their educational mission. Robert of Ketton, for instance, sent his translation of a work on astronomy to Peter the Venerable, Abbot of Cluny, evidently convinced that this must be relevant to the monastery's desire to improve the study of secular knowledge. As a reaction, the Abbot of Cluny ordered Robert of Ketton and his fellow translator Hermann of Carinthia to translate the *Quran* and other Muslim works from Arabic into Latin.

There were also secular patrons of the translation movement, in particular the Norman rulers in southern Italy such as Roger II, his son William I and Frederick II. There are a few characteristic features distinguishing the secular patronage of these rulers from the clerical patronage just discussed. The vicinity of Greek culture in southern Italy naturally gave a greater prominence to scientific and philosophical texts by Greek authors. Also individual preferences of rulers could affect the selection of texts to be translated, such as the passion of Frederick II for falconry, which led to the most advanced compilation of knowledge on the treatment of birds for hunting. More important was probably the fact that the court of the Norman rulers provided a place for the encounter between scholars from different cultures who could discuss and even cooperate. Yet, whatever the differences between secular and clerical patronage may have been or between patronage in Spain, France and Italy, its main motivation was, in any case, the hope of revealing the secrets of an alien culture and the riches of its knowledge.

Transmission of the exact sciences: the case of mathematical disciplines

The Latin West knew almost nothing of the numerous Arabic works of mathematics before the twelfth century. In fact, the influence of Arabic sciences in Latin works only became evident in the late eleventh century. However, only in the twelfth century and later was this influence widened and deepened, as is attested by the numerous translations of Arabic works of arithmetic, geometry and algebra whose results and methods were to exert a lasting influence on European mathematics for centuries.

Arithmetic

According to William of Malmesbury, Gerbert of Aurillac (d. 1003), the future Pope Silvestre II, was the first to introduce to Europe the abacus device for reckoning, made up of columns on which were placed counters marked or unmarked with figures.[19] The abacus represents the system of 'Indian reckoning' (*Al Hisab Al Hindi*), using nine figures and a zero as the basis of mathematical operations, which marked the major transfer of Arabic mathematics into Western Europe in the twelfth century.

After his work on algebra, about 825, Al-Khwarizmi (the father of algebra), wrote two arithmetical treatises; the originals are lost[20] but they survived in Latin in several versions.[21] One of them is the famous *Dixit Algorizmi*. André Allard recently published a summary of the relationships between this text and its principal influences in early European mathematics.[22]

The *Dixit Algorizmi* text, considered as the most ancient Latin version of Al-Khwarizmi's lost Arabic text, proves to be a hybrid text containing elements originating from different Latin authors. It was compiled towards the middle of the twelfth century and constitutes a precious piece of evidence of the birth of Indian reckoning in the West. Another text attesting the influence of Al-Khwarizmi's arithmetic, the

Liber Ysagorum Alchoarismi, is attributed by scholars to either Adelard of Bath or Petrus Alfonsus. It was compiled after 1143. Its arithmetical part contains elements recognized as coming from Arabic arithmetical Arabic works by Al-Buzjani or Al-Kindi.

The *Liber alchorismi*, another Latin version of Al-Khwarizmi's arithmetic, was compiled in Toledo around 1143. It is the most elaborate work on Indian reckoning prior to the *Liber abaci* of Fibonacci. Besides the parts attesting a different influence of Al-Khwarizmi's text, it also contains elements which are foreign to the latter and hence accentuates its character as a compilation of different influences, showing the elaborated character of the early Latin mathematical tradition in the light of the positive influence of its Arabic sources.

A fourth Latin version of Al-Khwarizmi's arithmetic is the *Liber pulueris* which contains long passages which are identical to those of *Liber alchorismi*. Yet, it also has many original sections. In fact, the extant Latin manuscripts of the four major Latin sources cited above reveal features related to the forms of Indo-Arabic numerals, which is interesting concerning the origin and diffusion of those numerals in Medieval Europe. These features relate to the differences between the figures, due to the evolution of the writing habits of the Latin copyists, to the variety of ways of writing some of the numerals and to the difficulties of transcription when writing in Latin from left to right.[23]

Thus, we note that the West clearly kept a trace of the forms of the numerals close to those which were discovered in the twelfth century in the Arabic works of arithmetic and astronomy. Afterwards, the Latin copyists gave these numerals the appearance most commonly noted and progressively the existence of a variety of forms shadowed the common source of those numerals in early Arabic influences. More generally, the first Latin treatises of Arabic arithmetic contributed to the diffusion of a technical vocabulary, of which the influence is evident in the widely diffused works of John of Sacrobosco (John of Halifax, fl. c.1256) and Alexander of Villedieu (d. c. 1240).

The diffusion of the influence of Arabic arithmetic in the Latin milieu in the twelfth century led to the genesis of influential Latin works that represented an important phase in shaping Latin arithmetic and showing the results of the Arabic sources. The calculation procedures using nine figures and a zero and practising the erasement of numbers during computing underwent its greatest diffusion due to two concise works published at the beginning of the thirteenth century: *Algorismus vulgaris* by John of Sacrobosco and the *Carmen de algorismo* by Alexander of Villedieu. However, another trend in calculating was represented by Fibonacci's abacus and its lasting influence after the publication of the first version of his *Liber abaci* in 1202. This fact is illustrated in particular by the example of multiplication.

John of Toledo, the author of the above mentioned *Liber Algorismi*, showed in the twelfth century that he was acquainted with procedures which do not use the erasement of figures, but rather the use of the addition of partial products, as $23.64 = 4.3 + 10(6.3 + 4.2) + 100(6.2)$. John of Sacrobosco operates the same way in his sixth rule of multiplication. Other authors limit this usage to numbers formed by units and tenths. The same method, extended to some number figures, is known in Arabic mathematics, such as in Al-Uqlidisi's (c. 952) arithmetic, under the name of 'method of the houses'. This method is precisely that proposed by Fibonacci in his *Liber abaci* of 1202 to multiply, for example, 607 by 607. The influence of this method lasted in European mathematics in later works until Luca Pacioli in 1494 and Nicolo Tartaglia in 1556. It is interesting to note that later Arabic mathematicians remained loyal to this method, as we see in the works of Ibn Al-Banna Al-Murrakushi (d. 1321), Al-Kashi (d. 1429) and Baha' Al-Din Al 'amili (d. 1622).[24]

This example suffices to show clearly the influence which was exerted on medieval European mathematicians by the early Arabic mathematical school of Indian reckoning represented by Al-Khwarizmi and his successors, from the first Latin versions of the twelfth century until the more elaborate Italian arithmetical works of the Renaissance. It is not easy to reconstitute this process in detail, by stating which texts come from which authors, nor even which contacts allowed the developments of the major stages to occur. It remains that historical investigation shows that the evolution was along those lines we emphasized.

Geometry

As in arithmetic, the West was also indebted to Arabic scholars for the discovery of true Enclidean geometry. Before the twelfth century, only some rare Euclidean definitions were in circulation, and the knowledge of geometry in the West was limited to rudiments of practical geometry and some summaries. The reason for this penury in the field of geometry can be found simply in the almost total absence of scientific texts containing demonstrative reasoning. The discovery by European scholars in the twelfth century of the Arabic translations of Euclid was a true starting point for intense scientific activity.[25]

Euclid's *Elements* was translated and edited into Arabic several times in the ninth century. Al-Hajjaj Ibn Matar (c. 786–853) completed two translations. Ishaq Ibn Hunayn (d. 910) made a third translation, which only reached us in the edition/revision of Thabit Ibn Qurra (d. Baghdad, 901). The medieval West made the greatest gain from these translations of the *Elements*. Three Latin versions of the Arabic Euclid are usually attributed to Adelard of Bath; another version is probably due to Herman of Carinthia; and Gerard of Cremona completed another translation. This translation constitutes the most complete version of the *Elements* known to the Latin West before the rediscovery of the Greek text. It includes numerous Euclidean elements, absent from the other translations cited above. Translated from a principal Arabic source of high quality, it displayed the version of the Arabic translation made by Ishaq Ibn Hunayn and revised by Thabit Ibn Qurra and was more faithful to the original Greek. All these features justify the superiority and diffusion of this translation by Gerard of Cremona, who also performed a Latin translation of the commentary by Al-Nayrizi on the first ten books of the *Elements*, a commentary of book X by Muhammed ibn 'Abd Al-Baqi and a fragment of the commentary of Pappus of Alexandria on book X, translated by Al-Dimashqi.

The existence of these treasures of geometry in Latin brought about a prodigious explosion of interest in the new vision of science in the ensuing decades, as is denoted by the study of the manuscripts of the thirteenth and fourteenth centuries, which Arabic sources introduced to the Latin West. An example suffices to prove this. On folio 49r of the Latin manuscript 73 in Bonn University Library (thirteenth century) and on folio 38r of the Latin manuscript 1268 in the Vatican Library, at the end of book VIII of the *Elements*, can be found a rule of proportions: 'For three given quantities the ratio of the first to the third is equal to the product of the ratio between the first and the second and the second and the third.'[26] When expressed geometrically, this demonstration corresponds to the fifth definition of book VI of the *Elements* in the Latin translation of the Arabic text of Euclid by Gerard of Cremona.[27] It can be found, without proof, in a translation by the same Gerard of *Epistola de proportione et proportionalitate* by Ahmad Ibn Yusuf (d. c. 912). This passage of Ibn Yusuf's Latin text was quoted by Campanus of Novara, Leonardo Fibonacci and Thomas Bradwardine.[28] The theorem and its demonstration also appear in the anonymous *Liber de proportionibus* attributed to Jordanus Nemorarius (d. 1237) and in the *Tractatus de proportione et proportionalitate* attributed to Campanus of Novara and in some notes by Roger Bacon on the *Elements*.[29] This is a striking example of the various ways of transfer, use and influence of a result of geometry originating in Arabic mathematics, until the *Quadripartitum* by Richard of Walingford (d. 1335), which is a continuation in Latin of a work on trigonometry by Nasir Al Din Al-Tusi, and in the *Tractatus proportionum* of Albert of Saxony (d. 1390).[30]

Given the different versions, translations and commentaries centred around Euclid's *Elements* in Latin, of which most were of Arabic origin, it is not easy to follow the influence of individual texts in specific authors or treatises. Yet, of all the works inspired by the Arabic version of Euclid, the *Commentary* of Campanus of Novara, which consists of the 'first edition' of Euclid in Latin (Venice, 1482), compiled very likely between 1255 and 1261, is clearly the one whose influence on Western science and its diffusion has been most determinative. The very high number of manuscripts of this work and the thirteen or so successive editions in the fifteenth and sixteenth centuries alone bears witness to the success of this work. However, owing to the lack of an exhaustive study of this subject, we do not have a precise picture of the diverse sources of Campanus, although among these we can cite the Latin works coming directly from Arabic sources or inspired by them. Among them: a version of Adelard of Bath's Latin translation of the *Elements;* the famous commentary of Anaritius (Al-Nayrizi); the *Epistola* of Ahmad Ibn Yusuf, mentioned several times by Campanus as Ametus filius Josephi; besides Latin works of the Jordanus Nemorarius school.[31]

More profoundly, the influence of the rediscovery of Euclid through the intermediary of translations and the original Arabic works of geometry extends beyond the framework of scientific literature to become the basis of the teaching of all sciences. It would be symptomatic of this general conclusion to emphasize the difference in quality which separates the *Practica geometriae* of Hugh Saint Victor (fl. c. 1068–1141), compiled on the basis of an old Latin work of Boethius (d. c. 524), from some contemporary Latin practical works, even from the *Practica geometriae* of Fibonacci (1220) or of Dominicus de Clavasio (fl. c. 1346), for example, where the influence of the Latin translations of the Arabic Euclid is always present.[32] In sum, the contribution to scientific progress in the Latin West represented by the knowledge of the *Elements* of Euclid was fundamental, and it intermingled with influences coming from other Arabic texts of geometry, from traces of old Greek texts (though we do not know exactly how they arrived in Western Europe in the high Middle Ages), and the results of rising scientific activity in the cultural centres of pre-modern Europe.[33]

Other important works of geometry were known in the West through their Latin translations. Hence, the works of Archimedes came to circulate among Western mathematicians after the endeavour of William of Moerbecke (c. 1215–86) who rendered into Latin the Greek text of the Syracusan scientist. However, the influence of the Arabic version of Archimedes carried on well beyond the twelfth and thirteenth centuries. As proof of this lasting influence, we can note that a work such as the *Liber de motu* of Gerard of Brussels (thirteenth century) is intimately linked to the Archimedean work *De mensura circuli* translated by Gerard of Cremona from Arabic. The same is probably true of the *Liber de curvis superficiebus* by Johannes de Tinemue (d. c. 1221). the The *De mensura circuli*, one of the most popular of the works inspired by Archimedes in the thirteenth and fourtenth centuries, together with the *Verba filiorum Moysi* of the Banu Musa, contributed to making known in the West the propositions of Archimedes first book, *De sphaera et cylindro*. They were used by European scientists from Nicholas Oresme (c. 1320–82) and Francis of Ferrara (1352) to the anonymous author of a commentary of *Liber de ponderibus* and the anonymous author of *Liber de inquisicione capacitates figurarum* (fourteenth or fifteenth century).[34]

The Arabic influence on the use of Archimedes' work in medieval science was large and multifaceted in the texts of authors mentioned above, as well as in the works of Jordanus Nemorarius, Leonardo Fibonacci, Roger Bacon, Campanus of Novara, Thomas Bradwardine, Albert of Saxony, Wigandus Durnheimer and numerous anonymous authors. The analysis of particular mathematical problems shows the influence of Arabic sources on the discussion of geometrical problems in the Archimedean framework in medieval Latin mathematics. Given its profound influence, a special mention should be made here of Gerard of Cremona's Latin translation of the *Book of the Knowledge of Measurements of Plane and Spherical Figures* by the brothers Banu Musa, known under the title *Liber trium fratrum* and most frequently as *Verba filiorum Moysi*. [35]

The examples and case studies discussed in detail by the historians of medieval science clearly show the progress of medieval science through the discovery of Arabic translations of Euclid and Archimedes. However, the status of Arabic science in Medieval Europe went above and beyond this transfer of Greek science and provided genuine texts of geometry of Ancient science. If, for example, the translations of Gerard of Cremona played a major role in the spread of geometrical knowledge from the works of Euclid, Theodosius, Archimedes, Menelaus and Diocles, much more numerous are the Arabic authors, compilers, translators, commentators and original scholars, from whom the medieval European scholars learnt a great deal through Latin translations: the Banu Musa, Ahmad Ibn Yusuf, Thabit Ibn Qurra, Ibn 'Abd Al-Baqi, Abu Bakr Al-Hasan, Al-Nayrizi, Al-Kindi and many other authors.

In this context, it is appropriate to refer to works such as *Liber de speculis comburentibus* and the *Liber de aspectibus* (or *Perspectiva*) of Alhazen, the Latin name of the famous Muslim physicist of the first half of the eleventh century Al Hasan Ibn Al-Haytham. Gerard of Cremona was the author of a translation of the first book and perhaps of the second, which brought conical sections to the attention of the medieval West. These two works were complemented by the translation of the *Liber de duabus lineis*, towards 1225, by John of Palermo, a member of the Sicilian court of Frederick II, then by the translations of Archimedes and Eutocius compiled by William of Moerbecke (1269) and at the end of the thirteenth century by an anonymous treatise *Speculi almukefi composition*. These works exerted a decisive influence on the texts of Witelo (1270), the editor of Ibn Al-Haytham's book on optics, John Fusoris (1365–1436), his contemporary Giovanni Fontana and Regiomantanus (1436–76), and on other fourteenth-century authors.[36]

Algebra

Algebra is the branch of mathematics concerning the study of the rules of operations and relations, and the constructions and concepts arising from them, including terms, polynomials, equations and algebraic structures. While the word *algebra* comes from the Arabic language (*al jabr*, restoration) and many of its methods from Arabic mathematics, its roots can be traced to earlier traditions, which had a direct influence on the mathematician of Baghdad Muhammad Ibn Musa Al-Khwarizmi (c. 780–850), the father of algebra who wrote *Kitab mukhtasar fi al jabr wa-'l-muqabala* [Concise Book of Algebra; or more precisely Concise Book of Calculation by Completion and Balancing], which established algebra as a mathematical discipline, independent from geometry and arithmetic.[37]

A little before the middle of the twelfth century, the West discovered this new science, different from arithmetic and much more efficient in treating equations. The link between the arithmetic of Al-Khwarizmi and his algebra can be attested in Medieval Europe by an important Latin manuscript, namely one of the Latin versions of his arithmetic, known under the title *Liber alchorismi de practica arismetice*, the most detailed and complete of all the ancient works stemming from the arithmetic of Al-Khwarizmi. In the unicum manuscript 7359 conserved in Paris, this text contains, besides various chapters of arithmetic, proportions and other mathematical subjects, a short chapter with the title *Exceptiones de libro qui dicitur gebla et muqabala*, which describes Al-Khwarizmi's three trinomial equations reduced to their canonical form, followed by numerical examples.[38]

It is known that Robert of Chester completed a translation of Al-Khwarizmi's *Algebra*, very likely in 1145. This translation was 'edited' by the German mathematician Johann Scheubel (1494–1570), who performed a revision in which he added several calculations to the text and replaced certain original terms by others better known at the time (for example *census* for *substantia*) and, more importantly, several paragraphs that did not appear in either other Latin versions or in the Arabic text and can only be attributed to Scheubel himself.[39] However, we have access to the text of Al-Khwarizmi's *Algebra* in a Latin version translated directly from Arabic by Gerard of Cremona.

Another early trace of Al-Khwarizmi's algebra in Latin can be found in the algebraic part of the *Liber alchorismi* of John of Toledo, which is contemporaneous with Robert of Chester's translation and, jointly, represents the first Latin manifestation of the work of Al-Khwarizmi, largely supplanted by Gerard of Cremona's later translation. These three versions of Al-Khwarizmi's work have not yet received an exhaustive comparative study; for the moment historians note their differences and the ways in which they treat some key parts of the content, such as the second canonical equation $x2 + q = px$, solved differently in the various texts and in the Arabic text which survived.[40]

In the period following the first Latin translations, Al-Khwarizmi's *Algebra* had differing effects and was selectively retained. This shows in Jordanus and Fibonaccio in the early thirteenth century, those two authors providing the basis of the Western appropriation of the tradition of algebra. Thus, in propositions IV, VIII, IX, X of his work *De numeris datis*, Jordanus explains, in his own way and with his own examples, the three trinomial equations reduced to their canonical form.[41] In the *Liber abaci* (1202), Fibonacci takes up the complete explanation of the three binomial equations plus the three trinomial equations together with Arabic demonstrations through the equality of areas and numerous examples; he even used a section title, *secundum modum algebra et almuchabale*, which clearly indicates the source.[42] Following these two scholars, the authors of pre-modern Europe continually reproduced the same proposition, sometimes with subtle subdivisions, which reached an extreme with Piero della Francesca (c.1419–92) and sixty one classes of equations.[43]

However, despite its influence and its various Latin translations, the book of Al-Khwarizmi was not rendered into Latin in its entirety, the first Latin authors were probably only interested in its algebraic part or they had at their disposal a text concerned only with algebra. The second and third parts, on the calculation of surfaces for surveying and on successions, were not translated in the twelfth century. But in the middle of the twelfth century, Plato of Tivoli translated the *Liber embadorum* of Abraham bar Hiyya (known as Savasorda). This text was written in Hebrew in 1116 and contained a form developed in the second part of Al-Khwarizmi's work. A work of the same nature attributed to Arabic author, Abu Bakr, was translated in the third quarter of the twelfth century by Gerard of Cremona, *Liber mensurationum*. Finally, an anonymous author translated into Latin, before the end of the twelfth century, the *Algebra* of Abu Kamil (c. 850–930). Abu Kamil forms an important link in the development of algebra between Al-Khwarizmi and Al-Karaji. With the Latin version of his work on algebra, medieval science received the remainder of Al-Khwarizmi's work, notably a better study of positive rational numbers.

The impact of Arabic algebra in the works translated into Latin and based on Arabic sources of Al-Khwarizmi and his successors, mainly Abu Kamil and Al-Karaji, is well known.[44] It was the mathematician Fibonacci who had a decisive role in transmitting the influence of Arabic algebra, since his innumerable borrowings from Arabic sources were studied thoroughly.[45] Among these Al-Khwarizmi, Abu Kamil and Al-Karaji appear regularly. From the author himself we know that he travelled to many places – North Africa, Egypt, Syria, Byzantia, Sicily and Italy – so one can imagine that his sources of information were many and varied. However, the answer to whether this information came from original Arabic texts or from Latin translations must remain unknown. Fibonacci made use of a Latin translation of Al-Khwarizmi's *Algebra* and the vocabulary he used shows that this was Gerard of Cremona's translation: thus the Latin words *regula* and *consideraction* translating the Arabic term *qiyas* (reasoning) are used by these two authors in the same circumstances. Also, one does not find any evidence in *Liber abaci* of Al-Khwarizmi's *Algebra* that is not perceptible in Gerard of Cremona's very faithful translation. Occasional studies have likewise shown the influence of Abu Kamil's *Algebra* in Fibonacci's work.[46] Although no systematic study on this direct influence exists, scholars have stressed the identical nature of a series of problems in the two works and the similarities in language, such as Fibonacci's translation of the Arabic words *mal* (*auere*, property, fortune) and *census* (square). This terminological aspect leaves no doubt as to the influence of Abu Kamil.[47]

In conclusion, based on our actual knowledge, historians of the intercultural transmission of mathematics between the Islamic world and pre-modern Europe stress the deep influence exerted by the Latin translations of Arabic sources. The *Algebra* of Al-Khwarizmi in Latin signified the beginning of algebra in the West and constituted the basis for the solution to problems of commercial arithmetic during the Middle Ages, especially in Italy and Germany where its use was more developed. Fibonacci's work *Liber de abaci* shows a more profound impact of Arabic sources, his work indicating the influence of several Arabic mathematicians, from Al-Karaji to Al-Khayyam and Ibn Al-Haytham. His work was an essential phase for the new bases of algebra laid down by François Viète (1540–1603), carrying Western mathematics into the modern era.

Transmission of the exact sciences: chapters of theoretical astronomy

We concluded in the previous section that the intercultural transmission of the branches of mathematics between the Arabic and Latin traditions in pre-modern times had a decisive fertilizing effect. Likewise, the influence of Arabic astronomy was fundamental in many of its constituent parts and provided the cradle and the matrix on both theoretical and practical fronts in the Middle Ages. This concerned the recording and classification of observations of celestial phenomena in observational astronomy, the formulation of hypotheses in theoretical astronomy, the explanation by theories of natural philosophy of the causes underlying the hypotheses, the compilation of tables of astronomical data and measurements, and the construction and use of astronomical instruments.

In each of these areas, the contribution of Arabic sources was essential to the birth and subsequent development of astronomy in the Latin West. Historians claim that prior to the penetration of Arabic works through translation in the twelfth century, there was indeed no astronomy of any advanced level in Europe.[48] The little knowledge of astronomy in Europe in the centuries up until the early Middle Ages lacked observations, geometrical analysis of celestial phenomena and reflections on the foundations of hypotheses. Moreover, astronomical tables were non-existent and basic instruments, such as gnomons and sundials, were of a very rudimentary sort.

The following section will present a synopsis of the changes produced on the Latin West in the field of astronomy by successive translations of Arabic works. It focuses on the problems of theoretical astronomy in order to reveal some essential aspects of Arabic influence on the growth and development of this theory in the medieval West, it will show the centrality of this influence on a fundamental chapter of astronomical science in Medieval Europe. For lack of space other aspects of this influence will not be dealt with, such as the influence of Arabic trigonometry on instruments and the Latin catalogues of stars.

Astronomical knowledge conveyed by the astrolabe

The first evidence of the penetration of Arabic astronomy in the Latin West relates to the stereographic astrolabe. In the absence of direct knowledge of the Latin text of Ptolemy's *Planisphere*, in which the properties and the advantages of the astrolabe are described, the West only acquired this knowledge in the twelfth century when a version of Ptolemy's text was translated into Latin by Hermann of Dalmatia (1143) from a critical Arabic revision by the Andalusian scholar Maslama Al-Majriti (c. 1000). However, astrolabes and treatises related to them were known to scholars from Andalus in the northern Iberian peninsula from the end of the tenth century. In this period, technical works appeared in Latin under the names of Gerbert of Aurillac (future Pope Sylvester II), Llobet of Barcelona and Hermann the Lame. These texts consisted of descriptions of the application or construction of astrolabes, extracted from earlier Arabic treatises.[49] A new series of translations in the twelfth century gave the Latin West definitive mastery of the instrument. These translations concerned the treatise of Ibn Al-Saffar (d. 1035) by Plato of Tivoli (Plato Tiburtinus, fl. 1134–45), and various original works based on Arabic sources, such as those of Adelard of Bath (c. 1142–6), Robert of Chester (1147) and Raymond of Marseilles (before 1141). This preliminary phase also saw the success of the Latin translation by John of Seville (fl. 1135–53) of a work attributed to the oriental astronomer Masha'allah (late eighth century).[50]

The astrolabe was an excellent instrument of calculation, permitting the rapid geometrical solution of the principal problems of spherical astronomy. It provided an easy demonstration of the daily and annual motions of the sun and of the combination of their effects, covering right and oblique ascensions, the duration of irregular hours, the heliacal rising of stars and so on. The treatises on the astrolabe dealt with only one main subject of astronomy, namely the description of the daily motion of the heavens, neglecting the causal approach to astronomy and planetary astronomy. This resulted in their containing little technical data. Apart from the positions of stars, the only technical details we find are related to the obliquity of the ecliptic, the location of the apogee of the sun and the position of the spring equinox in the calendar.

Raymond of Marseilles's treatise on the astrolabe,[51] the oldest Latin text on the subject that is not a pure adaptation from the Arabic, contains two tables of stars derived from Arabic sources, whether indirectly through the previous adaptation of Arabic data by Llobet of Barcelona and Hermann the Lame, or directly from the Andalusian astronomer Al-Zarqallu (d. 1100, the famous Arzachel of the Latins). We find in Raymond's text other data borrowed directly from his Arabic predecessor, such as the position of the apogee of the sun at 17;50° of Gemini and the value of the obliquity of the ecliptic estimated as 23;33,30°, which he prefers to that of Ptolemy (23;50°). This example already enables us to identify two notable aspects of Arabic influence on Latin astronomy: the major role played by the work of Al-Zarqallu and the questioning of Ptolemaic parameters in relation to the sun.[52]

Astronomical tables from Muslim Toledo

In the twelfth century, a considerable collection of Arabic texts were translated into Latin, which opened up to Latin astronomers a much wider field of study in the form of astronomical tables. This designation covers a huge variety of materials, which can be divided schematically into three groups: the first comprises elements relating more or less directly to astronomy of the prime mover (tables of right and oblique ascensions, of declinations, of the equation of time); the second comprises the planetary tables (chronological tables, tables of mean coordinates, tables of equations and tables of latitudes); the third group consists of disparate tables relating to conjunctions of the sun and moon, eclipses, parallaxes, the visibility of the moon and other planets and so on.

Three principal sources served to introduce the Latin astronomers to these subjects: first, the canons and tables of Al-Khwarizmi, as revised by the Andalusian astronomer Maslama Al-Majriti and translated by Adelard of Bath; second, the tables of Al-Battani (d. 929), first translated by Robert of Chester in a text that remains unfound, and then in a version by Plato of Tivoli, of which only the canons were preserved;[53] third, the tables of Al-Zarqallu, which form the basis of the collection known as the Toledan tables from their meridian reference. Translated by Gerard of Cremona, the Toledan tables achieved widespread diffusion throughout the Latin West.[54]

One of the first Latin scholars to use tables of Arabic origin was Raymond of Marseilles. In 1141, he composed a work on the motion of the planets, consisting of tables preceded by canons and an introduction in which he claims to draw on Al-Zarqallu. In fact, his tables are an adaptation of Al-Zarqallu's to the Christian calendar and the longitude of Marseille. As in his treatise on the astrolabe, Raymond utilizes the value of 23;33,30° for the obliquity of the ecliptic, which he took from Al-Zarqallu. Furthermore, he is aware of the proper motion of the apogee of the sun as demonstrated by Al-Zarqallu and he reproduces the Arab astronomer's table for the positions of the sun and other planets. Appearing some thirty years before the translations of Ptolemy's *Almagest* and the Toledan tables by Gerard of Cremona,[55] Raymond's work was the first to introduce to the Latin world, through the perspective of a borrowing from Al-Zarqallu, the Ptolemaic method of calculating planetary positions through algebraic calculations and finding equations of astronomical values.[56]

The adaptations of the Arabic tables, and particularly the Toledan tables, continued in various parts of the Latin world throughout the twelfth and thirteenth centuries. For example, the tables compiled around 1145 by Abraham Ibn Ezra for the meridian of Pisa, tables for the meridian of London in 1149–50 by Robert of Chester and in 1178 by Roger of Hereford, and further anonymous tables for London (1232), Malines, Novara, Cremona and so on. The tables for Toulouse seem to have been particularly well used, notably by astronomers of Paris, because of the proximity of the meridians of the two cities.[57]

The large number of manuscripts of the Toledan tables dating from the fourteenth and even the fifteenth century testify to their continued use, even after the Alfonsine tables had become the preferred source of astronomical reformers in Paris in the early fourteenth century. The Toledan tables also influenced the almanacs, which were designed to provide the planetary positions without the means of calculating them. We find this influence explicitly stated by Profatius (d. c. 1307) the author of the *Almanac* compiled for Montpellier, who himself records his debt to the Toledan tables.[58]

In the fourteenth century, Latin astronomy replaced the Toledan tables with the Alfonsine tables,[59] after that their Latin version appeared in Paris around 1320. These tables, a sign of a new stage in Latin astronomy after the direct reliance by Western astronomers on directly translated Arabic materials, dominated tabular astronomy until the publication of the *De Revolutionibus* by Copernicus in 1543. Yet, the link between the new tables and Arabic astronomy was not broken completely. To prove it, here are just two examples studied by historians. In his essay written in 1321, the *Exsposition tabularum Alfonsi Regis Castelle*, John of Murs considered that the Alfonsine tables represented, on the issue of the movement of precession, an attempt to reconcile the Ptolemaic theory of uniform precessional motion with the Arabic theory of the movement of accession and recession (*iqbal wa idbar*). As far as the planetary equations were concerned, the astronomers who compiled the Alfonsine tables made only slight modifications to the Toledan tables, except in the cases of the sun, Venus and Jupiter.[60]

Planetary theories and the geometrical analysis of phenomena

Although the astronomical tables could satisfy the practising astronomer by enabling him to find the position of a celestial body in longitude and latitude at any particular moment, they did not provide any direct information about the study of astronomical hypotheses and their causes. This important branch of astronomy was developed in the Latin West in the thirteenth century under the direct and decisive influence of Arabic sources. The development of this new field of research was made possible by the appearance of a new type of astronomical text, the *theoricae planetarum,* whose aim was to set forth kinematic models that would represent the celestial motions as faithfully as possible. Instead of the highly technical demonstrations in the *Almagest,* Latin astronomers preferred more basic descriptions of the world system according to Ptolemy, as epitomized in two Arabic treatises: the introduction to astronomy by Al-Farghani, translated in 1137 by John of Seville under the title *Differentie scientie astrorum,* and translated by Gerard of Cremona under the title *Liber de aggregationibus scientia stellarum*; and the treatise of Thabit Ibn Qurra *De his que indigent antequam legatur Almagesti,* translated by Gerard of Cremona.[61] In the same way as these two treatises, the *theoricae planetarum* (the Latin Middle Ages writings on the theory of planets) usually restricted themselves to explaining basic astronomical concepts and the general organization of the circles used to represent planetary motions. A notable example of this approach is the most widely known of all those medieval texts, the text called *Theorica planetarum Gerardi,*[62] whose author is unknown but which probably dates from the beginning of the thirteenth century. The geometrical models described in this work reveal the impact of Arabic sources, such as the translated work of astronomy of Al-Battani, the translations of the Toledan tables and those of the tables of Al-Khwarizmi. Different from the standard Ptolemaic methods, they were disseminated amongst Latin astronomers until the beginning of the fourteenth century.

In another vein, the *Theorica planetarum* of Campanus of Novara (composed between 1261 and 1264), combined a detailed theoretical exposé of the kinematics of planetary motions with a description of the appropriate equipment to represent those motions. Included in university programs during the fourteenth century, the *Theorica* of Campanus aided the widespread of ideas drawn from the work of Al-Farghani which was, after Ptolemy, its major source.[63]

Theoretical foundations of the hypotheses

Through the translations of Michael Scot of the commentaries of Ibn Rushd (Averroes, d. 1198), the West discovered works in which the Ptolemaic hypotheses were strongly criticized.[64] Aristotelian physics required that the celestial substance undergo no other movement than the uniform rotation of homocentric spheres. Ibn Rushd criticized Ptolemy's geometrical constructs by showing the contradictions between this physics and the astronomy of the eccentrics and epicycles. Simultaneously with the radical criticism by Averroes, the Latin West acquired Michael Scot's 1217 translation of the *De motibus celorum* of Al-Bitruji (fl. c. 1200), in which the author attempted to reformulate astronomy in accordance with the physics of Aristotle. In principle, the models of Al-Bitruji can be seen as a kind of reworking of the homocentric models of Eudoxus – accepted by Aristotle – with the innovation that the inclinations of the axes of the planetary spheres were made variable, the movement of each sphere being governed by that of its pole, which described a small epicycle in the neighbourhood of the pole of the equator.

The discovery of these texts initiated a lengthy medieval debate on the foundation of these hypotheses.[65] As early as 1230, echoes of the work of Al-Bitruji – albeit still confused – could be found in the writings of William of Auvergne (1180–1249), and a little later in the work of Robert Grosseteste (1175–1253). Albertus Magnus (d. 1280), for his part, was fascinated by a very simplified model of the theory of Al-Bitruji, that is the attempt to explain all celestial appearances by means of a single driving force that would carry all the celestial bodies in a more or less rapid motion towards the west, which would account for their apparent proper motions towards the east.[66] At the conclusion of his discussion, Albert rejects the criticism of Ibn Rushd concerning the eccentrics and epicycles, for the reason that celestial bodies differ from terrestrial bodies in matter and in form. He also rejects the astronomy of the homocentric spheres and finally gives prominence to the inability of this astronomy to account for appearances quantitatively, a failing that was constantly cited against the hypothesis of Al-Bitruji in the Middle Ages and which explains the indifference of astronomers towards it.[67]

The doubts and criticisms concerning Ptolemy raised by the works of Ibn Rushd and Al-Bitruji, by contrast, prompted a deepening reflection on the status of astronomical theory and led to the appearance of theses that would be studied anew in the sixteenth century as part of the polemic between Ptolemaic and Copernican hypotheses. Yet, before that, these theses were clearly articulated by another great Latin thinker, Thomas Aquinas (1225–74), who was deeply influenced by Arabic works, particularly those on the philosophical debate launched by Ibn Rushd.

In this Western debate between physics and astronomy in the aftermath of the Latin translation of Al-Bitruji's work, certain Latin scholastics found the germ of a solution in the work of another Arab author: the treatise on the *Configuration of the World* attributed to Ibn Al-Haytham (d. c. 1040), of which three anonymous Latin translations survive (one dated 1267).[68] The work contains a cosmographical scheme without any mathematical treatment in which the author presents a configuration of the celestial solid orbs similar to that imagined by Ptolemy in his *Planetary Hypotheses*. In this configuration, there is no need for eccentricity, a difficult device in ancient astronomy which separates it from Aristotelian physics. Presented by Roger Bacon (d. 1249) in his *Opus tertium* as an hypothesis created to avoid the difficulties of eccentrics and epicycles, it works as a physical interpretation that invalidates the objections of Ibn Rushd. Conversely, the variations of planetary distances and the non-uniformity of their motions appeared to the author of the *Configurationibus* to confirm the hypotheses of Ptolemy. This was also the opinion of numerous great medieval scholars, such as Bernard of Verdun, Richard of Middleton and Duns Scotus.

The inability of Al-Bitruji's system to account for astronomical observations, and the ability of the construction presented in the *Configuration* of Ibn Al-Haytham to respond to the criticisms of Ibn Rushd (opposition of physics and astronomy), ensured the triumph of the Ptolemaic hypotheses and their physical interpretation by means of the orbs of Ibn Al-Haytham. The most thorough exposition of this interpretation appeared at the end of the Middle Ages in the *Theoricae novae planetarum*, written in 1454 by Georg Peuerbach: the description of the celestial orbs contained in this treatise served as an authoritative account of the structure of the heavens until Tycho Brahe (1546–1601) rejected the very existence of the celestial spheres.[69]

The influence of Arabic astronomy on the medieval West did not reside only in these theoretical debates. Other themes were also part of this impact. This concerned technical problems of astronomy, such as the movement of precession, which refers to any of several slow changes in an astronomical body's rotational or orbital parameters, and especially to the Earth's precession of the equinoxes. On this very technical issue, Latin astronomers progressively shifted from the original values they found in Arabic sources, or the Latin parameters derived from them, and finished by building new astronomical values for the precession movement and its different parameters.[70]

Arabic astronomy in the Copernican revolution

Leading astronomers of the late Middle Ages worked on the analysis of kinematic models to describe the astronomical movements. This task was started by Peurbach in his *Theoricae novae planetarum* and *Epitome in Almagestum Ptolemaei* and completed by Regiomontanus. The latter work, which contained a highly detailed analysis of Ptolemy's *Almagest*, was the principal source for Copernicus concerning the results obtained by Arab astronomers, notably Al-Battani and Al-Zarqallu. In the former work Copernicus became familiar with the constitution of the solid spheres, as inherited by Ptolemy's *Planetary Hypotheses* and Ibn Al-Haytham's *Configuration of the World*. There he also found astronomical results contained in the Latin translation of the treatise *De motu octavae spherae* attributed to Thabit Ibn Qurra and the representation of the deferent of Mercury as an oval figure, the first mention of which occurs in the treatise on the equatorium of Al-Zarqallu, which had become known in the West through the Spanish translation in the *Libros del saber* compiled for Alfonso X[71] and which was probably Peurbach's ultimate source.[72]

The Arabic influence on Copernicus' texts focuses on two groups of problems which relate, on the one hand to astronomical calculations and observations (linked mainly to the theory of precession and solar theory) and, on the other hand, to planetary theory. In the rest of this section, we focus on the second of these issues.[73]

The analysis of Copernican texts, such as the *Commentariolus* and the *De Revolutionibus*, clearly show that the Polish astronomer was influenced by several waves of Arabic astronomers. The first wave was represented by the texts mentioned above of Thabit Ibn Qurra, Al-Zarqallu, and Ibn Al-Haytham. The second wave was more interesting since it comprised the works of major astronomers who worked in the thirteenth and fourteenth centuries: the astronomers associated with the observatory of Maragha (founded in northern Iran in 1259), such as Nasir Al-Din Al-Tusi (d. 1274), Muayyad Al-Din Al-'Urdhi (d. 1266) and Qutb Al-Din Al-Shirazi (d. 1311), as well as by the Damascene astronomer Ibn Al-Shatir (d. 1375).[74] It is true that we do not know of any Latin translation of their works, nor even of any reference to them in the Latin literature of the late Middle Ages. However, it seems that the transmission of certain of these Arabic texts to the Latin West may have been achieved through the intermediary of Byzantine sources. These reached Italy in the fifteenth century, where Copernicus accomplished his studies between 1496 and 1503 and was initiated into professional astronomy and to the latest results of astronomical research, including Arabic ones. Thus the manuscript Vat. Gr. 211, which was in Italy by 1475, contains a treatise dealing with planetary theory (in a Greek translation, made around 1300 by Chioniades from the original Arabic), Al-Tusi's lunar model and an illustration showing the Tusi couple. Further evidence of the use of the Tusi couple is found in the treatise of Giovanni Battista Amico entitled *De motibus corporum coelestium* (published in Venice in 1536), about the motions of celestial bodies according to the Peripatetic principles and without eccentrics and epicycles, in which the author endeavours to revive homocentric astronomy with the aid of models, which are all based on the use of Al-Tusi's mechanism.[75]

In his research into the avenues through which Copernicus became acquainted with the Arabic theorems on astronomy, George Saliba[76] indicated that these theorems were circulating in Italy around the year 1500, so Copernicus could have learnt about them during his stay in the Italian cities. Saliba demonstrated that the various collections of Arabic manuscripts preserved in European libraries contain enough evidence to cast doubt on the prevailing notions about the nature of Renaissance science, and to bring to light new evidence about the mobility of scientific ideas between the Islamic world and Renaissance Europe.

There was no need for Arabic texts to be fully translated into Latin in order for Copernicus and his contemporaries to make use of their contents. There were competent scientists around then who could read the original Arabic sources and make their contents known to their students and colleagues.

The modified Hellenistic astronomy and cosmology that was a product of Islamic astronomy was to have varying degrees of influence on the development of astronomy in several cultures. Starting at least as early as the thirteenth century, or perhaps earlier, one can detect the impact of Islamic astronomy in Byzantium, and there are even reports of Byzantine scholars travelling to Iran to study. The Greek *zīj* that is now known as the Persian tables is one example, as is a more theoretical tract containing the Tusi couple. These and other works reached Europe most likely in the fifteenth century and provide evidence for one means of transmission to Europe.

Of particular interest has been the discovery that Copernicus' models were virtually identical to those produced by Islamic astronomers as a result of their criticisms of Ptolemy. It has also come to light that his justification for the Earth's motion and a mathematical proposition needed to make the transformation from a geocentric to a heliocentric universe could well have had an Islamic provenance.[77]

The influence of Arabic astronomy on pre-modern Europe ended with Copernicus. He was the last to make constant use of observational results taken from Arab authors and who based his mathematical models on results previously discovered by them, as shown above. Shortly after Copernicus, the abundant and accurate observations of Tycho Brahe made all reference to ancient observations irrelevant; then Kepler put an end to the Ptolemaic geometrical models and their Arabic or Latin variations.

Technology, engineering and theoretical mechanics

Medieval Islam was a prosperous and dynamic civilization and much of its prosperity was due to an engineering technology that assisted in increasing the production of raw materials and finished products. In addition, the demand for scientific instruments, and the need to cater for the amusements and aesthetic pleasures of the leisured classes, was reflected in an original tradition of technology based upon delicate and sensitive control mechanisms. In the following section, I present instances of the Islamic contribution in the fields of technology, engineering and theoretical mechanics, and discuss the impact of these achievements on pre-modern Europe.

Some textual evidence

The translation movement from Arabic into Latin which started in the twelfth century had its impact on the transfer of technology. Alchemical treatises were full of industrial chemical technologies such as distillation. Arabic treatises on medicine and pharmacology included a large amount of technological information on materials' processing. Works on astronomy contained many technological ideas when they dealt with instrument-making. Within this framework, the inventions of the Islamic world and the theories of mechanics were transferred to the Latin West by many means, through direct borrowing or via the intermediary of translation from Arabic. For instance, the West was acquainted with the Muslim science of surveying through the Latin translations of Arabic mathematical treatises.[78]

In the field of technology proper, the *Libros del Saber de Astronomia*, compiled in the court of Alfonso X, includes several chapters on clocks and timekeeping (*Libros de los relojes*). Five booklets in the collection were dedicated to the construction of various types of clocks; one containing a weight-driven clock with a mercury escapement.[79] As we shall see below, such clocks were constructed by Muslims in Spain in the eleventh century, about 250 years before the weight-driven clock appeared in Europe.

Translations of technical materials from Arabic are evident in Adelard of Baths' edition of *Mappae Calvicula*, a compilation in Latin containing recipes for a number of crafts including metalwork, dyeing and mosaic, as well as several recipes relevant to painting.[80] Adelard resided in Arabic lands and was a noted translator from Arabic, as shown above. Another important text of Arabic origin is the late thirteenth-century work, the *Liber ignium ad comburendos hostes* [Book of Fires for the Burning of Enemies], a medieval Latin collection of recipes for incendiary weapons, including Greek fire and gunpowder. This text was allegedly written by a certain Marcus Graecus, whose existence is debated by scholars. An analysis of the text suggests that it was originally translated from Arabic, possibly in Muslim Spain. It is now acknowledged that gunpowder was first known to the West through this treatise.[81]

Besides the known Arabic works that were translated into Latin, and the Arabic manuscripts in Western libraries, there is ample evidence that there was an active traffic of recipes flowing from Spain into Western Europe. An Arabic literature of secrets arose, starting with Jabir Ibn Hayyan (early ninth century, the famous Geber of the Latins) in his book *Kitab al khawass al kabir,* which contains a collection of curious operations some of which are based on scientific principles, physical and chemical. Some secrets are called *niranjat*. Military treatises too, such as Al-Rammah's book, contain recipes as well as formulations for military fires and gunpowder.[82]

Arabic military texts and recipes found their way into Latin literature. All recipes in the *Liber ignium* corresponded to ones in known Arabic literature. Numerous other Latin works such as those of Albertus Magnus, Roger Bacon in the thirteenth century, and Kyeser and Leonardo da Vinci in the fifteenth, contain recipes of Arabic origin.

An explanation of how these Arabic recipes, military and secret, found their way into Latin literature has been suggested. In Spain there were persons with a knowledge of Arabic science and technology, who knew both Arabic and Latin and who embarked on compiling various collections of recipes from Arabic sources to meet the increasing demand in Europe. Jewish scholars were most active in this pursuit. These collections were purchased at high prices by European nobility, engineers and other interested parties. Some recipes were unintelligible, but were purchased in the hope that they would be interpreted at some future time.[83]

Mechanical engineering

Irrigation and water supply

With the westward spread of the Islamic Empire, agricultural and irrigation techniques were introduced into the western regions. The Umayyad rulers of Al-Andalus and many of their followers were of Syrian origin and the climate, terrain and hydraulic conditions in parts of southern Spain resembled those of Syria. It is hardly surprising, therefore, that the irrigation methods – technical and administrative – in Valencia closely resembled the methods applied in the Ghuta area of Damascus. On the basis of the available evidence, historians conclude that the present Spanish irrigation systems of Valencia and Andalusia are of Muslim origin.[84]

The irrigation system instituted under the Umayyad caliphs in Valencia was perpetuated over the following centuries and was adopted later when the Christian conquerors appeared in the thirteenth century. The Arabic names used in the irrigation systems give distinct proofs of the Muslim origin of these systems in eastern Spain (Valencia and Murcia) and in the kingdom of Granada, where the chief object of the local water supply was to distribute water to the fountains and baths of the capital.[85]

The Arabic irrigation systems were diffused from Muslim to Christian Spain. This accounts for irrigation traditions in Aragon. Subsequently, they migrated from Spain to America where we still find them practised in Texas. The story begins properly in the Canary Islands where, in the late fifteenth century, settlers from Spain introduced Islamic institutions of water distribution, then both the technology and institutional framework for irrigation and the distribution of water were taken to the American southwest.[86]

Qanats, dams and mills

The *qanat* technology, which originated in pre-Islamic Iran, was an efficient method for irrigation and water supply. It spread westward to North Africa, Spain and Sicily. The Andalusian agronomic writers provided practical advice on well-digging and *qanat* construction. From Spain, the *qanat* system was transferred to the New World and *qanats* have been found in Mexico, Peru and Chile.

In Sicily, a *qanat* system from Islamic times was used to bring fresh water to the city of Palermo and to irrigate its beautiful gardens. There are current plans to revive and reconstruct the Arabic *qanat* and use it to solve the acute needs of the modern city of Palermo for potable water. The project in hand is of great historical, archaeological, geological and hydro-geological importance.[87]

There are many Muslim dams in Spain, a large number of which were built during the tenth century, the golden age of the Umayyad caliphate in the peninsula. For example, many small dams, or *azuds,* were built on the 150-mile-long River Turia, which flows into the Mediterranean at Valencia. Note that the Spanish word *azud,* from the Arabic *al sadd* (dam), is one of many modern irrigation terms taken directly from Arabic. Eight of these dams are spread over six miles of river in Valencia, and serve the local irrigation system. Some of the canals carry water much further, particularly to the Valencian rice fields. These were established by the Muslims and continue to be one of the most important rice-producing centres in Europe. Because of their safe design and method of construction, and because they were provided with deep and very firm foundations, the Turia dams survived the dangerous flood conditions for 1000 years.[88]

Industrial water mills were built in Al-Andalus between the eleventh and thirteenth centuries. Fulling, steel and other mills, spread from Al-Andalus to Christian Iberia by the twelfth century.[89] The first windmills were built in Sistan, Afghanistan, sometime between the seventh and ninth centuries, as described by Muslim geographers. These were horizontal axis windmills with rectangular-shaped blades, geared to long vertical driveshafts. These were introduced to Europe through Spain.[90]

Water-raising machines

The *saqiya* was widely used in the Muslim world from the earliest days. It was introduced to the Iberian Peninsula by the Muslims, where it was massively exploited. Likewise, the *na'ura* (noria) is also a very significant machine in the history of engineering. It consists of a large wheel made of timber and provided with paddles. The large-scale use of norias was introduced to Spain by Muslim farmers and engineers. An installation similar to that at Hama, Syria, was in operation at Toledo in the twelfth century. The noria of Albolafia in Cordoba, which still stands, served to elevate the water of the river up to the Palace of the Caliphs. Its construction was commissioned by Abd Al-Rahman I, and it has been reconstructed several times. The noria was heavily exploited all over Muslim Spain. It diffused into other parts of Europe and, like the *saqiya,* has shown remarkable powers of survival into modern times.[91]

Five water-raising machines are described in Al-Jazari's great book on machines, *Al jami' bayn al 'ilm wa 'l'amal al nafi' fi sina'at al hiyal* [Compendium on the Theory and Useful Practice of the Mechanical Arts], completed in Diyar Bakr, Southern Turkey, in 1206. Al-Jazari's treatise is the most significant work on the Islamic tradition of mechanical engineering and is a groundbreaking text in the history of technology. One of Al-Jazari's water-raising machines is a water-driven *saqiya*, three of the others are modifications to the *shaduf*. These are important for the technological ideas they embody. The fifth machine, the most significant, is a water-driven twin-cylinder pump. Its important features are the double-acting principle, the conversion of rotary into reciprocating motion, and the use of true suction pipes. The hand-driven pumps of classical and Hellenistic times had vertical cylinders that stood directly in the water, which entered them through plate-valves in the bottoms of the cylinders on the suction strokes. The pumps could not, therefore, be positioned above water level. Al-Jazari's twin-cylinder pump could be considered as the origin of the suction pump. The assumption that Taccola (c. 1450) was the first to describe a suction pump is not substantiated. The only explanation for the sudden appearance of the suction pump in the writings of Renaissance engineers in Europe is that the idea was inherited from Islam, whose engineers had long been familiar with piston pumps throughout the Middle Ages.[92]

Evidence for the continuation of a tradition of mechanical engineering in the lands of Islam is provided by a book on machines, *Al-Turuq al-Saniya fī al ālat al rūhaniya* [The Sublime Methods of Spiritual Machines], written by Taqi Al-Din Ibn Ma'ruf about 1552. A number of machines are described, including a pump similar to Al-Jazari's, but the most interesting device is a six-cylinder pump.[93] The cylinders are bored in-line in a block of wood, which stands in the water; one-way valves admit water into each cylinder on the suction stroke. The delivery pipes, each of which is also provided with a one-way clack-valve, are led out from the side of each cylinder and brought together into a single delivery outlet. It is noteworthy that Taqi Al-Din's book antedates the famous book on machines, *Le diverse et artifiose machine* [The Diverse and Artifactitious Machines] written by Agostino Ramelli in 1588.[94] It is therefore quite possible that there was some Islamic influence on European machine technology even as late as the sixteenth century.

Fine technology

The expression fine technology, embraces a whole range of devices and machines, with a multiplicity of purposes: water clocks, fountains, toys, automata and astronomical instruments. What they have in common is the considerable degree of engineering skill required for their manufacture, and the use of delicate mechanisms and sensitive control systems. Many of the ideas employed in the construction of ingenious devices were useful in the later development of mechanical technology.

The tradition of pre-Islamic fine technology continued uninterrupted under Islam and was developed to a high degree of sophistication. Monumental water clocks in Syria and Mesopotamia continued to be installed in public places. The Abbasid caliphs were interested in clocks and ingenious devices. The well-known story of the clock that was presented by Harun Al-Rashid (786–809), to Charlemagne in 807 is a good testimony to the high quality of the mechanical arts among Muslims at this time.[95]

The Islamic tradition of clock-making technology goes back to the ninth century. It was transferred to Muslim Spain, where Al-Zarqali constructed, around 1050, a large water clock on the banks of the Tagus at Toledo in Spain. The clock was still in operation when the Christians occupied Toledo in 1085.[96]

Kitâb al asrâr fî natâ'ij al afkâr [The Book of Secrets about the Results of Thoughts] is a manuscript describing Andalusian monumental clocks written in the eleventh century by Ibn Khalaf Al-Muradi. The book is a priceless source for Andalusian engineering. It includes descriptions and drawings of more than thirty ingenious devices, covering mechanical apparatuses, water clocks, automatic calendars and war machines. The original manuscript of *The Book of Secrets* exists in a unique copy preserved in the Biblioteca Medicea Laurenziana in Florence (MS Or 152, folios 1r-48v). It was copied in 1266 in Toledo at the court of Alphonse VI, from an Arabic original dating back to the eleventh century.[97]

Most of the devices described in *The Book of Secrets* were water clocks, but the first five were large automata that incorporated several significant features. Each of them, for example, was driven by a full-size water wheel. The text mentions both segmental and epicyclical gears. In segmental gears one of a pair of meshing gear-wheels has teeth on only part of its perimeter; the mechanism permits intermittent transmission of power. The illustrations clearly show gear-trains incorporating both these types of gearing. This is extremely important: we have met simple gears in mills and water-raising machines, but this is the first known case of complex gears used to transmit high torque. It is also the earliest record we have of segmental and epicyclical gears. In Europe, sophisticated gears for transmitting high torque first appeared in the astronomical clock completed by Giovanni de Dondi about 1365.

In the Spanish work mentioned above, *Libros de Saber*, compiled for Alfonso X in 1277 and in which all the chapters are translations or paraphrases of earlier Arabic works, we find a description of a clock. It consists of a large drum made of wood tightly assembled and sealed. The interior of the drum is divided into twelve compartments, with small holes between the compartments through which mercury flows. Enough mercury is enclosed to fill just half the compartments. The drum is mounted on the same axle as a large wheel powered by a weight-drive wound around the wheel. Also on the axle is a pinion with six teeth that meshes with thirty-six oaken teeth on the rim of an astrolabe dial. The mercury drum and the pinion make a complete revolution in four hours and the astrolabe dial makes a complete revolution in 24 hours. Clocks incorporating this principle are known to work satisfactorily. This type of timepiece, however, with its effective mercury escapement, had been known in Islam since the eleventh century, at least 250 years before the first appearance of weight-driven clocks in the West.[98]

An important aspect of Islamic fine technology is the tradition of geared astronomical instruments described in Arabic literature. The most notable example is the astronomical geared mechanism that was described by Al-Biruni and called by him *huqq al qamar* ('Box of the Moon'). From Al-Biruni's text, we understand that these mechanisms were known in Islamic astronomy. A surviving example is the geared calendar dated 1221–2 that is part of the collection of the Museum of the History of Science at Oxford (Inventory number CCA 5).[99]

Derek J. de Solla Price, when describing the Antikythera mechanism dating from the late first century, remarked that: 'It seems likely that the Antikythera tradition was part of a corpus of knowledge that has since been lost but was known to the Arabs. It was developed and transmitted by them to medieval Europe, where it became the foundation for the whole range of subsequent invention in the field of clockwork.'[100]

Many of the ideas that were embodied in the mechanical clock in pre-modern and modern Europe had been introduced centuries before: complex gear-trains and segmental gears in Al-Muradi and Al-Jazari; epicycle gears in Al-Muradi; celestial and biological simulations in the automata and water clocks of Hellenistic and Islamic engineers; weight-drives in Islamic mercury clocks and pumps; escapements in mercury docks; and other methods of controlling the speed of water wheels. The heavy floats in water clocks may also be regarded as weights, with the constant-head system as the escapement.

The knowledge that Christians in Spain gained about Muslim water clocks was transferred to Europe. Water clocks in Europe became very elaborate with complications that were often a source of fascination and amusement. In a treatise written by Robertus Anglicus in 1271, it is mentioned that the makers of water clocks were trying to solve the problem of the mechanical escapement and had almost reached their objective.[101] The first effective escapement appeared a few years later.[102] This evidence, circumstantial though it is, points strongly to an Islamic influence upon the invention of the mechanical clock.

Practical chemistry

Other fields of technology transfer from the Islamic tradition to pre-modern Europe include whole chapters of practical and industrial chemistry. Arabic works on alchemy and chemistry were translated into Latin from the twelfth through the fourteenth centuries. As early as 1144, Robert of Chester translated the text of the dialogue between Khalid Ibn Yazid and Maryanus the Hermit. Since then there have been other translations of several works of Jabir Ibn Hayyan (Geber), Al-Razi (Rhazes), Khalid Ibn Yazid (Calid), Ibn Umayl (Senior Zadith) and others. Thus the Latin West became acquainted with Arabic chemistry and alchemy. This included the transmutation of theories as well as practical chemistry involving various chemical processes such as distillation, calcinations, assation and a multitude of others. It also involved the laboratory equipment that was used to carry out the chemical processes such as the cucurbit, the alembic, the aludel, and the equipment needed for melting metals, such as furnaces and crucibles. Knowledge of various materials was included such as: the seven metals; the spirits of mercury, sal ammoniac and sulphur; the stones; the vitriols; the boraxes (including the potassium nitrate)[103] and the salts.[104]

During their extensive experimentation Islamic chemists prepared mineral acids which they called sharp waters. They distilled the materials that produced nitric, sulphuric and hydrochloric acids. In the Latin translation of Al-Razi's book *Liber luminis luminum*,[105] we find a recipe for the preparation of nitric acid or aqua regia that involves distilling a mixture of sal nitrum, sal ammoniac and vitriol. We find a recipe for nitric acid also in *De inventione veritatis* [On the Discovery of Truth], which is a work in Latin ascribed to Jabir Ibn Hayyan that appeared at the end of the thirteenth century.[106]

Other transferred technologies include perfumes and rosewater, the fabrication and the making on an industrial scale of paper, sugar, glass and ceramics, tanning, the textiles industries, dyes and inks, the metallurgy of metals especially that of iron and steel, building methods and the influence of various styles of Islamic architecture, military technology, navigation and artisan crafts.

Theoretical mechanics and the science of weights

An important branch of Arabic mechanics is the theoretical one, which includes the problems of motion, the explanation of the functioning of machines and the application of theories and principles of natural philosophy to mechanical phenomena. The Arabic tradition of theoretical mechanics manifested a marked focus on balances and weights, these instruments being a sort of mental model for the problems of physics. We find these interests in a large corpus of writings unified under the denomination of *'ilm al-athqal* ('the science of weights'), in contrast to the problems of practical mechanics, encompassed under the header of *'ilm al hiyal* ('the science of machines').[107] This tradition of scientific and technical treatises is being reconstituted by the author[108] from manuscripts, most of which have never been published. The components of this corpus, amounting to more than thirty texts, cover the whole range of scientific activity in Islamic lands from the ninth to the nineteenth centuries. This group of texts is unified by a common theme: the spectrum of theoretical and practical problems related to the description, the functioning and the use of various types of balances, and especially of the steelyard, the balance with calibrated beam, unequal arms and moving weights.[109]

Some of these Arabic treatises were translated into Latin in the twelfth century and influenced the European science of weights. Indeed, the reconstruction of the Arabic science of weights yielded an unexpected result: a new understanding of the history of mechanics in terms of an intercultural history in which the Arabic and Latin tradition are successive phases of the same current of scientific problems. Hence, as we shall see below in brief, beyond cultural and linguistic boundaries, the Arabic science of weights afforded a foundation for the Latin *scientia de ponderibus* that emerged in Medieval Europe from the thirteenth century.

The historians of mechanics, from Pierre Duhem to Marshal Clagett, assumed that the foundation of the science of weights must be credited to the school of Jordanus in Europe in the thirteenth century. Now it appears that it emerged much earlier in Islamic science in the ninth century. Moreover, the first steps of the Latin *scientia de ponderibus* should be considered as a direct result of the Arabic-Latin transmission, and especially as a consequence of the translation of two major Arabic texts in which the new science and its name are disclosed, *Kitab fi 'l-qarastun* by Thabit Ibn Qurra and *Ihsa' al 'ulum* by Al-Farabi.

Indeed, the very expression *scientia de ponderibus* was derived from the Latin translation of Al-Farabi's *Ihsa' al 'ulum*. Versions of this text were produced both by Gerard of Cremona and Dominicus Gundissalinus. The latter made an adapted version of the *Ihsa'* in his *De scientiis* and used it as a framework for his own *De Divisione Philosophiae*, which later became a guide to the relationships between the sciences for European universities in the thirteenth century. In the two texts, Gundissalinus reproduced – sometimes verbatim – Al-Farabi's characterization of the sciences of weights and devices, called respectively *scientia de ponderibus* and *sciencia de ingeniis*.[110] The reason for this close agreement is easy to find: he could not rely on any scientific activity in this field in his times in Latin.[111] Among all the sciences to which Gundissalinus dedicated a section, the sciences of weights, of devices and of optics were obviously less known in the Latin West in the twelfth century. Even the antique Latin tradition represented by Boece and Isidore of Sevilla could not furnish any useful data for a sustained reflection on their epistemological status. It must also be added that Gundissalinus seems to ignore all their developments in the Arabic science, including Thabit Ibn Qurra's book on the theory of the balance and Ibn Al-Haytham's achievements in optics. Hence, the effort of theorization deployed by Gundissalinus, by showing the state of the sciences in the late twelfth century in Western Europe, throws the light on a considerable under-development in several sciences. This particularly concerns the different branches of mechanics.[112]

As mentioned earlier, *Liber karastonis* is the Latin translation by Gerard of Cremona of *Kitab fi 'l-qarastun* by Thabit Ibn Qurra. The general structure of both the Arabic and Latin versions is the same, and the enunciations of the theorems are identical, but the proofs show greater or lesser discrepancies. None of the Arabic extant copies of Thabit's *Kitab* seem to be the direct model for Gerard's translation. The Latin version was repeatedly copied and distributed in the Latin West until the seventeenth century, as it is documented by several dozens of extant manuscript copies. This high number of copies instructs us about the wide diffusion of the text. Further, the treatise was embedded into the corpus of the science of weights, which was understood to be part of the mathematical arts or *quadrivium* together with other works on the same topic, in particular the writings of Jordanus Nemorarius in the science of weights.[113] In addition, at least one version of Thabit's work was known in Latin learning as a writing of *scientia de ponderibus*. This version is the *Excerptum de libro Thebit de ponderibus*, a Latin text which appears frequently in the codexes. It is a digest of the logical strucure of *Liber de karastonis*, in the shape of statements of all the theorems.[114]

In the way of a conclusion

The transfer of scientific knowledge to pre-modern Europe between the Arabic-Islamic and Latin cultures, as outlined in this chapter, complies with a model of describing the dynamics of world history depicted in a recent global work by Nayef R. F. Al-Rodhan, *Sustainable History and the Dignity of Man: A Philosophy of History and Civilisational Triumph*.[115] Using an ocean model of a single collective human civilization, Al-Rodhan argues that we should think global history in terms of a common human story that is comprised of multiple geo-cultural domains and sub-cultures with a history of mutual borrowing and synergies. Considering that, all geo-cultural domains must succeed if humanity as a whole is to triumph. This collective triumph, for the author, will also depend on reason and on the recognition that a great deal of knowledge is indeterminate and may be temporally, spatially and perhaps culturally constrained.

Attempting to build a conceptual framework according to which human civilization is one human story marked by mutual borrowings, Al-Rodhan reasonably claims that the perfect example of this is the passing on of Arabic intellectual scientific excellence to the Latin West in the pre-modern period. Al-Rodhan argues, in this context, that cultures have risen in part because of an openness to cultural borrowing and exchanges. Raising his veto against the isolationist views of human cultural history, he claims that it is simply inaccurate and misleading to consider, as do some contemporary authors, that during most of human history, contacts between civilizations were intermittent or non-existent. The Arab-Islamic and Western-European histories, for example, cannot be understood in isolation from one another. There has, in fact, been a great deal of cross-fertilization between different geo-cultural forms. The technologies that enabled the European agricultural revolution, for instance, largely came from the East. The watermill, the windmill, the heavy mouldboard plough, particular types of animal harness and the iron horseshoe, all appear to have entered Europe from the East. Muslim communities drew on a Greek heritage. East of Egypt, the territories that came under Muslim rule in the seventh century once formed part of Alexander the Great's realm and were influenced by Greek philosophy. To Egypt's west, the Arab-Islamic caliphate included parts of North Africa, Iberia and southern France, which were once under Roman rule and equally influenced by Greek culture. As shown above, in the Middle Ages extensive stimuli from Muslim lands influenced philosophy, theology, mathematics, chemistry, medicine, music, literature, manufacturing and cuisine across Europe. Many of these borrowings helped to lay the foundations for Europe's later scientific and intellectual advances, but are often missing from the West's own historical accounts.

Al-Rodhan says in particular: 'Rather than thinking in terms of multiple civilizations, we need to think in terms of one fluid human story with internal characteristics linked to the time and place in which it manifests itself. Thinking in terms of the totality of human civilization requires an approach to history that allows one to conceive of a period of time that extends beyond that of the longue durée outlined by Braudel. A philosophy of history needs to encompass a span of human time that captures human nature and its mastery of its environment.' Rather than thinking of competing and separate civilizations, he continues, we should think in terms of only one human civilization, comprised of multiple geo-cultural domains that contain sub-cultures. Thus, into collective human civilization flow rivers, representing different geo-cultural domains, into which flow tributaries, representing sub-cultures. At the points where rivers (geo-cultural domains) enter the ocean of human civilization, there is likely to be a concentration or dominance of that culture. Over time, all rivers become one. Thus, in the middle of the ocean an equal mix of all cultures exists, although it may be weighted towards the dominant culture of the day. A fluidity at the centre of the ocean exists, nevertheless, which means that the weighting will alter depending on whichever culture happens to be globally more dominant, or on the particular balance that is found between cultures. Borrowing between cultures occurs, particularly between geographically adjacent geo-cultural domains. However, proximity can also generate friction between different cultures. The size and influence of the dominant culture of the day is subject to change and may decline as the influence of another rises, or as other cultures are better accommodated. Efforts to help facilitate a better understanding of such specificities have taken a number of forms in recent years and are based on the notion that common ground exists with regards to fundamental values on which to base a dialogue. Al-Rodhan considers that such efforts are positive, because they help to avoid assuming a hierarchy among cultural achievements, assuming that diverse cultures are viewed as different expressions of a broader human experience.

Notes

1. In writing this chapter I was greatly helped and inspired by the works of expert historians about the Arabic-Latin transmission movement. Special mention should be made here of the works of the following authorities in the field, whose learned works constituted the basis for the sections on mathematics, astronomy and technology. See, respectively, A. Allard (1996), 'The Influence of Arabic Mathematics in the Medieval West', in R. Rashed and R. Morelon (eds) *Encyclopedia of the History of Arabic Science*, Vol. 2 (London: Routledge), pp. 539–80; H. Hugonnard-Roche (1996), 'The Influence of Arabic Astronomy in the Medieval West', in Roshdi Rashed (ed.) *Encyclopedia of the History of Arabic Science*, Vol. 1 (London: Routledge), pp. 284–305; and A. Y. Al-Hassan (2005), 'Transfer of Islamic Technology to the West', in E. Ihsanoglu (ed.) *Cultural Contacts in Building a Universal Civilization: Islamic Contributions* (Istanbul: IRCICA), pp. 183–223.
2. To get an idea of the wide scope of the massive reconstruction of the Islamic tradition of science, technology, medicine and arts, see the following general bibliography: M. Abattouy (2007), *L'Histoire des sciences arabes classiques: une bibliographie sélective commentée* (Casablanca: Publications de la Fondation du Roi Abdulaziz pour les Sciences Humaines et les Etudes Islamiques).
3. A. Castro (1954), *The Structure of Spanish History*. English translation by E. L. King (Princeton, NJ: Princeton University Press).
4. *Mudéjar* is a Medieval Spanish corruption of the Arabic term *mudajjan* ('domesticated'). It was applied specifically to individual Muslims of Al-Andalus, who remained in Iberia after the *Reconquista*.
5. The *Mozarabs* (from the Arabic *musta'rib*, Arabized) were Iberian Christians, who lived under Islamic rule in Al-Andalus.
6. See M. de Epalza (1994), 'Mozarabs: An Emblematic Christian Minority in Islamic Al-Andalus', in S. Jayyusi (ed.) *The Legacy of Muslim Spain* (Leiden: Brill), pp. 148–70; and H. Kassis (1994), 'Arabic-Speaking Christians in Al-Andalus in an Age of Turmoil (fifth/eleventh century until A.H. 478/A.D. 1085)', *Al-Qantara*, Vol. 15, pp. 401–50.
7. A. Ahmad (2000), *History of Islamic Sicily* (New York: Columbia University Press) and F. Gabrieli and Umberto Scerrato (1993), *Gli Arabi in Italia. Cultura, contatti e tradizioni* (Milan: Garzanti Scheiwiller).
8. On some instances of the transfer of science and technology from the Islamic world to Byzantium in the medieval period, see A. Jones (1987), *An Eleventh-Century Manual of Arabo-Byzantine Astronomy* (Amsterdam: J. C. Gieben); E. Gerland and F. Traumüller [1899] (2000), 'Die Byzantiner und Araber', reprinted in *General Technology. Texts and Studies* (Frankfurt: Institut für Geschichte der Arabisch-Islamischen Wissenchaften).
9. E. Barker (1931), 'The Crusades', in T. Arnold and A. Guillaume (eds) *The Legacy of Islam* (Oxford: Oxford University Press), pp. 40–77; C. Singer, E. J. Holmyard, A. R. Hall and T. I. Williams (eds) (1979), *A History of Technology*, Vol. 2 (Oxford: Oxford University Press), pp. 764–5.
10. N. K. Singh and M. Zaki Kirmani (eds) (2005), *Encyclopaedia of Islamic Science and Scientists*, Vol. 1 (New Delhi: Global Vision), p. 777. See also the detailed study by A. Y. Al-Hassan, 'Gunpowder Composition for Rockets and Cannon

in Arabic Military Treatises in Thirteenth and Fourteenth Centuries', published online at: http://www.history-science-technology.com/Articles/articles%202.htm#_Ednref10, accessed November 2011.
11. Singer et al., *A History of Technology*, p. 328.
12. Al-Hassan, 'Transfer of Islamic Technology to the West'.
13. J. Taylor (2003), *Muslims in Medieval Italy: The Colony at Lucera* (Lanham, MD: Lexington Books), pp. 114, 203–4.
14. Al-Hassan, 'Transfer of Islamic Technology to the West'.
15. See sub-section 'Some textual evidence'.
16. G. Saliba (2007), *Islamic Science and the Making of European Renaissance* (Cambridge, Mass.: MIT Press), p. 218; F. Secret (1998), *Postel revisité: nouvelles recherches sur Guillaume Postel et son milieu* (Paris: S.É.H.A).
17. For more details on the interest in Arabic learning during the Renaissance in Italy and Europe, see R. Jones (1994), 'The Medici Oriental Press (Rome 1584–1614) and the Impact of its Arabic Publications on Northern Europe', in G. A. Russell (ed.) *The 'Arabick' Interest of the Natural Philosophers in Seventeenth-Century England* (Leiden: E. J. Brill), pp. 88–108; G. J. Toomer (1996), *Eastern Wisdome and Learning: The Study of Arabic in Seventeenth-Century England* (Oxford: Clarendon Press).
18. Most of the material in this section is summarized from an article I co-authored: see M. Abattouy, J. Renn and P. Weinig (2001), 'Transmission as Transformation: The Translation Movements in the Medieval East and West in a Comparative Perspective', *Science in Context*, Vol. 14, pp. 1–12.
19. However, Indo-Arabic numerals did not spread to the West via abacus counters, but rather through the manuscripts on Indian reckoning.
20. Al-Khwarizmi wrote at least two works, both lost: one specifically devoted to Indian reckoning (*Hisab Al Hind*) and the other dealing with arithmetical problems (*Kitab Al Jam' wa 'l tafriq*).
21. See M. Folkerts (2001), 'Early Texts on Hindu-Arabic Calculation', *Science in Context*, Vol. 14, pp. 13–38.
22. Allard, 'The Influence of Arabic Mathematics in the Medieval West', pp. 540 ff; the results of this publication are summarized hereafter.
23. See ibid., pp. 542–3.
24. This method is known in the texts of Arabic mathematicians as the *shabaka*, translated as the 'fisherman's net': See ibid., p. 550 and n. 54.
25. M. Caveing (1991), 'Les traductions latines médiévales des *Eléments* d'Euclide: A propos de deux publications récentes', *Revue d'histoire des sciences*, Vol. 44, No. 2, pp. 235–9.
26. Allard, 'The Influence of Arabic Mathematics in the Medieval West', pp. 554–5.
27. See W. R. Schrader (1961), *The Epistola de Proportions et Proportionalitate of Ametus filius losephi*, PhD thesis, University of Wisconsin, p. 125; B. Boncompagni (1857–62), *Scritti di Leonardo Pisano, matematico*, Vol. 1, Roma, p. 119; and T. Bradwardine (1955), *Tractatus de proportionibus*, edited and translated by H. L. Crosby (Madison: University of Wisconsin Press), p. 74.
28. See M. Clagett (1976), *Archimedes in the Middle Ages*, Vol. 2 (Philadelphia: American Philosophical Society), pp. 13–15; and Bradwardine, *Tractatus de proportionibus*, p. 76.

29. M. Curtze (1899), *Anaritii in decem libros priores Elementorum Euclidis Commentarii*, in J. L. Heiberg and H. Menge (eds) *Euclidis Opera omnia, Supplementum* (Leipzig), pp. 1–252.
30. H. L. L. Busard (1985), 'Some Early Adaptations of Euclid's *Elements* and the Use of Its Latin Translations', in M. Folkerts and U. Lindgren (eds) *Mathemata. Festschrift für Helmuth Gericke* (Stuttgart: Franz Steiner), p. 140.
31. See for this tradition G. Van Brummelen (1988), 'Uber den lateinischen Euklid im Mittelalter', *Arabic Science and Philosophy*, Vol. 8, pp. 97–129; and J. E. Murdoch (1968), 'The Medieval Euclid: Salient Aspects of the Translations of the *Elements* by Adelard of Bath and Campanus of Novara', *Revue de synthèse*, Vol. 3, pp. 67–94.
32. H. L. L. Busard (1965), 'The *Practica Geometriae* of Dominicus de Clavasio', *Archive for History of Exact Sciences*, Vol. 2, No. 6, pp. 520–75.
33. For example, the part of Fibonacci's text on inheritances: see Allard, 'The Influence of Arabic Mathematics in the Medieval West', p. 556.
34. See the fundamental work of M. Clagett (1964), *Archimedes in the Middle Ages*, Vol. 1 (Madison: The University of Wisconsin Press), Vols 2–4 (Philadelphia: American Philosophical Society, 1976–1980). The seventh chapter of volume 1 (*The Arabo-Latin tradition*, pp. 558–63) summarizes the conclusions of the author on the Arabo-Latin tradition of Archimedes. See also pp. 439–557.
35. See Allard, 'The Influence of Arabic Mathematics in the Medieval West', pp. 557–9.
36. See J. E. Murdoch (1971), 'Euclid: Transmission of the *Elements*', *Dictionary of Scientific Biography*, Vol. 4 (New York: Charles Scribner's Sons), pp. 437–59.
37. On Al-Khwarizmi and his work, see R. Rashed (2009), *Al-Khwarizmi: The Beginnings of Algebra* (London: Saqi Books).
38. Allard, 'The Influence of Arabic Mathematics in the Medieval West', pp. 561–2.
39. L. C. Karpinski [1915] (1997), *Robert of Chester's Latin Translation of the Algebra of Al Khowarizmi*. With an introduction, critical notes and an English version (Frankfurt: Institut für Geschichte der Arabisch-Islamischen Wissenchaften), pp. 88–9.
40. Allard, 'The Influence of Arabic Mathematics in the Medieval West', pp. 562–3.
41. J. de Nemore, *De numeris datis*, edited by Barnabas B. Hughes (Berkeley: University of California Press), pp. 100–1.
42. See Boncompagni, *Scritti di Leonardo Pisano, matematico*, pp. 406–9.
43. G. Arrighi (ed.) (1964), *Paolo Dell'Abbaco: Trattato d'Aritmetica* (Pisa: Domus Galileana), pp. 85–91. See also Piero della Francesca (1970), *Trattato d'abaco*, edited by G. Arrighi (Firenze: Nistri-Lischi).
44. This impact is summarized in Allard, 'The Influence of Arabic Mathematics in the Medieval West', pp. 562–5.
45. On this point, see K. Vogel (1971), 'Fibonacci, Leonardo or Leonardo of Pisa', in C. C. Gillispie (ed.) *Dictionary of Scientific Biography* (New York: Charles Scribner's Sons), Vol. 4, pp. 604–13, especially the bibliographic references on p. 613.
46. Shuja' Ibn Aslam Abu Kamil (1966), *The Algebra of Abu Kamil: Kitab fi al-jabr wa 'l-muqabala*. Translated by Martin Levey, commentaries by Mordecai Finzi (Madison: The University of Wisconsin Press), pp. 217–20.

47. Allard, 'The Influence of Arabic Mathematics in the Medieval West', pp. 567–8, concedes the same influence by analysing a mathematical problem in Abu Kamil's *Algebra* and Fibonacci's *Liber abaci*.
48. For a synthesis on the astronomy of the Middle Ages before the arrival of Arabic science in the West, see O. Pedersen (1975), The *Corpus Astronomicum* and the Traditions of Medieval Latin Astronomy: A Tentative Interpretation', in O. Gingerich and J. Dobrzycki (eds) *Colloquia Copernicana III* (Wroclaw: Ossolineum), pp. 59–76; and a short summary in Hugonnard-Roche, 'The Influence of Arabic Astronomy in the Medieval West', pp. 284–5.
49. See for these sources the classical studies of J. M. Millas Vallicrosa (1931), *Assaig d'historia de les idees fisiques i matematiques a la Catalunya medieval* (Barcelona: Estudis Universitaris Catalans) and (1960) *Nuevos Estudios sobre Historia de la Ciencia Española* (Madrid: CSIC), pp. 79–115.
50. Hugonnard-Roche, 'The Influence of Arabic Astronomy in the Medieval West', pp. 285–6.
51. See the edition of the treatise in E. Poulle (1964), 'Le traité d'astrolabe de Raymond de Marseille', *Studi medievali*, 3rd ser., Vol. 5, pp. 866–900, with a list of existing editions of Latin treatises on the astrolabe, pp. 870–2 and E. Poulle (1975), 'Raymond of Marseilles', in *Dictionary of Scientific Biography*, Vol. 11, pp. 321–3.
52. Hugonnard-Roche, 'The Influence of Arabic Astronomy in the Medieval West', p. 286.
53. There is no modern edition of Plato of Tivoli's translation, which was published in Nuremberg in 1537 under the title *De scientiis astrorum*.
54. There does not exist a critical edition of the Toledan tables, but see their detailed analysis in G. J. Toomer (1968), 'A Survey of the Toledan Tables', *Osiris*, Vol. 15, pp. 5–174. See also J. Samsó (1992), *Las Ciencias de los antiguos en Al-Andalus* (Madrid: Mapfre), pp. 147–52.
55. See R. Lemay (1978), 'Gerard of Cremona', *Dictionary of Scientific Biography*, Vol. 15, pp. 173–92. For the Arabic-Latin tradition of the *Almagest*, see P. Kunitsch (1974), *Der Almagest: Die Syntaxis mathematica des Claudius Ptolemaüs in arabisch-lateinischer Überlieferung* (Wiesbaden: Otto Harrassowitz).
56. Hugonnard-Roche, 'The Influence of Arabic Astronomy in the Medieval West', p. 287.
57. J. M. Millas Vallicrosa (1943–50), *Estudios sobre Azarquiel* (Madrid-Granada), pp. 365–94.
58. For the analysis of the impact of the Toledan tables, see G. Toomer (1973), 'Prophatius Judeus and the Toledan Tables', *Isis*, Vol. 64, pp. 351–5 and Hugonnard-Roche, 'The Influence of Arabic Astronomy in the Medieval West', pp. 289–91.
59. The Alfonsine tables were drawn up in Spanish between 1252 and 1272 by astronomers sponsored by Alfonso X of Castile, and only the original canons survive in a unicum manuscript (Madrid, Biblioteca Nacional, MS 3306, folios 34v-73v). See the recent thorough study and edition of the tables in J. Chabás and B. R. Goldstein (2003), *The Alfonsine Tables of Toledo* (Dordrecht: Kluwer Academic Publishers).
60. Hugonnard-Roche, 'The Influence of Arabic Astronomy in the Medieval West', p. 297.

61. This translation is published in F. J. Carmody (1960), *The Astronomical Works of Thabit b. Qurra* (Berkeley and Los Angeles: The University of California Press). The original Arabic text, with French translation and commentary, is in R. Morelon (1987), *Thabit Ibn Qurra. Œuvres d'astronomie*. Texte établi et traduit par R. Morélon (Paris: Les Belles Lettres).
62. See the English translation of this text by Pedersen published in E. Grant (ed.) (1974), *A Source Book in Medieval Science* (Cambridge, Mass.: Harvard University Press), pp. 451–65.
63. For more details on this point, see Hugonnard-Roche, 'The Influence of Arabic Astronomy in the Medieval West', pp. 292–3.
64. The passages of his works in which Averroes criticizes Ptolemaic astronomy are collected in F. J. Carmody (1952), 'The Planetary Theory of Ibn Rushd', *Osiris*, Vol. 10, pp. 556–86. On the criticism of Ptolemy by the Arabic scholars of Muslim Spain, see A. I. Sabra (1984), 'The Andalusian Revolt against Ptolemaic Astronomy: Averroes and al-Bitruji', in E. Mendelsohn (ed.) *Transformation and Tradition in the Sciences* (Cambridge, Mass.: Harvard University Press), pp. 133–53.
65. P. Duhem (1913–59), *Le Système du Monde. Histoire des Doctrines cosmologiques de Platon à Copernic*, 10 vols; Vol. 3 (Paris: Hermann), pp. 241–498.
66. On the work of Al-Bitruji, see F. J. Carmody (1952), *Al-Bitruji: De motibus coelorum. Critical Edition of the Latin Translation of Michael Scott* (Berkeley; Los Angeles: The University of California Press).
67. Hugonnard-Roche, 'The Influence of Arabic Astronomy in the Medieval West', pp. 294–5.
68. One of these translations, which seems to have been made from a Spanish version compiled for Alfonso X, has been published by J. M. Millas Vallicrosa (1942), *Las traducciones orientales en los manuscritos de la Biblioteca Catedral de Toledo* (Madrid), pp. 285–312.
69. Hugonnard-Roche, 'The Influence of Arabic Astronomy in the Medieval West', pp. 295–6.
70. See E. Poulle (1973), 'John of Sicily', in *Dictionary of Scientific Biography*, Vol. 7, pp. 141–2; E. Poulle, (1976), 'William of Saint Cloud', *idem*, Vol . 14, pp. 389–91; E. Poulle (1973), 'John of Murs', *idem*, Vol. 8, pp. 128–33; Hugonnard-Roche, 'The Influence of Arabic Astronomy in the Medieval West', pp. 296–8.
71. *Libros del Saber de Astronomía* de Alfonso X el Sabio [The Books of the Wisdom of Astronomy by Alfonso X the Learned] is a work that contains Arabic and Jewish scientific texts translated into Latin, and from the Latin into Castilian. *The Books* draw primarily from texts dating from 1254 to 1259. These sources were later compiled in the 1270s to form the present work, which is divided into 16 sections. The books' principal themes were astronomy and astrology, the king's primary interests: the movement of the celestial bodies, the construction of astronomical instruments and, finally, the measurement of time. Among the major sources used for this project, we find the writings of Al-Zarqallu and 'Abd Al-Rahmân Al-Sûfî (tenth century). Furthermore *The Books* served as the groundwork for the Alfonsine tables. See M. Comes, R. Puig and S. Julio (eds) (1987), *De Astronomia Alphonsi Regis: Proceedings of the Symposium on Alfonsine Astronomy Held at Berkeley (August 1985)* (Barcelona: Instituto 'Millás Vallicrosa' de Historia de la Ciencia

Árabe); M. Comes, H. Mielgo and J. Samsó (eds) (1990), *'Ochava espera' y 'Astrofísica': Textos y estudios sobre las fuentes árabes de la astronomía de Alfonso X* (Barcelona: Instituto 'Millás Vallicrosa' de Historia de la Ciencia Árabe); O. Gingerich (1990), 'Alfonso X as a Patron of Astronomy', in F. Márquez Villanueva and C. Vega (eds) *Alfonso X of Castile, the Learned King, 1221–1284: An International Symposium (Harvard University, 17 November 1984)* (Cambridge, Mass.: Dept. of Romance Languages and Literatures of Harvard University), pp. 30–45; and E. S. Procter (1951), *Alfonso X of Castile, Patron of Literature and Learning* (Oxford: Clarendon Press).

72. Concerning solid spheres and the representation of the deferent of Mercury according to Peurbach and his Arabic sources, see W. Hartner (1955), 'The Mercury Horoscope of Marcantonio Michiel of Venice: A Study in the History of Renaissance Astrology and Astronomy', *Vistas in Astronomy*, Vol. 1, pp. 84–138, reprinted in W. Hartner (1968), *Oriens-Occidens* (Hildesheim: Georg Olms), pp. 440–95.
73. For the first group of problems, see Hugonnard-Roche, 'The Influence of Arabic Astronomy in the Medieval West', pp. 299–301. An overall survey of the influence of Arabic astronomy on Copernicus can be found in N. Swerdlow and O. Neugebauer (1984), *Mathematical Astronomy in Copernicus's De Revolutionibus*, 2 vols (New York: Springer-Verlag), pp. 41–8.
74. An abundant historical literature exists on this important topic, of the major results of a rigorous and patient investigation of the history of science, conducted in an international environment and dynamic discussion by several generations of historians since 1950. For a short survey, see Hugonard-Roche 1996, pp. 298–303. A set of representative studies include the following selected publications: W. Hartner (1975), 'The Islamic Astronomical Background to Nicholas Copernicus', *Ossolineum, Colloquia Copernica* III, Nadbitka, pp. 7–16. Reprinted in W. Hartner (1968–84), *Oriens-Occidens: Ausgewählte Schriften zur Wissenschafts- und Kulturgeschichte Festschrift zum 60. Geburtstag*, 2 vols (Hildesheim: Olms), pp. 316–25. W. Hartner (1974), 'Ptolemy, Azarquiel, Ibn Al-Shātir, and Copernicus on Mercury. A Study of Parameters', *Archives internationales d'histoire des sciences*, Vol. 24, pp. 5–25. F. J. Ragep (2001), 'Tūsī and Copernicus: The Earth's Motion in Context', *Science in Context*, Vol. 14, Nos 1–2, pp. 145–53; F. J. Ragep (2007), 'Copernicus and his Islamic Predecessors: Some Historical Remarks', *History of Science*, Vol. 45, No. 1, pp. 65–81. V. Roberts (1957), 'The Solar and Lunar Theory of Ibn al-Shātir: A Pre-Copernican Copernican Model', *Isis*, Vol. 48, pp. 428–32. G. Saliba (1984), 'Arabic Astronomy and Copernicus', *Zeitschrift für Geschichte der Arabisch-Islamisch Wissenschaften*, Vol. 1, pp. 73–87; G. Saliba (1987), 'The Role of Marāgha in the Development of Islamic Astronomy: A Scientific Revolution before the Renaissance', *Revue de Synthèse*, Vol. 108, pp. 361–73; G. Saliba (1994), *A History of Arabic Astronomy: Planetary Theories during the Golden Age of Islam* (New York/London: New York University Press); G. Saliba (1998), *Al-fikr al-'ilmī al-'arabī: nash'atuhu wa tatawwuruhu* [The Scientific Arabic Thought: Its Genesis and Its Development] [in Arabic] (Balamand, Northern Lebanon: Center of Christian and Islamic Studies, Balamand University); Saliba, *Islamic Science and the Making of the European Renaissance*.

75. See Swerdlow and Neugebauer, *Mathematical Astronomy in Copernicus's De Revolutionibus*, pp. 47–8. On Amico, see M. Di Bono (1995), 'Copernicus, Amico, Fracastoro and Tusi's Device: Observations on the Use and Transmission of a Model', *Journal for the History of Astronomy*, Vol. 26, pp. 133–54.
76. G. Saliba, 'Whose Science is Arabic Science in Renaissance Europe?' online at: http://www.columbia.edu/~gas1/project/visions/case1/sci.1.html. See the printed version: (1999) *Rethinking the Roots of Modern Science: The Role of Arabic Manuscripts in European Libraries* (Washington: The Centre for Contemporary Arabic Studies, Georgetown University).
77. See for more details Ragep, 'Copernicus and his Islamic Predecessors: Some Historical Remarks', pp. 65–81 and Ragep, 'Tusi and Copernicus: The Earth's Motion in Context', pp. 145–63.
78. D. R. Hill (1996), 'Engineering', in R. Rashed and R. Morelon (eds) (1996), *Encyclopedia of the History of Arabic Science*, Vol. 3 (London: Routledge), pp. 766–9.
79. J. Vernet and J. Samso, 'Development of Arabic Science in Andalusia', in Rashed and Morelon, *Encyclopedia of the History of Arabic Science*, pp. 260–1. See also A. A. Mills (1988), 'The Mercury Clock of the *Libros del Saber*', *Annals of Science*, Vol. 45, No. 4, pp. 329–44 and J. A. Sánchez Plaza (1955), *La personalidad científica y los relojes de Alfonso X el Sabio* (Murcia Academia de Alfonso X el Sabio).
80. C. Burnett and L. Cochrane (1987), 'Adelard and the *Mappae clavicula*', in C. Burnett (ed.) *Adelard of Bath: An English Scientist and Arabist of the Early Twelfth Century* (London: The Warburg Institute), pp. 29–32.
81. J. R. Partington (1998), *A History of Greek Fire and Gunpowder* (Baltimore: The Johns Hopkins University Press), p. 42; C. E. Dana (1911), 'Notes on Cannon; Fourteenth and Fifteenth Centuries', *Proceedings of the American Philosophical Society*, Vol. 50, p. 149; I. A. Khan (2006), 'The Indian Response to Firearms, 1300–1750', in B. J. Buchanan, *Gunpowder, Explosives and the State: A Technological History* (Farnham: Ashgate Publishing), pp. 51–2.
82. Hassan Al-Rammah (d. c. 1295) is a Syrian scholar, author of *Kitab al-Furusiyya wa-'l-Manasib al-Harbiyya* [The Book of Military Horsemanship and Ingenious War Devices, written in 1280], edited by A. Y. Al-Hassan, Aleppo, 1998. See also A. Y. Al-Hassan (1987), 'Chemical Technology in Arabic Military Treatises', *Annals of the New York Academy of Sciences* (New York: New York Academy of Sciences), pp. 153–66; pp. 159–60. 'Transfer of Islamic Technology to the West. Part 1: Avenues of Technology Transfer', http://www.history-science-technology.com/Articles/articles%207.htm.
83. Al-Hassan, 'Transfer of Islamic Technology to the West', pp. 183–223.
84. T. F. Glick (1970), *Irrigation and Society in Medieval Valencia* (Cambridge, Mass.: Harvard University Press), pp. 169–70, 186, 214, 230, 264–5.
85. Ibid., ch. 8, p. 149 ff.
86. Al-Hassan, 'Transfer of Islamic Technology to the West'.
87. K. Grewe (1998), *Licht am Ende des Tunnels. Planung und Trassierung im antiken Tunnelbau* (Mainz: Verlag Philipp von Zabern), pp. 94–6; D. R. Hill (1984), *History of Engineering in Classical and Medieval Times* (London: Croom Helm), p. 36; A. Aureli and S. Carrubba (2001), 'The Hydrogeological Exploitation of the Calcareous Mountains around Palermo through the *qanat*', *Sciences et*

techniques de l'environnement (Mémoire hors-série, *7th Conference on Limestone Hydrology and Fissured Media*), Vol. 3, pp. 17–21. See for a general history of *qanats*, H. Goblot (1979), *Les Qanats* (Paris: Mouton).
88. N. A. F. Smith (1971), *A History of Dams* (London: Peter Davies), p. 91.
89. A. R. Lucas (2005), 'Industrial Milling in the Ancient and Medieval Worlds: A Survey of the Evidence for an Industrial Revolution in Medieval Europe', *Technology and Culture*, Vol. 46, p. 11.
90. A. Y. Al-Hassan and D. R. Hill (1986), *Islamic Technology. An Illustrated History* (Cambridge/Paris: Cambridge University Press/ United Nations Educational Scientific and Cultural Organization (UNESCO)), p. 54.
91. For a general history, see T. Schioler (1973), *Roman and Islamic Water-lifting Wheels* (Odense: Odense University Press).
92. S. Al-Hassani and M. Abattouy (2008), 'La pompe hydraulique d'al-Jazarī (début du XIIIe siècle)', in A. Djebbar (ed) *Les découvertes en pays d'Islam* (Paris: Editions Le Pommier), pp. 130–5. See also Al-Hassan and Hill, *Islamic Technology*, pp. 45–9.
93. A. Y. Al-Hassan (1976), *Taqī al-Dīn wa-'l-handasa al mīkanīkiya al-'arabiya. Ma'a Kitāb 'Al-Turuq al-Saniya fī 'l-ālāt al-rūhāniya' min al-qarn al-sādis 'ashar* (Aleppo: Institute for the History of Arabic Science), p. 38.
94. M. T. Gnudi and E. S. Ferguson (1976), *The Various and Ingenious Machines of Agostino Ramelli. A Classic Sixteenth-Century Illustrated Treatise on Technology* (New York: Dover Publications).
95. D. R. Hill and D. A. King (author and editor) (1998), *Studies in Medieval Islamic Technology: from Alexandria to Diyār Bakr* (Coventry: Ashgate-Variorum), p. 179.
96. Al-Hassan and Hill, *Islamic Technology*, p. 57.
97. Among the many studies published on *The Book of Secrets*, see A. I. Sabra (1977), 'A Note on Codex Medicea-Laurenziana Or. 152', *Journal for the History of Arabic Science*, Vol. 1, pp. 276–83; J. Vernet (1978), 'Un texto arabe de la corte de Alfonso X el Sabio', *Al-Andalus*, Vol. 43, pp. 405–21; J. Vernet, R. Casals, M. V. Villuendas (1982–3), 'El capitulo primero del *Kitâb al-asrâr fî natâ'ij al-afkâr*', *Awraq*, Nos. 5–6, pp. 7–18. See also the recent electronic edition of the manuscript containing Arabic transcription, with Italian, English and French translations, in the form of a facsimile and a DVD-ROM sponsored by the Qatar Museums Authority, Doha: L. Massimiliano, M. Taddei, E. Zanon (2008), *The Book of Secrets in the Results of Ideas [*sic*]. Incredible Machines from 1000 Years Ago, Ibn Khalaf Al-Muradi* (Milano: Leonardo 3).
98. Al-Hassan, 'Transfer of Islamic Technology to the West'.
99. J. V. Field and M. T Wright (1985), 'The Early History of Mathematical Gearing', *Endeavour*, Vol. 9, pp. 198–203.
100. D. J. de Solla Price (1959), 'An Ancient Greek Computer', *Scientific American*, Vol. 200, p. 67.
101. Robertus Anglicus was an English astronomer of the thirteenth century. He is known as the author of a 1271 commentary on the *De Sphera Mundi* of Johannes de Sacrobosco. See L. Thorndike (1943), 'Robertus Anglicus', *Isis*, Vol. 34, No. 6, pp. 467–9.
102. L. White (1966), *Medieval Technology and Social Change* (Oxford: Oxford University Press), pp. 119–27; C. M. Cipolla (1967), *Clocks and Culture, 1300 to 1700* (London: Collins), p. 31.

103. See A. Y. Al-Hassan, 'Potassium Nitrate in Arabic and Latin Sources', published online at http://www.history-science-technology.com/Articles/articles%203.htm# _ftnref1, accessed January 2012.
104. For an extensive study of this subject, see A. Y. Al-Hassan (2009), *Studies in al-Kimya': Critical Issues in Latin and Arabic Alchemy and Chemistry* (Hildesheim: Georg Olms Verlag).
105. *Liber luminis luminum*, attributed to Al Razi, was translated from Arabic by Gerard of Cremona: see E. Grant (ed.) (1974), *A Source Book in Medieval Science* (Cambridge, Mass.: Harvard University Press), p. 38. A treatise of a similar title is attributed to Michael Scot, but Thorndike presumed that it is the same as the *Lumen luminum* ascribed to Al-Razi in the manuscript preserved in Paris, Bibliothèque Nationale, MS 6517. In MS Riccardian 118, folios 35v–37v the following text appears: 'Incipit *liber luminis luminum* translatus a magistro michaele scoot philosopho', implying that Michael Scot was not the author. See L. Thorndike (1947), *A History of Magic and Experimental Science,* Vol. 2, 4th edn (Columbia University Press), p. 308.
106. R. Russell (translator), with an introduction by E. J. Holmyard [1678] (1997), *The Works of Geber* (Whitefish, MT: Kessinger Publishing), p. 201 ff. See also A. G. Debus (2004), *Alchemy and Early Modern Chemistry* (Huddesfield: Jeremy Mills Publishing).
107. On this distinction and its consequences, see M. Abattouy (2007): 'The Arabic Tradition of *'Ilm al-athqal* (Science of Weights): Texts and Context', in *Etudes d'Histoire des Sciences Arabes,* Textes réunis et présentés par M. Abattouy (Casablanca: Publications de la Fondation du Roi Abdulaziz pour les Sciences Humaines et les Etudes Islamiques), pp. 43–82.
108. M. Abattouy (forthcoming, 2014), *The Corpus of the Arabic Science of Weights (9th–19th centuries): Critical Editions of the Texts, English Translations and Historical and Analytical Commentaries.*
109. For a detailed description of the Arabic science of weights, see M. Abattouy (2001), 'Greek Mechanics in Arabic Context: Thābit ibn Qurra, al-Isfizārī and the Arabic Traditions of Aristotelian and Euclidean Mechanics', *Science in Context*, Vol. 14 (Cambridge University Press), pp. 179–247; and M. Abattouy (2008), 'The Arabic Science of Weights (*'ilm al-Athqâl*): Textual, Tradition and Significance in the History of Mechanics', in E. Calvo, M. Comes, R. Puig and M. Rius (eds) *A Shared Legacy, Islamic Science East and West* (Barcelona: Universitat de Barcelona), pp. 83–114.
110. Dominicus Gundissalinus (1903), *De Divisione Philosophiae.* Herausgeben und philosophiegeschichtlich untersucht von Dr. Ludwig Baur. *Beiträge zur Geschichte der Philosophie des Mittelalters*, 4.2–3, (Munster: Druck und Verlag der Aschendorffschen Buchhandlung), pp. 121–4 and Domingo Gundisalvo (1932), *De Scientiis.* Texto latino establecido por el P. Manuel Alonso Alonso (Madrid-Granada: Impressa y Editorial Maestre), pp. 108–12.
111. It is to be noted that Hughes de Saint Victor, who, in his *Didascalicon de studio legendi*, provided the most complete Latin classification of the sciences before the introduction of Arabic learning, just overlooked the two mechanical arts. On the *Didascalicon*, see J. Taylor (1991), *The Didascalicon of Hugh de saint Victor. A Medieval Guide to Arts* (New York: Columbia University Press).

112. This was noted by H. Hugonnard-Roche (1984), 'La classification des sciences de Gundissalinus et l'influence d'Avicenne', *Etudes sur Avicenne.* Dirigées par J. Jolivet et R. Rashed (Paris: Les Belles Lettres), p. 48. Other Arabic works on the classification of the sciences translated into Latin might have been a source for the distinction of the science of weights and its qualification as the theoretical basis of mechanics. For instance, Al-Ghazali's *Maqasid al-falasifa*, translated as *Summa theoricae philosophiae* by Gundissalinus and Johannes Hispanus in Toledo, and Ibn Sina's *Risala fi aqsam al-'ulum*, translated by Andrea Alpago: *In Avicennæ philosophi præclarissimi ac medicorum principis.... De divisione scientiarum*, Venice, 1546, folios 139v-145v.
113. The *Liber karastonis* is edited with English translation in E. Moody and M. Clagett (1952), *The Medieval Science of Weights (Scientia de Ponderibus). Treatises ascribed to Euclid, Archimedes, Thabit Ibn Qurra, Jordanus and Blasius of Parma* (Madison: The University of Wisconsin Press), pp. 88–117. For more details on its codicological tradition, see F. Buchner (1922), 'Die Schrift über den Qarastûn von Thabit b. Qurra', *Sitzungsberichte der Physikalisch-Medizinischen Sozietät zu Erlangen*, (Chicago: University of Chicago), pp. 141–88 and J. E. Brown (1967), *The Scientia de Ponderibus in the Later Middle Ages*, PhD Dissertation (Madison: The Wisconsin University Press).
114. Brown, *The Scientia de Ponderibus*, pp. 24–30 and W. R. Knorr (1982), *Ancient Sources of the Medieval Tradition of Mechanics: Greek, Arabic and Latin Studies of the Balance* (Firenze: Istituto e Museo di Storia della Scienza), pp. 42–6, 173–80.
115. N. R. F. Al-Rodhan (2009), *Sustainable History and the Dignity of Man: A Philosophy of History and Civilisational Triumph* (Berlin: LIT Verlag). See especially the introductory chapter of the book, in particular the section 2 entitled 'The Ocean Model of One Human Civilisation'. The quotations I refer to here are taken from pp. 29–36.

9

Way Forward: Implications for Contemporary Trans-cultural Relations

Nayef R. F. Al-Rodhan

The development of human civilization is built on foundations to which everyone has contributed. Many of the great achievements in history that are commonly attributed to one geo-cultural domain often owe a great debt to those from others. In this sense, some of the greatest achievements of human civilization have been collective efforts and are part of the same human story.

Instead of thinking in terms of competing and separate civilizations, we should think in terms of only one human civilization, comprised of multiple geo-cultural domains that contain sub-cultures. When we do so, we can see that each high point in the history of human civilization has occurred where the conditions were ripe and, moreover, achievements that have taken place have borrowed and built on the advances made by other cultures whose golden age may have passed.

The rise of Europe needs, therefore, to be viewed as part of a global history. Once this is done it is possible to see its linkages to civilizations, other than that of Ancient Greece, that disturb the historical trajectory commonly attributed to it – one running from Ancient Greece through the Renaissance to modern Europe. As the foregoing chapters have shown, the Arab-Islamic world and the wider East, as well as Ancient Greek civilization helped to lay the foundations of modern Europe, whether it be in the area of science, law, trade and finance, philosophy, humanism or religious reform. Seen in this light, the Renaissance was not a miraculous rebirth premised solely on the rediscovery of Greek knowledge, as is often assumed. In fact, Arabs and Muslims played a critical role, not only as the guardians of this corpus of Ancient Greek knowledge, but also as contributors in their own right to the areas of science and philosophy from which Europeans borrowed for the advancement of their own knowledge. As Goody notes in his chapter, 'they developed their own tradition in astronomy, in medicine, in geography and timekeeping'. As always happens, they did so by drawing on the contributions of others – classical, Indian, Chinese and Persian traditions. Indeed, all advances in knowledge are in some way inspired by ideas developed earlier in other geo-cultural domains. In this sense, Europe is no exception.

Almost every golden age of geo-cultural domains has been characterized by good governance, exchanges, borrowing, innovation and the adaptation of earlier contributions to forms of knowledge and rationalism. A contemporary challenge that we face is to uncover the many examples of coexistence and cross-cultural fertilization that represent parts of our common history, not always marked by conflict but often by a tolerance of diversity and by mutual sharing.

A close look at the history of relations between the Arab-Islamic and Latin Christian worlds calls into question the notion that their relations have been marked by blood and conquest. Conflict certainly existed, but there have also been mutually enriching exchanges that have helped to shape the world we live in today. We need, therefore, to engage in individual and collective efforts to salvage these more hopeful parts of our common history in order to construct a narrative that is not marked by an us and them division, but is testimony to our capacity to coexist peacefully.

As an example of misperceptions, the requirement of non-Muslims to pay a special tax called *jiziah* is often cited as a form of discrimination by Muslim authorities against non-Muslims. A closer examination of this, however, reveals the opposite. Rather than a discriminatory act, this was viewed at the time as a respectful act because Muslims pay a similar tax called *zakat* and Muslim authorities, out of respect for non-Muslim communities, sought to avoid imposing the Muslim *zakat* on non-Muslims and decided to devise an equal yet different tax in order to avoid any perception of imposing Muslim customs on non-Muslims.

My own cursory examination of the golden ages of the Arab-Islamic world suggests that good governance, a high value placed on learning, an openness to criticism, toleration and respect for diversity are vital ingredients for enabling innovation of all forms to flourish. A lack of historical memory is partly linked to the response to the influence of the Arab-Islamic world on Medieval Europe at a time when the Islamic faith and Arab-Islamic culture had a considerable appeal.

As Goody points out, advances in Muslim medicine made use of Persian knowledge that had itself been catalysed by the contributions of earlier geo-cultural domains and from the Indian tradition. Through their pioneering hospitals, Arabs and Muslims passed on their own tradition to Europe, the resurrection of classical knowledge already forming part of an Islamic renaissance, before both classical and Muslim knowledge became part of a European renaissance.

In his chapter, Abattouy amply demonstrates the transmission of Arabic science and technology to Medieval Europe. The Arabic to Latin translation movement led to a transformation of science and medicine and, in so doing, helped to lay the foundations for the advancement of science in pre-modern Europe. The translation of scientific texts from Arabic to Latin brought serious scientific knowledge to Europe in the twelfth century, with the greatest impact in mathematics, astronomy, chemistry and medicine. Indeed, that influence was not short-lived; Europeans continued to demonstrate interest in scientific knowledge coming from the East right up to the seventeenth century.

The contribution of the Arab-Islamic world to the European Enlightenment also disrupts the self-imposed European historical trajectory running from Classical Antiquity to the Renaissance. As Ould Mohamedou argues, this is rarely acknowledged, forming part of the general historical amnesia from which the collective memory of the West tends to habitually suffer. Yet, approaches to the acquisition of knowledge that were fundamental to the rise of the West have Arab-Islamic origins. A strong tradition of reasoning that invited individual judgement, and thus enlightenment, developed within the Islamic Empire that long predated the European Enlightenment. Indeed, this point is particularly well-highlighted by Attar's discussion of Ibn Tufayl's *Hayy Ibn Yaqzan*, a novel, written in the twelfth century, that specifically dealt with the importance of individual reasoning, and contributed to the development of rationalist philosophy in its own right as well as through its replication in the works of prominent European philosophers, such as Descartes. Another innovation within the Arab-Islamic tradition was the use of reason as well as observation in the development of scientific knowledge. This went beyond the Hellenic tradition of observation. It also freed the study of nature from religion and politics. European humanists were influenced by this tradition and, in many ways, carried it on. Indeed, this freedom of thought partly contributed to the rise of secularism in Europe, something that may seem counterintuitive given the dominant assumption in the West that Islam is, by its very nature, incompatible with enlightenment through the use of individual reason.

As we have seen, not only did the Arab-Islamic world contribute to the intellectual foundations of the rise of the West, but also to its material and institutional bases. As outlined by Hobson, Europe may not have pioneered the growth in trade and finance upon which its rise was partly built. Indeed, the notion that the modern capitalist world was created solely by Europeans has to be problematized, since the East in general and Muslims in particular did a great deal to lay the path to modern capitalism. As Hobson notes in his chapter, 'Islam acted as the bridge of the world, serving to diffuse all manner of Eastern and Islamic resource portfolios into Europe, from which it benefited immeasurably'. This point is also highlighted by Goody, who emphasizes that commercial and industrial activities in the Near East and India helped to fuel the Industrial Revolution in Europe and the rise of European capitalism. He makes the interesting point that the Near East's importation of precious metals helped to fuel the growth of Venetian trade and, by so doing, the Italian Renaissance. The notion that capitalism could only have emerged in Europe as the result of a particular kind of ethics or due to the emergence of a rule of law also needs to be revisited. In relation to rationality and the rule of law, Watanabe suggests that rational procedures that underpinned the emergence of a rule of law in Europe, and played a critical role in creating an environment conducive to the emergence of capitalism, may have some of their origins in Islamic legal institutions. This also implies that the idea the rational, impersonal state in Europe may not have stood in such stark contrast to oriental despotism, as has often been claimed within European historiography. Indeed, Islamic institutions may have played a role in enabling the development of the modern, impersonal European state and, in so doing, the separation of church and state in Europe, most notably in England, as well as the breakdown of feudal relations and the eventual emergence of capitalism in Europe.

Islam may have even influenced the reform of Christianity, as Guerin argues. Within mainstream European historiography the Reformation is viewed as instrumental in bringing about the emergence of Western modernity. Specifically, it is thought to have been influential in the rise of the nation state in Europe, as well as in liberating European political and social institutions from ecclesiasticism, generating religious tolerance and freedom of conscience, and propelling the rise of modern capitalism. The very identity of Europe is, therefore, intertwined with the processes put in motion by the Protestant Reformation. However, as Guerin notes, exchanges of ideas between East and West merit greater attention from historians. She argues that Islam played an important role in the construction of Protestant theology and confessional identities, albeit often through a process of polarization. Religious tolerance and freedom of conscience in the Ottoman Empire was directly experienced by Protestant communities in Ottoman-ruled Christian lands. Protestant travellers and preachers also witnessed this permissive environment. This generated a cultural affinity between Protestants and Muslims that is not acknowledged in conventional European accounts of their own history. The Arab-Islamic world was also at the centre of developments associated with the Reformation, such as the establishment of universities and the use of paper and block printing, which were imports from the East. Reformation history may, therefore, reveal a great deal about the role of Islam in the emergence of modern Europe.

When the contribution of the Arab-Islamic world to the emergence of the modern West is acknowledged, the foundations of European cultural identity are radically disturbed. The division between the European Self and the oriental Other suddenly appears more problematic than before. This should not, of course, be surprising given the myriad of exchanges that took place between Europe and the Arab-Islamic world as a result of the movement of people, ideas and goods. Even during times of adversity, cultural exchanges occurred. Crusaders were transmitters of ideas and institutions from the Arab-Islamic Empire to Europe. Indeed, this fits with my previously published 'ocean model of one human civilization' outlined in the introduction to this book, in which all geo-cultural domains, like rivers, feed into a broader and deeper ocean or human civilization. There is an element of the East in the West. This not only problematizes the construction of European identity, but also the European or Western Self in relation to the oriental Other. Qualities customarily attributed to Europe and the West – that propelled its phenomenal rise – no longer appear as inherently European. This in itself also suggests that the question posed by so many students of European and Western history, namely 'Why Europe?' needs to be revisited. Intellectual curiosity and rationality were not, as we have seen, specific to Europe as is often posited.

Another consequence of Europe's Eastern heritage is that the position of the East is no longer so reassuringly inferior to that of the West in global history. Indeed, the Arab-Islamic world's contribution to the rise of West, as Ould Mohamedou points out, undermines the assumption generated by the dominant narrative of the West that universal principles belong to Europe and the West alone. This has very real political consequences, since the Arab-Islamic world in particular and the East in general are, for the most part, viewed as the domains of particularism and, as such, relegated to a peripheral and subordinate role in the onward march of history, which, if we are to believe Francis Fukuyama, is the march toward Western-style liberal democracy.[1] It is far from the case that the East has contributed nothing to the West or that the West has a monopoly on characteristics frequently associated with modernity. It is, thus, not the case that the West occupies a unique position from which to bring civilization to non-Western areas of the world.

Above all, the foregoing chapters urge us to acknowledge and to better comprehend the complex nature of different geo-cultural domains, to move beyond stereotypes that do not stand up to closer inspection, but are so convenient for those who are intent on sowing the seeds of discord. Closure and intolerance are not the basis upon which sustainable advances can be built. It is useful to recall that the triumph of the Arab-Islamic world was in no small way due to openness and tolerance that characterized its golden age, when advances in knowledge were embraced regardless of the race, religion or ethnicity of the scholar. We have much to learn from this in today's world. Cultural and ethnic diversity needs to be thought of as benefiting humanity's future, survival, strength and excellence, rather than as a threat to be feared and controlled. In our present era, Islam is viewed as a foreign and threatening presence in Europe, whose Enlightenment history is seen as setting it radically apart from the Muslim world. It is true that conservatism and retrenchment did take place in the Arab-Islamic Empire and prevented the continuation of the achievements of the golden age of the ninth and tenth centuries. Yet, at least part of what Europe represents today is due to the renaissance and enlightenment tradition that developed in the Arab-Islamic world and was inherited by Europe. Recognition of this transmission is a foundation upon which mutual respect may be built. After all, we cannot respect others if we do not acknowledge their achievements. Indeed, respect and recognition are critical to improving intercultural relations.

Despite its importance for harmonious relations, culture has tended to be neglected as an important dimension of global security, except in negative and even apocalyptic terms, Samuel Huntington's clash of civilizations thesis being one of the most prominent examples of this.[2] It is true that as people are increasingly connected to each other and able to access information about what is happening elsewhere in the world, negative cross-cultural exchanges do have the capacity to make a significant impact on the domestic affairs of states as well as on world affairs. Yet, this does not mean that a clash is inevitable. What this does imply is that we need to take culture seriously. We have seen that positive exchanges can have a profound impact on history too. Contact and exchanges today are marked by their unprecedented intensity and scope of relations. This offers up tremendous opportunities. Indeed, decisive contributions to humanity's collective knowledge have historically occurred as a result of borrowing and exchanges.[3]

Trans-cultural security, nevertheless, needs to be actively pursued. The notion of trans-cultural security suggests that cross-cultural relations may be viewed as a legitimate subject of security. Elsewhere, I have put forward 'a multi-sum security principle' that, along with justice, is a prerequisite for global security. This principle states that: 'In a globalized world, security can no longer be thought of as a zero-sum game involving states alone. Global security, instead, has five dimensions that include human, environmental, national, transnational, and trans-cultural security, and, therefore, global security and the security of any state or culture cannot be achieved without good governance at all levels that guarantees security through justice for all individuals, states, and cultures.'[4] Trans-cultural security is, thus, essential for overall global security, as depicted in Figure 9.1.

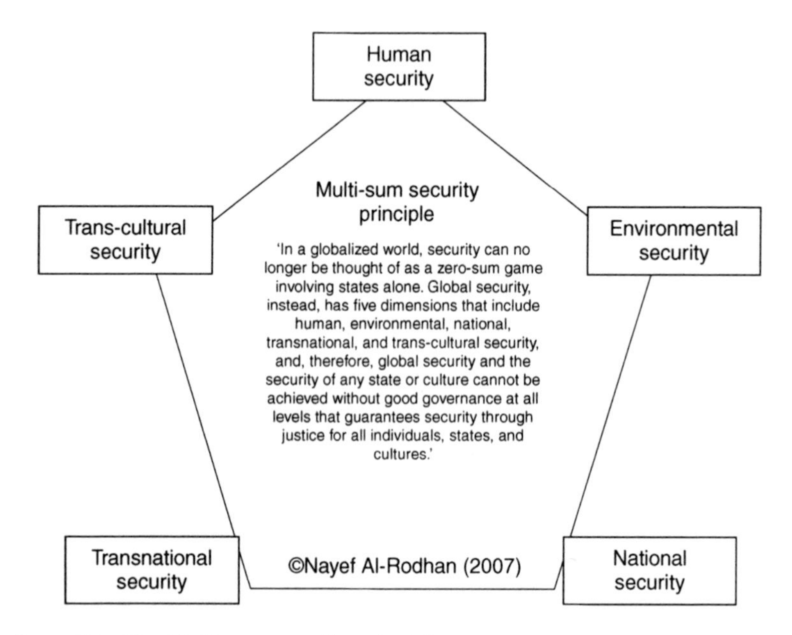

Figure 9.1 The Multi-sum security principle

Source: N. R. F. Al-Rodhan (2007), *The Five Dimensions of Global Security: Proposal for a Multi-sum Security Principle* (Berlin: LIT), p. 31, reproduced with the permission of LIT.

Trans-cultural security requires an awareness of the cross-fertilization of ideas, techniques and institutions that have taken place between diverse geo-cultural domains, enriching a broader human civilization. As the chapters of this book have shown, there is a rich heritage of exchange that needs to be more broadly recognized among the general populace. This can only be achieved through efforts to generate a more holistic view of history, as well as a re-orienting of Western historiography, which itself will require a great deal more research to be carried out in a number of domains, including those discussed in the chapters of this book. Not only would this help the West in general, and Europe in particular, to understand their own heritage, but it would also help to illuminate the foundations of aspects of a shared consciousness and common action that exist but have been obscured.

Yet, recognizing a common and richly intertwined heritage is not enough to ensure trans-cultural security. It also has to be generated through good governance that specifically aims to promote positive intercultural relations. Good governance, which is at the heart of human dignity and the triumph of human civilization, does not, however, imply the need for a uniformity of political systems.

Rather than assuming the end of history in Fukuyama's terms (the triumph of Western liberal democracy), which itself can be counter-productive to harmonious relations between peoples of different cultures, we should aim for a sustainable history. Sustainable history does not presuppose that Western liberal democracy is the end towards which all peoples are working. Although Western-type liberal democracies have been very successful, there are still persistent inequalities in some sections of these societies. In other words, freedom alone is not enough and, according to my sustainable history theory, the guarantee of the nine human dignity needs for all, at all times and under all circumstances (mentioned below) is essential for the sustainability and prosperity of these societies in the long term. In the case of the Arab-Islamic world, where religion is central to people's lives, endogenous good governance paradigms, need to be developed in keeping with local cultures and histories, while meeting minimal global criteria. These governance models will also need to be acceptable, appropriate and affordable by the local populations for them to be sustainable. The imposition of governance models from elsewhere will be rejected at three levels: the political elites will reject them due to the fear of external geopolitical control and influence; the cultural elites will reject them due to the concern of cultural hegemony; while the masses will reject them because they will equate them with the perceived West's effort to de-Islamize the Arab-Islamic world. These cultural frameworks for governance cannot and should not be used by autocratic regimes to stall or avoid the speedy development of accountable and transparent governance models that cater for the people's dignity, needs and aspirations. An evolutionary approach is preferred in most instances, except in situations where brutality is rampant, in which case the international system will need to intervene collectively. One challenge that we face is to agree on the minimum criteria for good governance that are not perceived as a threat to cultural traditions, and to draw on moral concepts that are indigenous to specific cultural settings while meeting the minimal global criteria of governance and human rights and diversity to ensure maximum and sustainable moral and political cooperation.[5] In my own sustainable history theory, I argue that any sustainable political order, whether national or global, will be mediated through good governance paradigms that balance nine

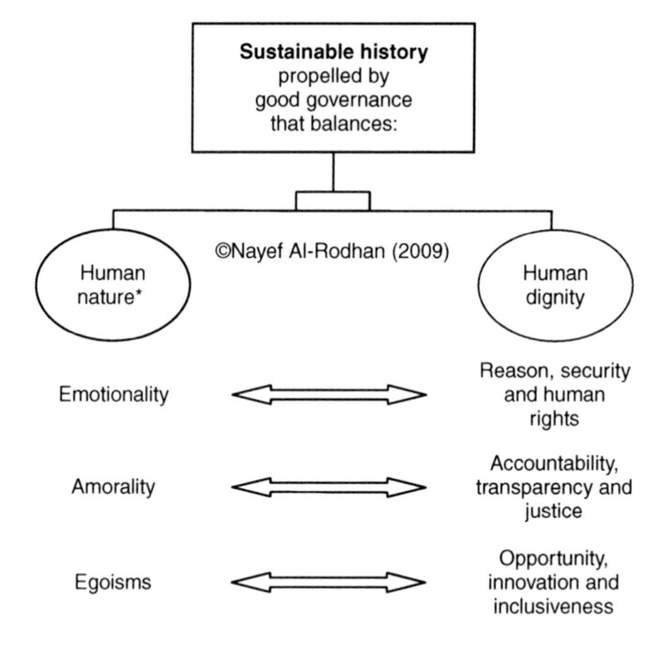

Figure 9.2 Sustainable history

Note: *See N. R. F. Al-Rodhan (2008), *'Emotional Amoral Egoism': A Neurophilosophical Theory of Human Nature and its Universal Security Implications* (Berlin: LIT).

Source: N. R. F. Al-Rodhan (2009), *Sustainable History and the Dignity of Man: A Philosophy of History and Civilisational Triumph* (Berlin: LIT), p. 15, reproduced with the permission of LIT.

fundamental human dignity needs (reason, security, human rights, accountability, transparency, justice, opportunity, innovation and inclusiveness) with three central human nature attributes (emotionality, amorality and egoisms),[6] as shown in Figure 9.2.

Prerequisites for sustainable history may include: (1) the triumph of *all* individual geo-cultural domains; (2) a minimum criteria of human needs and dignity; (3) a minimum criteria of global justice; (4) a minimum criteria of inclusive, good national and global governance; (5) the multi-sum security principle; (6) symbiotic realism; (7) neo-statecraft and meta-geopolitics; and (8) trans-cultural synergy and universal axiology.

The sustainable history theory is relevant to the idea of trans-cultural harmony, synergy and a more dignified, inclusive and just global order, because these can only be achieved through good global governance paradigms that ensure an equilibrium between human nature attributes and human dignity needs. Minimum criteria of inclusive and effective good global governance may include: (1) effective multilateralism; (2) effective multilateral institutions; (3) representative multilateral decision-making structures; (4) dialogue; (5) accountability; (6) transparency; (7) burden-sharing; and (8) stronger partnerships between multilateral organizations and civil society.

Moreover, future advances in human knowledge will depend on allowing individual judgement and intellectual freedom to be freely exercised and this will need to be ensured not only by governance structures that create opportunity, innovation and inclusiveness, but also by those that allow individual reason, security and human rights. Civilizational triumph is important because if it is not actively sought, conflictual relations between members of geo-cultural domains may become a self-fulfilling prophecy.[7]

In this regard, education is of major relevance in achieving trans-cultural synergy and global security. To be effective, any education program must include: (1) empowerment and development; (2) global knowledge of histories and cultures; (3) cultural respect and understanding; (4) communication, exchange, and exposure; (5) global citizenry through responsible media and political statements; (6) global values and equality; (7) abuse of knowledge; and (8) other truths and views.

This will also require the success of individual geo-cultural domains if humanity as a whole is to triumph. The idea of regional triumph in a globalized, connected and interdependent world will not be sustainable. Prerequisites for the triumph of individual geo-cultural domains may include : (1) good governance; (2) cultural borrowing; (3) innovation;

(4) more reason; (5) less dogma; (6) respect and tolerance of diversity; (7) inclusiveness; and (8) the success of other individual geo-cultural domains.

A sustainable progressive trajectory also depends on our collective triumph. For this to occur, trans-cultural synergy is essential. This is because the success of any one geo-cultural domain is likely to be dependent on that of another; a geo-cultural domain cannot excel in isolation from others. Greater inclusiveness needs to be promoted through policies and governance structures aimed at reducing structural inequality and promoting inter-civilizational understanding and dialogue.

Civilizational triumph is therefore not a zero-sum enterprise that favours one geo-cultural domain over another. Justice is paramount to civilizational triumph because of its centrality to the need for human dignity, to the success of individual geo-cultural domains and to the well-being of human civilization. While contact and exchanges have taken place between people of different cultures for millennia, the present is marked by the unprecedented intensity and scope of relations. This offers up great opportunities on a number of levels. Historically, decisive contributions to humanity's collective knowledge have often occurred as a result of borrowing and exchanges.

In today's world, a focus purely on extremism, whether in the Arab-Islamic world or the West, will not alleviate the root causes of tensions between members of different cultures. It will only alienate those who do not recognize themselves in those stereotypes and generate fear and misunderstanding. Cultural essentialism is, thus, intimately tied to power relations. Fixity, homogeneity and separateness are prioritized within an essentialist framework. Therefore, part of any effort to resist essentialism is recognizing diversity within difference, contingency, mutability and connectedness. One of the key ingredients of coexistence and successful cooperation is trust.

A universal axiology would therefore need to identify the common normative ideals that we have in the diverse moral languages that underpin our fundamental values. This is likely to take place through communication, exploration and an increased awareness of cultural and religious diversity, making dialogue as well as research, education and exchanges critical. Given that our moral codes are normative ideals, it ought to be possible to develop a global moral code on the basis of common universal values. Trans-cultural synergy and universal axiology could be achieved through: (1) dialogue; (2)

agreed upon rules and ethics of dialogue; (3) mutual understanding; (4) tolerance and respect; (5) mutual learning; (6) identification of a moral minimum; (7) reduction of the technological gap; and (8) fair representation.

One means of breaking down essentialist conceptions of geo-cultural domains and highlighting their interconnectedness within a much broader human civilization is to research and raise awareness of the many and varied instances of exchanges and borrowings that have taken place between different geo-cultural domains. This is important not only for diminishing cultural arrogance, but also for building greater understanding, respect and trust among members of the world's cultures. All relationships of trust and respect are premised, among other things, on reciprocity, and that includes a recognition of the achievements of others and our debts to them.

Indeed, collective triumph will also depend on both the application of reason and the recognition that a great deal of knowledge is indeterminate and may be temporally, spatially and perhaps culturally constrained.

In order to ensure a well-educated, tolerant and peaceful world, it is critical to realize and teach that there are all kinds of moral truths that see the world from different perspectives and none of them have to be necessarily more right than the other. Therefore, in my view, there is no reason why a clash of civilizations is inevitable. However, if civilizations are securitized and become intertwined with geopolitical interests, it is likely that we may experience what appears to be a clash between civilizations. In some instances, ideology, identity and geopolitical issues may become entangled. Yet, differences between civilizational forms do not have to constitute a cause for fear or insecurity and, therefore, conflict.

Cultural and ethnic diversity needs to be thought of as benefiting humanity's future, survival, strength and excellence. It promotes what I call cultural vigour similar to the way in which molecular/genetic diversity promotes hybrid vigour in nature and thus strength, resilience and a higher potential for a problem/disease-free future. Therefore, what I call 'the natural selection of ideas', which is comparable to nature's way of selecting genetic traits, will result in what I term 'the survival of the fittest ideas in the long run'.[8] Thus, in the end, the best ideas and ideologies will prevail, because they are the most just and dignified, and the most likely to appeal to sustainable and conflict-free self-interest in the form of emotional egoism, which is a powerful motivating factor for humankind.[9]

Notes

1. See F. Fukuyama (1992), *The End of History and the Last Man* (New York: The Free Press).
2. See S. P. Huntington (1996), *The Clash of Civilizations and the Remaking of World Order* (London: Simon & Schuster).
3. N. R. F. Al-Rodhan (2009), *Sustainable History and the Dignity of Man: A Philosophy of History and Civilisational Triumph* (Berlin: LIT Verlag), p. 385.
4. N. R. F. Al-Rodhan (2007), *The Five Dimensions of Global Security: Proposal for a Multi-sum Security Principle* (Berlin: LIT Verlag), p. 115.
5. Al-Rodhan, *Sustainable History and the Dignity of Man*, pp. 172–3.
6. See ibid.
7. Ibid., p. 219.
8. Ibid.
9. N. R. F. Al-Rodhan (2008), *'Emotional Amoral Egoism': A Neurophilosophical Theory of Human Nature and Its Universal Security Implications* (Berlin: LIT Verlag).

Index

CPSIA information can be obtained at www.ICGtesting.com
Printed in the USA
BVOW042042081212
307618BV00003B/20/P